STRONG FAMILY

THE FAMILY MANUAL
HOW TO BUILD A
STRONG FAMILY
A FOUNDATION OF ROCK

R Lindemann

Aleph Publications
Wisconsin, USA

Aleph Publications
Manitowoc, WI

Paperback Edition
ISBN-13: 978-1-956814-18-7

32 31 30 29 28 27 26 25 24 23   1 2 3 4 5

Dedication

All around us there is both beauty and horror. Many of us live lives filled with trouble; and with all of our energy, we try to overcome these problems. Yet nothing that many of us encounter will allow us to be free from the chains that bind us. It is my hope that those who are feeling these pains and chains of trouble are drawn to this book so that they too can forever break free of the chains that bind their lives and the lives of their families.

It is to those who have gone through these troubles, to those who have overcome these troubles, and to those who have not yet heard this message to whom this book is dedicated. It is my hope that those who have been lied to, or been given misinformation, will draw near to the light of truth; and through that light, gain the strength to overcome those who bind them in the chains forged of lies and misinformation.

To every person who has ever had to struggle, to every person who is now struggling, and to every person who will someday see struggle, this book is dedicated to you. You deserve a life that is better than what you have been sold. You are in the hearts of those who truly know *Love!*

Disclaimer

All information, views, thoughts, and opinions expressed herein are those of the author(s) and are being presented only for your consideration and should not be interpreted as advice to take any action. Any action you take with regard to implementing or not implementing the information, views, thoughts, and opinions contained within this published work is your own responsibility. Under no circumstances are distributor(s) and/or publisher(s) and/or author(s) of this work liable for any of your actions.

Anyone, especially those who have been victim of misdirected explanation and understanding, may be best served seeking wise counsel before deciding to implement any information, views, thoughts, opinions, or anything else that is offered for your consideration in this work. All information, views, thoughts, and opinions in this work are not advice, directive, recommendation, counsel, or any other indication for anyone to take any action. All information, views, thoughts, and opinions offered herein are offered only as suggestions for your personal consideration, which is done of your own free will. Your life is your own responsibility; use it wisely.

Any use of trade names or mention of commercial sources is for informational purposes only and does not imply endorsement or affiliation.

Contents

Acknowledgements

Putting together one's own thoughts into a comprehensive work takes more than one lone author. In the process there are many people involved, ranging from editors and reviewers all the way to those involved anywhere the work is distributed. In that process are hundreds of unnamed people who all do a wonderful job of fulfilling the mission to get helpful information to those readers who seek it. I would like to take this opportunity to thank every one of you involved with the creation and distribution of this work, for your efforts to swiftly get it into the hands of the readers. Thank you! And special thanks to Lisa A. Miller and Chris Van Den Berg for your thoughts on the manuscript and for pointing out where further clarity was needed. Without the efforts of all those people, no author could ever hope to share with the world their insight, ideas, and stories.

Introduction

Having grown up witnessing much trouble and strife in the lives of those around me, I often wondered why things are the way they are.

Finding, and then sharing, the answers to why things are the way they are has been my deepest quest for most of my adult life. After years of my own observations and experiences, I felt compelled to write this book to share the simplicity of creating a family of children who are strong, loving, self-assured, and kind. I also want to share how easy it is to experience joy within your own family when you know the simple secret that few truly know.

Growing up, I got my dose of parenting techniques and advice from all of the usual "experts." Some of this advice is now debunked. In my early years, this information came through my parents and some of the reading they did; and in the years of my own awareness that followed, the information came from TV talk shows and other such programs, and from books found and read on my own. Through observation and listening I have seen and heard enough contradiction in the parenting techniques and family advice to last anyone a lifetime.

Most of us are now, or have been, witness to parenting gone bad, either in our own childhood families, or in our current families with our very own offspring. We are also witness to the seemingly endless parade of trouble that we hear and read about from friends and family, and in the news. Why do some families do so well while others cannot seem to conquer the toil and strife that infect their homes? Why do so many families lack the joy that they deserve?

Many problems come from bad parenting techniques—a statement that hurts many of us at our very core. But, to pass the buck a bit, much of what we suffer from today is due to the contradictions from our past that we have heard, seen, and learned from our parents and from others—contradictions that we have subsequently accepted and duplicated. In other words, no one instructed us as to how proper parenting should be done. Instead, through our environment, we learned our parenting techniques without specific intent to do it right. To address this, we will be discussing some of the more prominent contradictions that we experience in life and how to remove those contradictions from our thinking and from our lives.

If there are contradictions in our current or past information, it does not mean that the information is one-hundred percent wrong. We can witness the Sun rising and setting from day to day and make the wrong conclusion that the Sun circles the Earth, but that does not change the fact that we see the Sun rise and set every day. However, believing that the Sun circles the Earth affects your ability to see the truth about what is really occurring.

Information about making our lives better, more robust, and more joyful is no different than the example just given. Part of our human nature and innocence is that we have *preconceived* ideas and beliefs that cause us to overlook important details. Our problem comes in when we refuse to consider ideas and solutions that are new to us that others provide. When their ideas and solutions are solid, it can quickly elevate us out of our troubles and make our lives very joyful!

If you have older children, the problems you may have experienced, or are currently experiencing, *and* what to do about those problems are addressed in this book. If you are planning to have children, or already have them, then this book will guide you and help you to avoid the problems that you have been observing in other families and the world around you.

Think of *Strong Family* as *The Family Repair Manual*. It is not meant to pump you up and excite you when you are done reading, only to have you be let down again when things go wrong. This book is written to enable you to understand the source of your problems so that *you* can repair or replace what is broken in your life and in your family. This book shows you *why* your family is or was broken to begin with. Reading *Strong Family*, before problems occur, can allow you to avoid the troubles before they have had a chance to take root in your life. Unless we can remove the cause, or the *why*, of something that has been broken, it will unnecessarily keep breaking over and over again throughout the remainder our lives. This will have us needlessly going in circles in attempt to repair the damage each time the problems reoccur.

Strong Family is meant to be read and then used as a reference book and a reminder of how to stop the problems *when* they occur, and, better yet, often *before* they occur. This *Family Repair Manual* is for parents of all ages, and for parents with children of all ages—including adult children who are well into their fifties, sixties, and older. *Strong Family* busts through many myths of the past to get you on the right track. This is not your typical parenting book that gives you step by step feel-good instructions. It is not a quick or temporary fix. It is a dig-into-the-problems-and-get-your-hands-dirty kind of book that reveals the root of your troubles, allowing you to swiftly remove those troubles. We *will* suffer the consequences when we fail to do this.

The point of *Strong Family* is to get our heads in the right place so that parenting comes easy! Doing so allows us to see through the inconsistencies that currently exist in each our lives, and the inconsistencies that we will encounter in our own family's future. Your view of life can be hopeful and confident when you finish reading *Strong Family*. Your added understanding will give you an advantage to see things more clearly; thus allowing you to breeze through life with little concern, and with much joy in your spouse, in your children, and in yourself!

Chapter 1

Building the Foundation

Just about every new parent wonders, "Will my children turn out to be good, or did I get "bad-egg" children? Will my kids be spoiled little brats at age two? Will they choose the slippery slope of drugs and alcohol when they're teenagers? Are they going to be overweight and unhealthy? Or, did we get lucky and have really great children who will be sweet, happy, loving, hard-working, responsible people when they grow up?"

Some of us don't give this much thought because everything in our lives is fine right now, but suddenly, our children start getting into trouble, rebelling, or maybe hanging with the "wrong crowd." Some parents are dealing with problems with much older children who are at "midlife" age and are *still* troublesome, or are *becoming* troublesome.

Every parent wonders what they need to do to raise good children who will not disappoint them. Is there any hope, or are we stuck with what we've got? Is it a role of the dice, or can we deliberately make things better? Do we wait and see what happens, or can we do something *now* to change our dismal future?

The solutions to the seemingly inescapable problems of life are a mystery to most of us. We spend a great deal of time and money listening to and/or reading books about parenting, but nothing seems to help the troubles that we see and feel coming our way. When we're fully and deeply immersed in our troubles, it often takes all of our efforts just to maintain our sanity, leaving us with none of our will left to fight the actual problems.

The mysteries of having a strong family are not secret to those who want the best for their families and are willing to make a few simple changes to implement those "mysteries". The solutions, or "mysteries", to many child-rearing problems are right here in these pages for your consideration, and are far simpler than you might think! This book has many views, thoughts, and opinions for you to consider, but *your* situation is unique to your circumstances, so what you read here are not instructions for what you *must* do, but rather it is merely views, thoughts, and opinions for you to consider. Doing so can help you to better understand your situation. The decisions you make are yours alone and because your situation has details that only *you* know, it is your responsibility to properly consider what you read and then decide how and if that applies to your own circumstances. When you take the time to do so, you will be better equipped to decide what direction and what steps to take as you move forward. It is also important to gather all information *before* deciding your next step, so reading this *entire* book *before* making any changes is another thing to consider doing.

Strong Family is your *Family Repair Manual*, and in it, you will learn the secrets of strong families. This book goes into great detail about the *why* of the way things happen, and discusses the stumbling blocks that our society has so eloquently laid out before us all. It's common for us to start to read a book and not complete it, this book must be read in its entirety for someone to be able to come to the full understanding required in order to correct the problems we face in life.

While there are some parenting books that should not be read or considered—*ever*—due to their inaccuracy, many and maybe most books are helpful and have many wonderful parenting tips that have been of use to multitudes of people. Yet, within the multitude of books, even with having read some of the better parenting books, many families still experience far too many problems and far too much family strife. Even after using much of the advice that we read, we often fail in this regard. Why is this?

Many of the ideas in parenting books end up being nothing more than temporary patches, never really getting to the core of our problems. We have become a society that tends to focus on the symptom, rather than on what caused the symptoms to begin with. Putting a bandage on a rash will not stop you from getting a rash the next time you unknowingly walk through a patch of poison-ivy. What we all need to know is exactly what poison-ivy looks like and where it is located so that we can simply walk around it, thereby avoiding its poisonous effects in our lives.

Implementing techniques without understanding *why* they work is of little value to you in the long run when your circumstances change slightly and produce yet more trouble for you. A slight change in our life can make problems temporarily appear to go away, but then an entirely new problem shows up. Typically, the new problem is merely just another similar problem stemming from the same root-source that the original problem was from. When we understand what the root causes of our problems are, then we can easily accommodate the adjustments needed in order to remove these problems whenever the problems come back into our lives in their newly mutated form.

What the World Keeps Forgetting
Does Your Family have a Good Foundation?

If you've faced problems with your own children, if you're a new parent, or if you're planning to be a parent, and you want to avoid unnecessary future pain in your home, then you probably have questions about how to deal with past problems or potential future problems that are answered in this book.

If you had family problems growing up, or if you had or now have problems with your own children, then don't feel alone, because you are not! The world seems to keep forgetting its past. And for some reason, over the centuries, we have continuously failed to bring the mysteries, solutions, and lessons like those discussed here to each new generation. Though, there are some families who have succeeded at doing so and joyfully reap the benefits of their success!

So let's start at the very beginning, the **foundation**. The words *family* and *familiar* are from the same root. In its ancient form "*fam*" means: shared, the *same seed,* or *from the same seed.*

No matter what you do in life, the foundational portion of any task is *always **the*** most important.

Have you ever seen news clips of houses plunging to their destruction because the hill or land that they were built on washed away in a flood? We see this all the time during major flooding and in mudslides. If you want your home to be able to stand through the rains of troubles, then you need to have a foundation made of rock, rather than a foundation made from vulnerable, weak dirt that will wash away during the rains of trouble.

Where, then, do you start to look for a rock foundation to build your home, your family, upon?

Why Understanding is Important to You

The answer to the last question is, **Understanding!** Your foundation starts with *understanding.* It doesn't matter what you're doing, because if you do it and you don't understand what you're doing, then you are getting by on instruction and luck alone. Going through life having to depend upon instructions and luck will always lead to disaster and disappointment in the long run. Let's take a computer as an example: If you use a computer, then you can function well and get much done with it; but, when problems occur with the computer, then you're lost unless you *understand* the details of the computer.

When we don't understand, we take our computer to someone, who hopefully does understand, and *they* correct the problems for us. This is fine and it serves the world well. But, things are different with our families, because families last a lot longer than computers. While you can bring your family member into the doctor to stitch up a wound, much like bringing your computer in for repair, the matters of the behavior and mind or heart are considerably more evasive in the people in a family in comparison to a computer problem.

Many people live, survive, and go about their lives, and everything is roses until... *it happens!* Problems creep into your family and home, and you don't understand what or how it all happened. After all, "Everything was going along just fine." But, much like computers, problems in life do occur from time to time, and when you don't understand those problems, then they are very mysterious indeed! The next thing that happens is that we seek guidance for ourselves or for our children who are experiencing the problems. The guidance usually comes in the form of a counselor, psychiatrist, or some other type of therapist. In many cases, these people do much good for the troubled person. The troubled person and their family are often assigned tasks or goals to complete before their next therapy session, and these tasks may or may not be of any help. In some cases, the person is still troubled even after many years of therapy and much unwanted expense. Once a person understands, then therapy is generally no longer needed.

Are You Over-Thinking It?

Though there are therapists who are in it only to get the client back again for the sake of more money, many therapists are decent upstanding people who truly want to help you. But there can be a problem in too much scrutiny of our lives. We can repeatedly analyze a situation and never actually solve anything. Some people even end up going to their therapist only because the therapist actually listens to them. Listening is a very attractive quality, but merely listening can be a trap that will keep you coming back to the therapist for many years. The bottom line with therapy or any other help is the actual *result*. If you are doing something to remedy your problems, then there should soon be a positive result. If there is not a positive result in a reasonable amount of time, then you're not getting to the real problem.

Over-analysis is of little help to anyone, and at a certain point, more discussion will not change anything for you and sometimes it makes matters worse. Do not over-think life. Find the problem and take prompt decisive action to properly correct the problem, and then be done with it and move on.

You Build Children

This chapter is titled *Building the Foundation*, but it is not discussing *what* the foundation is to be built of. We will cover that in another chapter, but for now, know this: **Understanding** is key.

As mentioned in our earlier example, with the house on the hill during a flood, the house washed away *along with* its foundation. The person who chose to build in that particular location, ignored, and likely did not *understand* the reality of the potential dangers of a problem, such as a rare occurrence of a major flood. When the builder built the house, they failed to adequately explain the risks of building in that particular chosen location.

We must not rely on others to teach our own children. It is the *parents* who build a child much the way the builder builds the house. If the builder does not make absolutely sure that the base foundation is on solid ground, then, at some point, the rains of trouble *will* pour down and the house *will* fall—period! **You** are the builder of your children. Let's repeat that:

> " **You**—are the builder—of **your** children"

This is a bit Biblically proverbial with houses, foundations, rain, and all, but the truth is that we do build our children; be courageous and adopt these truths. Often, when we read a book that exposes our shortcomings, and we begin to realize our own errors, it is at that point of realizing our internal conflicts that we often put a book down and fail to pick it up again; thus, *never* solving our problems. Don't let this happen to you. Press through those things that are difficult to hear, and then eradicate them from your life, because those are the things that are holding you back in life.

We cannot solve problems by ignoring our own internal conflicts. What you are reading can make you stronger and give you absolute control and power over your troublesome situations and over life in general, even though it may sting somewhat during the adjustment process. Keeping that in consideration, our problems are almost always *our own fault.* Trying to place our responsibilities onto others will not make things better. In fact, it generally tends to make matters worse—much worse—often ending in disaster and a broken family. Even if someone else is behaving in a poor and unfair manner, it is still our own responsibility to properly deal with the unfair situation to protect ourselves and our families.

There are many broken families out there who succeed very well, but few, if any, wish that their family was broken. Most people would like to have one loving mother and one loving father—till death do us part, and have their children in the house until the children are grown and strong enough to survive on their own.

Children **Need** a Solid Foundation.
But How Solid is Your Foundation?

Most cultures have been on the fast-track to having all families become "broken" families. But these cultures cannot manage to get some families to go along with the Master Plan of destroying family. What is the secret of the families who are immune to family destruction?

> No matter what you do in life, from the smallest to the greatest, the foundation is the single most important part.

The secret is their foundation! There is nothing more important than what you build your family upon. Consider using a plowed field as a roadway. This would not be a good foundation for the wheels of your car; it simply is not proper and is best suited for tractors. Sure you can do it, but consider the problems and damage that *will* occur to your car. Or take for example, placing a boat on a highway for a foundation. The foundation for a boat is meant to be water, and anything that is not a liquid will render the boat useless and cause it a great deal of problems. Or consider plans for dinner, where your foundation is the money that you will use to pay for the meal; what will happen to your dinner plans if your wallet and financial accounts contain no available funds?

A foundation has two parts: first, is the part that you are building upon, it is the ground or earth part of the place where you choose to build. And second, is the base that you lay down to make things level and straight, on top of which you will build your life. With an actual house, the first part of the foundation is the earth or ground, and the second part is the basement and/or footings. Both of these parts, the *ground* and the *base* are extremely important to the strength, integrity, and long-term durability of your home.

Think of *understanding* as the first part of your foundation— the earth or ground part. If you don't want to understand everything properly, then **expect** problems—and a whole lot of them. If you don't want to understand, then **you** have made a choice for trouble. But, if you seek to understand, then you will quickly see that all other things become far simpler and more expeditiously handled by you.

The second part of a proper foundation is the ideas or information that you are understanding, which is what this book is all about. You realizing that you need to put forth the effort to understand, and then actually understanding the foundation, is the ground or earth that you build upon. *What* you understand, is the blocks of your foundation that you put in place one by one—this book contains those blocks. So what is it that we need to understand?

What Did You Expect?

To start with, we need to understand people. The most important person for each of us to understand is our own self. Yes, I know it's sometimes scary, but let's do it anyway. We'll discuss *understanding* in-depth in a later chapter; but for now, just know that understanding *is* important to you and your family. Understanding is a skill that is seldom taught. Most of our parents do not, or did not, understand people or their relationships; and their parents did not understand; and their parents did not understand, all the way back to the dawn of mankind.

Sure, we picked things up here and there over the centuries, only to have the next generation forget some of those things and/or fail to pass them along down the line. After doing a good deal of reading about ancient and modern history, it seems that we have forgotten a great deal over the centuries. It is often said that those who fail to learn from history's mistakes are bound to repeat them. The problem that occurs is, we make assumptions; and none of us are exempt from this—not one.

When we pass information on to our children, we usually *assume* that they understand what we are trying to tell them. With eyes glazed over, a blank stare, and a nod, they acknowledge our explanation. Then *we* believe *they* understand, and, generally, so do they. However, just because we believe it, does not make it so.

Imagine this: If a young child sees a yummy candy bar sitting on the kitchen table, then that's what they will be thinking of. Now, if you say to them "Would you some candy?" They will most certainly be picturing their most recent encounter with the candy (an assumption) which is *their* favorite yummy candy bar sitting on the kitchen table. However, instead, *you* are thinking of the dinner mint that you brought home from your lunch appointment at a local restaurant. When you produce that lint covered mint from your pocket and hand it to the child who is picturing the perfectly wrapped, full-sized candy bar, then you are likely going to experience a very disappointed child. This is because some *expectations* had been made based upon assumptions, and those expectations were *not* met.

The situation in this example is a classic misunderstanding. You failed to specify the type of candy, and the child assumed that the object of their affection, which is their most recent encounter with the candy bar on the table, would be the candy referred to in your question, "Would you like some *candy?*"

This is an understandable problem that was unanticipated by you. You didn't know about the candy bar, or simply did not have any thought of it in your mind when making the offer to them about candy. If you had thought about the candy bar, then you would likely have presented the mint first, and then asked if they would like to have the mint candy.

This might seem to be a petty problem; I mean, it's only candy, right? Wrong! The candy has absolutely nothing to do with the problem that we're discussing here. What happened is that the child's *expectation* was crushed. Now, most parents would pick up on the fact that we disappointed our child in this situation, so we often find an in-between point that will, at least, partly remedy our child's disappointment. However, if the situation is not remedied, then what will the child be left to think after their crushing disappointment?

The lesson here is that other people do not necessarily understand you or know *exactly* what you mean when you say something to them. You coming to this understanding will help you alleviate and head off potential disappointment that others will have when you communicate with them.

What Did You Label Your Child As?

Parents are the creators and/or molders of the thoughts of their young children. Of course we can add to that the things you allow them to be exposed to on television or on the internet. This is to say that, in general, the child will think what you taught them to think, especially in their earlier years of life. A child who is called a "cry baby" or "spoiled rotten" by their parent(s) might end up living up to the labels that the parents cast for them.

If you have been treated unfairly and, in front of your young children, you have voiced your opinions about the situation, then they will certainly pick up those opinions and adopt them as their own. This might seem good, provided that you are being fair in your assessment and judgment about the situation for which you have expressed your views. But, as illustrated with the candy misunderstanding, it is likely that your children will not understand the complexities of the problem about which you have voiced your thoughts and opinions while they were within listening distance.

They simply will not understand the details. They will be much more connected to the *level* of emotion that you express yourself with than they will the details of the problem.

What this means is that if you're overreacting, they will think something to be far worse than it actually is. Additionally, children are very tuned in to their parents' emotions. And to the children, *everything* is a far bigger deal than it is to you. So, if you're overreacting and crying or screaming about an unfair or bad situation, then they will relate your overreaction to the pain they may feel when *they* cry and scream. This is the level of empathy that will be shown by them for your situation. Your emotional overreaction can make a situation that's not really all that bad, seem to them, to be very traumatic.

If you're angry and you are name-calling because you were treated badly or were greatly disappointed by someone, then you are placing labels on things attached to those emotions and emotional levels. When doing so, you can be certain that your children will eventually repeat these labels in the same way you used the labels. This gets many children in unwanted and unneeded trouble throughout life.

Name calling is only one kind of label. Labels are not bad in themselves, but they do cause many problems. For instance, if you refer to someone as an "idiot" when you are angry at them, then it is likely that your children will do the same, even if the one they are calling an idiot is the Creator of the entire universe or maybe even you. In this case, the label is a misapplied description. All labels are descriptions, but we typically don't use labels as the abbreviated descriptions that they were originally meant to be. Instead we use labels in anger and/or in ignorance as emphasis to express our immediate feelings of outrage.

You must understand that labels are descriptions, and you must accurately use them as such. If you do not, then you are dooming your children to being subject to things that are not true.

If, in frustration, you call someone an "idiot" when they truly are not, then you have misused that label and have taught your child to do the same. Now, think about how much worse this is if we should happen to call our own child an idiot, bad, or naughty. With you being the parent, your children will often *believe* whatever *you* tell them. If you tell your children that they are idiots, then they will eventually believe you, and they will usually do so sooner rather than later.

We also label conditions and diseases. Disease labels work similarly. If someone says that a child is hyperactive or depressed, often the parents, and therefore the children, accept this stigma and run with it. Labels are labels and they are intended to describe something, *not* dictate something.

Part of your rock foundation of understanding is to understand that labels are meant to **de**scribe and not **pre**scribe. Labels do not tell you what you are or what to do; but rather, labels tell you what you did. *Did* is past tense. It already happened. It is over and done with.

Your children will adhere to labels like a cheap bumper sticker in the hot summer sun adheres to your car. Understand that **labels are descriptions**. Unfairly accepting and/or pasting labels onto your children (who never deserve to be labeled) is a dangerous and damaging parental error that we parents make all too often.

Beginning to Get Control of a Spoiled Child

The only way to correct or avoid a problem is to approach it head-on and fully understand it—and then correct it. Blaming someone or something else will only serve to lock you in your current or future problems, and it will keep you there as long as you continue unjustly blaming. It's our failure to address problems head-on that has been our core problem throughout the entirety of human history. And it is this same failure to address problems head-on that continues to keep all of humanity locked within our own problems.

Spoiled children come from only one source—that source is an oversight or breech in parenting. We'll get deeper into *Beginning to Get Control of a Spoiled Child* later, but for now, let's understand that spoiled children are not randomly handed out to you by some cruel god. All of your children are built brick by brick by you and by your spouse, with a little substandard mortar from society.

Certainly there will be some readers who have experienced a great deal of problems at the hand of a very unfair spouse who likely is seldom in the picture or not in the picture at all. If this is your case, then it is true that the person might have treated you very badly, and you feel that all of your problems are their fault. To a point this could be true, but today you are reading this book, and *today* your life is beginning to change for the better because you are now understanding some things that you didn't know or consider before! For everyone else who does not have someone deliberately trying to destroy their life, all of the same understanding still applies.

This cannot be said strongly enough: *If our children are spoiled, it is our own fault!* The sooner we grasp this, then the sooner we can easily and quickly correct our problems and make our heartache disappear forever.

Quickly grasping things is ultimately what this book is about and it goes far beyond that. As parents, it's not just an unspoiled child that we are seeking. We also want children who are self-assured and will live joyful, robust lives and bring themselves, us, and everyone around them a great deal of joy! If we fail to raise joyful children, then we have failed our children. That means it's time for us to stop and reevaluate our situation and make the needed changes to accommodate our new understanding.

A critically important point to know and remember is that every moment of realization that you have is the beginning of your new life. If you find a useful morsel of wisdom right now at this very moment, then you can implement it into your family and change the rest of your lives for the better, forever! Then, if you find a morsel of wisdom right now at this next moment, you can also implement *it* into your family and change the rest of your lives for the better from this moment forward. And if you find another morsel of wisdom next week, then you can implement that morsel into your family and change the rest of your lives for the better from that point on as well. In fact, this never ends. Every moment is a new moment to make changes moving forward and improve your life.

Understanding is the first critical piece of a strong family foundation. Without it, expectations *will* be violated, and disappointment *will* be inevitable within your family. If we have not understood in the past, then we must not let that stop us from understanding in the future. Every day is a new day to add to your life's wisdom, and to then live by that truth. Failing to do this *will* cause your family much strife and trouble in the long run. This is one of the simple secrets of bringing joy into your family.

Chapter 2

Making Choices

The first step in making choices is to understand that everything in life is either true or it is false—it is good or it is bad. If it is true, then it is good information. If it is false, then it is bad information.

The next step is to always choose the information that is true and good. This simple task gets obscured and perverted when people who choose false information are leading others. This is because the leaders' perception of what is true and good is obscured and perverted, and they deceive themselves and others through ignorance, though, sometimes it's deliberate.

If a person who is adhering to false information tells us something that *they believe* to be true (but it is not true), it tends to misdirect our focus and leads us to wrong conclusions, even if the person doing the telling is you. For instance, if your child has temper tantrums and they are ten years old, then the truth is that they are too old for that behavior and the tantrums are your own fault. We must choose truth, but this does not mean that it dictates the long-term outcome of our lives. A person who is ignoring facts, or a person who is a liar, will accept the "truth" that the child has tantrums, but then believe that's just the way the child is—spoiled!

It is our own choice, of what we believe, that determines our future and our child's future in this or any other situation. Embracing and accepting a child as a "spoiled child" and then treating them as such, with no attempt to correct them, will get you varying degrees of a *permanently*-spoiled child, often referred to as a bully or a terrorist. People might get offended at the notion of saying that a spoiled child could be referred to as a "terrorist", but when a child uses their poor behavior to torment other children, or even adults, they are in fact terrorizing those children. And, as is all too often witnessed, some of these children will go on to become adults who behave the same way. Some will even go as far as physically harming others. If you doubt this, then simply read the daily news.

You have the choice to know that the truth is that your child is acting out and behaving badly. You have the choice to accept that something in your child's life is not right. You have the choice to know that *you* can and must make the difference *if **you*** choose to do so.

Other people cannot make the choice to accept *truth* for you—not your friends, not your family, not even your spouse. We each must accept the truth for ourselves, and then face it and deal with problems appropriately. If we do not, then we will pay the heavy and grievous price for our own wrong choices.

Guiding people in how to make good choices does not work well until we are able to relate these choices to their life situations. This book illustrates a good number of negative situations in order to help you connect and fully understand the life-troubles that most of us seem to experience at some point. And in doing so, you will find it to be one of the most positive books you will ever read. You're not going to get a bunch of arbitrary rules to follow. When you're done reading, you should find choosing what is *true* and *good* to be the only thing needed, and you will find that choosing what is false or bad is the obvious wrong choice for you or anyone else in your family.

Why are Statistics are Important to You?
What You Don't Want to Overlook

I've watched many people needlessly struggle because they chose to be too mentally lazy to think about the things that cause trouble in their own lives, causing themselves a great deal of unnecessary and unwanted work and pain. When we are unwilling to take on the responsibility of *understanding* within our own lives, then we *will* suffer the consequences—Of this, you can be certain!

Most of us never think to attempt to understand— **understanding** (that is to say, to understand what *understanding* is.) If we don't understand the understanding mentioned in the last chapter it will cloud much of our perception of the information we receive on a daily basis. And along with understanding—*understanding,* we also need to understand statistics. Why is it so important to understand statistics?

When we follow the often skewed or misrepresented statistics offered to us by profiteering people and sensationalized headlines, it does *not* help our families. The way we read statistics, or the way we understand statistics, is critical in our own understanding of life. Statistics would not matter, but because so much of the way that we interact with life is guided by statistics, the importance of understanding statistics and their use cannot be understated.

The following are some critical areas where understanding statistics is very important to you and your family.

If I ask, "What percent of people get divorced?" the common answer typically is, "About fifty percent" or "half of them." But while it is true that "About half of all marriages end in divorce", it is *not* true that half of all people who get married get divorced. "How is this?" you ask?

People are not marriages—people are people. When one person has been divorced three times, then, statistically, it means that there are three other people in the statistics that will never divorce—**ever!** That is to say, of the six marriages total, three marriages from the first person and one from each of the three couples that are married for life, that half of the *marriages* ended in divorce. Assuming that the person who divorced had married three separate people and did not marry any one of them twice, this scenario would involve ten people total, and only four would have divorced. This particular group has a rate of divorce for *people* set at forty percent, and a *marriage* divorce rate set at fifty percent.

Statistically, you can take comfort in your own marriage when you know someone who has been divorced twice. This means that you and another friend and both of your spouses will not ever get divorced, right? Ah, not so fast!

Divorce is in your head, not in statistics. If you have it in your head that your marriage has a fifty percent chance of ending in divorce, then the chance that your marriage will end in divorce is probably closer to ninety to one-hundred percent.

Inversely, if you and your spouse have it in your heads that you will *never* divorce, then the chance that you will divorce is about ten percent to no chance of divorce at all. You can easily verify this by simply discussing divorce with people to do your own simple survey. Divorce is a choice that a couple makes early in their relationship, but it is **you** who needs to make the choice that you will stay married and forget the statistics when you're angry with your spouse. Entertaining the idea of divorce will most certainly bring divorce into your life.

Another primary reason that understanding statistics is important is because, in general, our world has a tendency for greedy and self-serving behavior. When companies, for instance, have a need to make money, they often are not going to take the time to get in-depth as to why you should or should not use their products; this includes medicine or pharmaceutical products. Instead they just offer you manipulated statistical information that makes you believe that you *need* their products. Then in a sheep-like manner, we have a tendency to believe whatever the companies' advertisements tell us. Thus, we are subservient to them of our own free choice and free will. This does not make the companies bad or evil; but often, they certainly do border on irresponsible. It is each our own responsibility to research and decide if their claims apply to our own lives. This is true whether it is a medical issue, or just a product for our own vanity or enjoyment.

Behavioral statistics for children are some of the most horribly abused statistics that have ever been presented to mankind. Never follow statistical trends unless you want to be the negative subject of those statistics. Many parents quickly embrace behavioral statistics that claim to explain the poor, odd, or erratic behavior of their own children. This is a cop-out used by those of us who refuse to choose the *true* information mentioned earlier.

Statistically, whichever "disease" happens to be the new "*in*" disease or trend will be embraced by the pharmaceutical companies. Then their new medicine will be promoted as an ongoing cure for your child's behavioral problems. When your child's behavior problems become a problem for the school system, then the school system encourages *you* to utilize what, to them, seems to be the fastest route to solving your child's behavioral problems—their easiest route often is prescription drugs because it quickly puts a patch on a problem but it doesn't deal with actually solving the problem.

The statistical increase in children's disease is unfounded and it is proliferated by doctors who are overzealous, profiteering, and/or foolish. "Diseases" and some "Disorders" such as ADHD and Autism are often overblown. First, labeling diseases and conditions does your child no good whatsoever. Secondly, in speaking of labels, the word "*disease*" means "*dis*" or "*not*" plus "*ease.*" In other words, a "*disease*" brings *discomfort* to the person. So, by definition, a person who is harmful to others is also a disease or a disorder. It's a pity that we do not have a medication that we can take to be rid of foolish people who torment our lives. Be judicious as to what you choose to call a "disease," because the disease label that we accept for our children is often pointing the finger of blame at our own selves, because in many cases it is us parents who are disordered and we often eagerly accept the erroneous conclusions of "Doctors" who blame those disorders or diseases on our innocent children. Your children are what you make them.

Admittedly, people whose children are diagnosed with these and other behavioral "diseases" might not see it this way. If your child has been diagnosed with ADHD or Autism, know that it is in your power to accept this as true or false. These descriptive labels are not "diseases" but rather, they are results of actions.

If you currently have children, or if you are planning to have children, then know that it is in your power to quickly place your child back on a straight path that does not traverse through the desolate abyss of ADHD, modern Autism, and other such behavioral disease labels. The ever-increasing statistics, with regard to reading the survey results of these diseases, should set off statistical alarms for you and your family. It is only when we understand how the basics of statistics work that we can clearly see how often those statistics are manipulated for the financial and agenda-driven benefit of those who use them. Often, us not understanding statistics properly, ends in horror for our own families. For the purposes of this book, this is enough of an explanation about statistics. If you would like a further explanation of how misrepresented statistics affects your life, the cornerstone books *Hot Water* and *Red Hot Marriage* explain more.

Then we also have to account for family eating habits and the effect that it has on the children. It is truly an unfair and tragic situation when a child is not eating healthy meals. There are many family situations where the children are eating foods that will spike and then deplete the child's blood sugar levels, causing them to have bouts of energy and lethargy clouding their focus and their will. In some cases, when this occurs and the children are acting unruly with high energy, some people will attribute it to ADHD. This unfair and dangerous analysis puts everyone in harm's way. It does your family and child no good to allow and support poor eating habits, and then, due to the food-induced attention issues, to medicate the child for a "disease" that is typically questionably diagnosed to begin with. If such a diagnosis feels forthcoming in your family, first consider thinking about a proper meal plan and sticking to it. Many families are pleasantly surprised at the positive effect this typically has in those situations, and let us not forget loving discipline.

Make Some Choices

All of the choices surrounding you and your family-life are the responsibility of you and your spouse. A society that believes diseases, like those just mentioned, are unavoidable is a society that has chosen to hand their children over to an uncaring world that will do what it can to rob them of their dignity. Accepting responsibility for the choices regarding your family is a personal choice, and only you can make it.

I encourage you to embrace this true information. If your child has been diagnosed with such a disease, then understand that it is not a disease. Rather, know that it is a description of their behavior. This behavior should always be handled with proper and loving care, by you—the parent(s) of the child.

Do not short-change the brilliance of a so-called "autistic" child. Their underlying peculiar behavior is typically a gift that other people do not understand, thus causing it to be labeled as a "disease." Similarly, the boredom of, or parental distance from, a child with "ADHD" is also labeled as a disease. Children need the *proper* attention, care, and understanding of their parents. Too often, our world demands too much of each of us, to a point where we inadvertently end up neglecting the deeper needs of our children. We end up only fulfilling the superficial needs, such as food, clothing, and to be occupied with things like video games, sports, etc. You, as a parent, must make the decision as to how you will spend time with your children and what you will allow into their lives.

You Must Drive Out Bad Influences from Your Life

Another set of choices that you need to consider are those that include bad influence to your family. A bad influence can be anything from your job, to the people in your childhood family (the family you grew up in), and it can include everything and everyone in between.

As a parent, it is imperative that you eradicate damaging things from your family as soon as possible. If you have a co-worker, friend, or even a birth- or adopted-family member who is causing undue stress on you, it is best to cut ties with them. They are doing no good for you or your family if they refuse to stop their harmful behaviors.

In general, a stressed parent makes a bad parent. It's not fair to your spouse or children to come home to them stressed because of how people are behaving badly in your life *outside* of your home. It is important to note that, and as discussed in the cornerstone book *Understanding Prayer - Why Our Prayers Don't Work*, when we continue to tolerate the bad behavior of others, and then bring that stress home to our family, our stress increases the chances that our children will be the ones causing others stress when the children are grown up. This is *not* your goal.

We will get deeper into this later, but for now consider the effects of the influence on your children when they observe you, and also the effects while they are being entertained by video games, TV, movies, radio, music, and the internet. If there is any doubt that these forms of media have an effect on your children, then consider this simple perspective: If these forms of media had zero effect on children, then they would never *ever* repeat or emulate a single line or joke from any of it. Don't misunderstand this, it is not bad to repeat a line from a program or song; just be careful with what lines they are exposed to, and thus, will repeat.

If children indulge in any form of media, then the likelihood that they have not, do not, or will not repeat things that they have seen and heard is about zero. Driving out these bad influences is easy when it is in your control, but when the influences are from their time at school then it's nearly impossible. While changing schools sometimes helps, bad influence will still exist no matter what school they attend.

It is the foundation that *you* choose and build that provides them with an adequate filter to rid *themselves* of the bad influences they *will* encounter in their lives. Your family foundation guides them in their choices no matter what that foundation is. If it is a poor foundation built on false information, then their choices will include false information because you have trained them that way by your example of what you allow in their lives. But if it is a good foundation built on truth, then that will be reflected in your children.

Making Your Internal Choice About God

Fear not, I am not going to ask you to accept Christ as your personal savior. That is not the purpose of this book. Most of us claim to believe in God, or some power bigger than ourselves, but we often stop at that.

For many who have chosen to believe that God exists, or even for those who have chosen to believe that there is no god, life still goes on. Whether the existence of a God/god is true or not, our problems still exist. And unless you embrace the basics of this book, you *will* continually suffer from your problems with or without the belief in a God or a god, or no g/God at all.

Many people are able to make themselves feel as if they have escaped the problems of life by becoming aggressive and stepping in front of others by taking things out of proper turn. This gives them the appearance that all is well. But is it?

There are not many people that have sacrificed family for money, who are pleased with their choices while lying on their death beds. Those who have done so are usually filled with a lifetime of tremendous regrets at the point of death.

We see self-proclaimed godless people with problems, and we see God-fearing people with problems. So it's apparent that *proclaiming* that God does or does not exist has little bearing on our problems.

Personally, I have not yet had the experience to meet a godless person who was not bitter in that regard; though, it is true that many God-fearing people are also bitter. So where does this leave us?

Our decision of the belief of whether or not there is a God seems of little consequence to most people; this is because most people believe in a superior being of some sort. And that's about as far as it goes because many people typically don't want to discuss it or think about it much further than that.

Believing in God is a choice that each of us must make. But as a parent, you had better have a well nailed down understanding of your belief system, because regardless of which belief you hold, God or no god, your children are only as strong as the information that you give them.

Lies are weak and they create weak children. If there is a God, then denying it will eventually end in problems for your children. If there is no god, then insisting that there is one will also end in problems for your children. We are weak only when we are wrong; and our *beliefs* have no bearing on whether we are right or wrong. What has bearing on being right or wrong is the—*what*— we have chosen to believe. If *what* someone believes is false, then their foundation is weak, but if *what* they believe is true, then their foundation is strong—nothing will ever change this basic truth. So if you believe there is no God and you're wrong, then you will have to deal with the consequences of your choice. But as we have seen through the centuries, even if there is a God, believing so improperly can have devastating results. The battle within us on this subject is a good thing. The very fact that you would ponder the question is also a good thing. If this "God" does exist, then we have to assume that God would be pleased that we would work to verify the existence. If God does not exist then it simply does not matter. It's not my place to tell you what to believe. That can only be your own decision either way. The most important part to understand is this: No matter what you decide to believe about the existence of "God", it will not change the truth about the existence of God no matter what that truth is.

How You Denied Reality

Since this book is about building great children and a great family, it would be ridiculous to not speak on the subject of religion in our lives. Whether you claim that there is no god, or if you are deeply immersed in your religion, or if you are anywhere in-between, the true information is that "religion" is an enormous part of our world's culture and society. So it does matter, at least to that extent. There is a deep reality that many people choose to deny, and doing so will gain you nothing in the end.

The religions of our world permeate every aspect of our societies and of our cultures, ranging from our eating and clothing, to our songs, our architecture, and just about everything else you can think of. This is true whether we know it or not. It is true whether we admit it or not. And it is true even if we choose to describe our religion differently and call it something else such as "science." Interestingly, even the darker factions of "religion" acknowledge the existence of God and Creation. The question then is, exactly who or what is it that *you* have chosen to serve?

Chapter 3

Does Religion Really Matter?

If you have not decided to make a choice about God, then does religion really matter to you? Of course it does! I suppose we could debate about the level of importance that religion has in our lives, but it's a good idea to at least consider the following information in this chapter before drawing any further conclusions. Whether or not a God exists, our *understanding* of religion causes many of the problems in the world and in our families. Getting a firm grasp on how deeply religion has affected the world, our personal world cultures, and *especially our own families,* is imperative to properly building your family's foundation.

When discussing the state of religion throughout history, the "Church" is often painted negatively. But in truth, it is not the Church that is the problem; rather it is *some* of the people who lead the Church who are responsible for the negative behavior. Let us keep in mind that "The Church" is the people, and only some are a problem, most people are good.

What is Religion and How Have Labels Affected It?

Religious labels have a profound impact on families, and this impact persists whether or not the labels are disconnected from their source. This is true regardless of whether the source is good or bad.

For many people, "religion" is the scourge of mankind. It is something that they can blame all of their woes upon. However, since many people have chosen to have no religion, and yet still have problems, it is a clear indication that religion itself has little to do with our personal problems.

With this line of thinking, it would, of course, be expected to be pointed out that religion has caused many deaths over the centuries. Some of these deaths are from all of the wars done "in the name of the Church." But in this, we must realize that "religion" is nothing more than a label like the labels discussed earlier.

Religion is a label that simply means to *re-bind* or to *bring* or *tie together*. Few people take the time to try to understand this, which is where the true danger of labels actually resides—in our lack of understanding. The term "religion" is from an older language and dialect, and the term has been adopted as a label or condition. The underlying implication of the term "Religion" is "that which joins us", which are the things we think or believe.

It is virtually impossible to do anything without having that thing you are doing *labeled*. Such as: What do you do for a living? The response is usually, "I am a [*fill in the occupational label*]" doctor, teacher, scientist, fast food worker, etc. These are all labels that we allow to be placed on ourselves. Not only do we allow labels to be placed on us by others, but each one of us typically labels ourselves.

When we ask someone what their religion is, what we are truly asking them is, what *group* do you belong to and associate with, or what do you believe or think about God and The Christ? Since religions are somewhat complex in their doctrine, most of them are quite quickly summed up in their own fundamental creed. Even if someone says, "I am a... [*Catholic, Jew, Muslim, Lutheran, or other Protestant sect*]" all are still *labels* of something. While these particular religion labels are not, in themselves, describing labels, they still do indicate that you "belong" to a group or a way of thinking or a set of beliefs which is referred to by that particular name label.

A sizable quantity of people throughout the world have heard the term "The God of Abraham, Isaac, and Jacob." It is a description that has survived throughout the years without really becoming a label as we think of the term "label." Let's not blame the word *religion* or the names of those religions, Catholic, Jew, Muslim, Lutheran, etc. for the ills of the world.

The phrase "The God of Abraham, Isaac, and Jacob" *has* been able to stand the test of time and has not become a label because it contains a list of specific names. If we only referred to God as "the God of Abraham", then it may have ended up in much the same manner as the Lutherans with Martin Luther as their perceived leader. If the phrase had only been, the God of Abraham, then a religion would likely be called Abrahamites or Abrahamians

There are underlying meanings, even within each word, in the phrase "The God of Abraham, Isaac, and Jacob," but we won't get into that in this book, as it is a subject in itself. This description does a very good job of *not* becoming a "label." The problem with most labels is that they lose their descriptive nature, mostly through translation.

As we introduce religion to our children we typically tell them what religion we are without actually understanding our own religion ourselves. We do this because when a label, religious or otherwise, is brought from a different culture, or even just a different generation, then the label often loses its descriptive value, blinding us from its actual meaning. This is similar to the word "*car*," which when you get down to its source means to *carry*, run, or transport. A "*car*" is not the thing with four wheels we all drive around in; a car is what the thing with four wheels does. But to most people the label carries an assumed understanding of being a thing with four wheels.

The phrase "The God of Abraham, Isaac, and Jacob" is descriptive in a manner where it is unlikely to ever lose that value. In other words, the *what* of *who* or, if you prefer, the *who* of *who,* where with Lutherans it is stating a person, with "Muslim" it is means to *submit to* (the God part is assumed), and the word "Catholic" means *universal.* The latter two are lost in translation and the first is lost in generations.

Properly understanding religious labels can quickly propel us beyond the "whitewash" that we have allowed labels to become (whitewash, which hides the label's true description and original intent.) *Properly* understanding the labels of religion allows us to see through the stereotypes that we associate with any given label. An additional thought to keep in mind regarding labels is that what we just discussed applies to *all* labels of every kind, not just those pertaining to the major religions.

When we divide our children by making such religious distinctions we run the risk of having them misunderstand religion. This typically causes tension with other people in their adult years. Please understand that I refer here to the many religions that reference the Creator of *all*, who is also the God of Abraham, versus some other obscure unfounded and arbitrary belief system.

Understand Your Own Religion

We often want to force others to believe as we ourselves believe within our own religious labels. "Religion," as we think of it, is the invention of man. It was not intended to become as it is; but because we utilize labels in the way that we do, religion has become a set of rules. People often wrongly believe that if you don't follow *their* religion, then *you* will be eternally damned. This is not true! What we call "God" and this God's Christ are for *all* people to embrace; we need not attach a label to it. Labels typically serve to divide people into *us* and *them* groups.

> **There are only two groups in this world:**
> those who accept truth, and those who do not
> accept truth.

Your children will fall into one of the two groups when they are adults; and regarding religion, that choice typically is made by the parents in their children's early years.

In much the same way the earlier described candy bar scenario of *misunderstanding* that happened with the child, understanding religion is no different. What the organization's (Church's) doctrine actually states, is generally somewhat different than the way any one of us typically chooses to understand the religion. Some of us think that we are getting a candy bar when we are actually getting a linty mint, and some of us think we are stuck with a linty mint when, in truth, there is a perfect and fresh yummy candy bar waiting for us in the Church *if* we understand how and where to look.

Your religion is the set of beliefs that you have chosen or were born into. Those who have chosen to believe that there is no god also have a religion or a tie that binds them, and that tie is the common belief that there is no god. The label placed on the particular belief set of "no god" is often a descriptive label that is used to describe those beliefs in a single word—"atheist", meaning no god or without god. We create such labels so that others do not need to re-explain the details of their belief-set every time that concept's label is mentioned or every time the subject comes up.

We can make the claim that there is no religion, or that religion does not exist. In a sense this is true, but a set of beliefs is more readily described with the label "religion" and its sub-labels, Jewish, Catholic, Lutheran, Muslim, atheist, etc. The word "religion" is a label but does not even need to be mentioned when stating the name of a given religion; for instance, just saying *Catholic* brings to mind *religion* and all of the traditions and beliefs that accompany that particular label. The same is true for those who choose to believe in a godless existence.

It is important to understand that what Lutherans believe about the Catholic religion is not necessarily the same as what Catholics believe about the Catholic religion. The inverse is true as well. Catholics will often hear from Lutherans that the Catholics are wrong, for instance, for worshiping or praying to the Virgin Mary; however, many, and maybe most, Catholics do not do this. This would be similar to if a small group of people from some other religion went on a murderous rampage and then we made the dangerous broad assumption that *everyone* from that religion was the same as the small rampant group. That's what labels do, they often *unfairly* stereotype and group people, as opposed to *fair* stereotyping, such as: women are better physically equipped to care for infants because a woman gives birth to a child and is able to feed that child from her own body.

The problems with religion are not the label or even the underlying doctrine or creed. In general, those are all very well stated and very harmless; and truthfully, they generally are very kind, loving, and correct. The problems come in with *our own* personal *understanding* or interpretation of our own religion and of other religions. For this reason, *religion* and *understanding* matter more to any family than most people will ever realize. This is especially true with your children as they form their long-term life opinions. Always keep the candy bar example in mind; meaning that they might not be understanding the various religions in the same way that you intend them to while you explain the various religions to them. In addition to that, any biases that you have will be readily received by them even if you intend those biases to be hidden or you believe that the biases are true or if you think you have no biases but actually do.

Eventually children grow and become adults (that's us) and we now carry the misinformation learned during our childhood. So, to make the point a bit sharper with regard to our interpretation not necessarily matching the Church's interpretation: how is it that two people from the same *religion* **and** *church* can have a debate about the meaning of anything within that church or religion? After all, aren't they both supposed to believe the same exact things about their own religion, church, and religious doctrine? If we all understood things equally, then we would all agree, and thus problems would seldom occur in our world. But this is not the case, and this issue affects all of us.

It's common for any two people within any given religion to have some disagreement about their religion's doctrine or Biblical interpretation. Not understanding things in the same exact way is normal. We are all subject to the possibility that *we* are not understanding something completely and properly as it was intended for it to be understood. Even in this book, where the point is to promote understanding, some readers may require hearing or reading parts of it several times before fully grasping the message the way it is intended to be understood. When we fail to put forth the effort to understand religion and its role in our families, we then become susceptible to believing the many inaccuracies that are hurled at us about "religion". These incorrect bits of information can be from us and from Church *leaders* or from Church *opponents*. Following these people causes us to believe the wrong things, and, in turn, believing the wrong things *will* hinder our families.

There are holes in our communications that are caused from everyone's lack of understanding; and these holes are extremely dangerous. Those holes are the single most important area of our life to try to master and eliminate in order to be able to have the robust life, family, and children with the strong foundation, that we are all born for. Seeing through the labels of religion will help us to avoid those holes.

Be Careful With How You Wield Your Religion

Religion starts at the family level, and it really **does** matter *what* and *how* you teach your children. If *all* of us would take the time to get to know and understand *other* religions properly, and, even more so, *our own religious doctrine*, then we would all live in a very different world today.

"Religion", in itself, is not the problem. It is our understanding of religion that causes many of our problems. An interesting part of people's understanding of the God-based religions is that each sect, group, or religion lays claim to salvation, so that you and your family can only be "saved" *if you* follow *their* doctrine and obey the commands of *their* church and leaders. This is an attitude that is held by many people regardless of what the actual doctrine says. This makes little sense because then it will only be a fairly small group of people who would have a *chance* to ever see salvation. Thus, if you do not believe what *they* believe, you are going to suffer the consequences of the fiery pits of hell! In the name of the salvation of mankind, past societies would go out to conquer other peoples and try to teach, or force on to others, what the conquerors believed "salvation" to be. Attempting to enlighten others is *not* a bad thing—unless it is done through force, rather than through truth. This also applies to your own family.

Forcefully imposing our views on other societies has brought about the following handful of major religions: The Jew, who is wrongly thought to be the original major religion, attempted to crush the followers of the Christ. Then after the death of the Christ the Catholics emerged. Then, several hundred years later, Mohammed was visited by the angel Gabriel to warn the Jews and Christians to behave. It is stated that Mohammed warned the Christians to disregard the trinity and was instructed to tell them that God has no partners, and that there is only one God (Muslims call "God" "Allah".) Then later, Martin Luther came along and was displeased that the Catholic leaders were *selling* salvation in order to pay for a fancy cathedral and cover other expense shortfalls of the Church. Luther believed that salvation only comes through accepting Christ.

Via Martin Luther's protestant rebellion, many other protestant (*Protest*-ant) religion sects were emboldened and sprang up. It is important to note that much of the customs of the Catholics, Mormons, Lutherans and other Protestant sects, and the Muslims are identical. And further, much of what they do and believe is identical to what the Jews believe, with the important exception of who the Christ actually was, is, or will be. To top that all off, the Muslims believe in the virgin birth and the importance of the Christ. An important thing to note here is that few people seem to know that the "Jewish" Torah (first five books) and Tanakh (The old testament) are the same as the old testament of the Christian Bible; and that the Koran (Quaran) mentions the Bible with a great deal of respect. In more recent centuries, religions such as Mormon and Jehovah's Witness have sprung up, and they also use the Bible as their primary or preliminary guide book.

Because of the *way* that we all understand, our choice of religion can be very damaging if we choose the wrong one. If you get involved in a peculiar cult that focuses on self-destruction, then it is likely that you and your children will suffer the consequences of that foolish decision. If we actually understood the word *religion* as the label that it is, then our world would be far more peaceful and safe. Few of us ever take the time to discover the actual truth about our own or other peoples' religions.

So how does all of this fit in with building a great foundation for your family? In a word—*Index*!

Index is the thing that you measure things with. Our religion is our measuring stick. We have a given set of ideas that we use to indicate good and bad behavior. Throwing our religion by the wayside removes that indexing measuring stick. We are then left trying to figure out what is right and what is wrong on our own. Though, to be truthful, there are very few of us who actually do not understand right and wrong on our own. It seems to be inherent in our human nature to understand right and wrong. If you have already had the opportunity to raise a child, you will recall times where your children had "the guilty look" because *they knew* that they did wrong even though not doing the particular thing was never specifically discussed with them.

Without a reference point in life, anyone can make up anything and call it true. *You* might not do this, but many others will do it, and do. When your children interact with the other people who *will* do it, and if your family has a weak foundation, then you *will* have to deal with the fallout that follows.

It's not religion that is the index of good and bad, but rather, your understanding of the doctrine and creed of that religion and its label—and *that* understanding is up to you. But further, it is the religions' interpretation of the Bible that we must all diligently observe, and ask ourselves, is the interpretation correct? For instance, when we take the time to look, then we can clearly see the purpose for the illustrations set forth in the Bible and the recounting of the historical events listed therein.

In truth, there very are few people mentioned in the Bible whose behavior we actually should emulate.

This does not make the Bible wrong or bad, but it does make it honest depending upon your understanding or interpretation of the Bible. Whether or not we choose to believe it, we cannot ignore the Bible with regard to our understanding. This is because the Bible, in the past and still now, has a deep and lasting impact on the entire world and on the way many people think and/or see the world and people. The Bible's influence and effects will continue for the remainder of your life and beyond, regardless of your opinion of it.

Other people's beliefs or non-beliefs regarding it *will* affect your family.

Your Religion is Your Choice

To begin to get a full grasp of religion and its effect upon our own families, we must all understand that religion is each our own responsibility. A belief is a belief no matter what that belief is.

One day, I was listening to someone discuss the roots of disbelief, or the "disbelief movement," and the person was hoping to impress the point that we can choose to have no belief and that we need not even consider any sort of God (or god) whatsoever. What he failed to realize, however, is that the thought of no belief is, in itself, a *belief*. A belief means to hold something dear or to love it— to exist in the perception that something is a certain way. So, if someone chooses to have no belief, then that is what they hold dear and therefore is their belief—it is their religion. By definition alone, it binds them to others who feel similarly, thus, it is a religion.

The creed you choose to follow is your own choice even though you were likely born into it. You can, at any point, decide that you are going to choose a different creed to follow. Regardless of the religion you choose, it is highly likely that you will *not* completely understand the religion's doctrine as it is stated in the doctrine itself. In fact, few people do fully understand such doctrine. Even two people who are proclaimed "experts" will disagree with each other within their own same religious sect. This is clearly demonstrated by all of the continuing divergence of the various protestant sects over the centuries. Where then does this leave those of us who do not have PhD's in religious doctrine when even the "experts" can't agree?

As families, we need not get caught up in any of the petty arguments of a religion in order to raise a great family with a strong foundation. In fact, *not* being a so-called "expert" is very much an advantage to us. The experts were told what to believe by their education and their perception of that education, which is where their blind-spot typically resides.

The rest of humanity has the option and luxury to be open-hearted and eager to understand what the *true* information actually is. While we don't need to get caught up in the petty arguments of the experts, we do need to make some choices about our own understanding of religion in general.

The first place to start in understanding religion well enough to make proper choices for ourselves and for our families is to root out our bitterness. Most of us have experienced arguments amongst ourselves about religion. The most entertaining is the various protestant groups' bitterness towards Catholic doctrine. The protestant sects hold a bitterness that was born into those religions at their root with Luther's well-placed and accurately focused anger and bitterness toward the Catholic Papacy and Clergy. It is not surprising that the bitterness still exists today, since the rebellion is *why* any protestant religions still exist to begin with; that is their doctrine—"Catholics are wrong!" While the *Universal* or "Catholic" church *did* need to be corrected on the issues of selling salvation, Luther's protestant bitterness seed has caused this world a great deal of unintended trouble even though Martin Luther clearly indicated that he did not intend or desire such *separation*. In brief, his intention was *correction*, but the social climate was prepared for *rebellion* that could not be stopped. This type of religious behavior is seen and felt in families throughout the world, especially throughout Europe and Eurasia. And it has affected your family regardless of whether or not you attend any church, regardless of if you believe, and regardless of if you care. It *has* affected your family, so it *does* matter.

Make Your Life a Whole Lot Easier

We need not agree with the assessment the experts have of our own religion. If the experts were correct, then nothing in the religion's belief system would change—*ever*. But since it *does* change, we can safely infer that someone may now be, will be in the future, or has been in the past, wrong at some point. Thus, changes are necessary, and thus, changes are made.

Changes are also being made *because* someone is steering the religion in a wrong direction. This is what caused Martin Luther's justified anger at the Catholic Church in the first place. The Church was moving in a direction of selling salvation, but salvation is something which cannot be bought or sold; and clearly, Luther understood that. This is why he attempted to persuade the Church to adjust its direction, and that problem has since been corrected.

So, do you need a religion that at its core has a belief in God? That choice is up to you, but *properly* believing in a Creator has proven to benefit many people in many ways.

Science and religion have been at odds for centuries about a Creator. Why is this? It is because of how we each understand our own religion and how we understand science. In addition, personal biases are also at stake. When it became obvious that the Earth moved around the Sun, rather than the Sun moving around the Earth, some in the "Church" did not want to hear the news, so those who were in charge suppressed the information and tried to make Galileo, who made those statements, recant. Why? Why would anyone not want to embrace this new, correct information?

It's because they understood things a certain way and did not want to make mental changes or admit to their own errors and be shown to have been wrong all along. Additionally, there were other financial risks of such information being known by the public. These risks were to their own status and the Church's status. So why then? It was their fear and their greed. If the reality is that the Earth moves around the Sun, then what good does it do for us to deny this fact?

All of this past turmoil has produced an education system that is outright hostile towards any religion that serves the God of Abraham. For most people reading this, your children will at some point attend a school that is likely funded in part by public tax funds. This means that the educators are limited in what they can teach, thus they cannot teach in an honest upright manner even if they want to.

Only personal motives of fear or greed will trip us up. We have no other reason to deny what is true. Make your life easier and follow what is true and teach your children the same.

You Judged Yourself

Often, we hear people pinning the blame on the Creator for our own shortcomings. For instance, "How could a 'loving God' destroy an entire city with fire and brimstone?" It's common for our children to become embittered towards religion when we hold such shortsighted perspectives. This area is a blind-spot for many people. In the Bible, the city was said to be so entirely corrupt and evil that it was not doing any good for anyone in the city or for anyone passing through it.

Taking the position of "How could a 'loving God' do that?" is a cop out. That is the sort of thing that people say when they refuse to make changes within their own lives. In other words, we want to be able to do whatever we want to do, regardless of how we hurt others *and* without any consequence to ourselves. We humans are self-righteous!

A belief is a belief, and the choices of which religious beliefs you are going to adopt are up to you and your family. As a matter of single-minded consistency however, recall your purpose for reading this book before making any decisions regarding religion—even minor religious belief changes. Gather, first, the information, and conclude later *after* the information is collected. Consider that the Creator may have destroyed the city to protect the innocent and as act of mercy in order to stop the violators from adding to their own errors with even more evil actions against the innocent, which would have resulted in bringing even more guilt upon their own heads.

What is true is true, and what is not true is not true. When you embrace what is true, then you are living righteously. When you embrace what is *not* true, then you are believing what is *not* true and you are living a lie. It is a choice, and it is yours alone to make. Will you believe the lies, or will you believe the truths?

You are not *forced* to believe any particular thing, nor am I asking you to believe any particular thing; that is your freewill choice and it is up to you to make the choice that you desire. However, use caution when deciding what you are going to believe, and know *all* of the information thoroughly before drawing your conclusions. All decisions made with less than all of the information have a tendency to be incorrect. And know this: your consistency in your choices of religion, when contrasted with your actions in your everyday life, matter. They carry considerable weight with regard to your children's life direction. You do not get to choose what is right and what is wrong, you only get to choose to agree with right or wrong.

What good will it do you or your family if you are believing anything that is not true? Man was not made with wings, so if you believe you can fly without an apparatus and you decide to jump from a roof, then will you be able to fly? If someone convinces you that you can fly, to the point where you actually believe it, then will you be able to defy the effects of what we call "gravity"?

Believing things that are wrong or that are a lie will not benefit us or our families, and when we choose to do so, we judge ourselves. For instance: If you believe you can step off the roof and fly, which I strongly advise against, and I tell you that you will plummet to the ground and injure yourself, then, am *I* responsible for *your* bad decision? No, against my wise counsel, you made the choice to proceed with your belief, and you will pay the price for doing so. The proof and truth will be shown in the result of your actions. If you are able to gain altitude and control your way in the air, then you believed rightly; but if you plummet to the ground, then you believed wrongly and you will find yourself injured and with many broken bones.

Teaching our children to blame the Creator, or the messenger, for our own shortcomings will *not* help them in life. In the example above, it was your decision, your action, and your stubbornness that allowed you to follow the belief that you could fly without an apparatus as you stepped off of the roof. You judged and punished yourself.

Rethink Your Long-Term Thinking If You Have It,
and
If You Don't have Long-Term Thinking, Then Start Now

When we choose wrong thinking and decide to jump off the roof, when wisely advised against such a foolish action, we are not thinking about the long-term ramifications of living with a crippled leg that was damaged from hitting the ground. Far too many of us are living *for* the moment, rather than living *in* the moment. We plan for today, but fail to see that what we do today will cause the troubles of our tomorrows. And when it comes to our long-term future, we don't even give it the slightest thought. What we do today *will* impact the rest of our lives to some extent.

People who have much joy in their lives plan life decades in advance, that is to say, they make choices today based upon the effects those choices will have later in life. Those who fail to look ahead and instead only see the current moment will, and do, suffer the consequences of their deliberate ignorance. If you follow a trend in clothing today, you can change those clothes tomorrow. But when you do something that permanently affects you or those around you, then you will pay for many years to come. *You* will suffer the consequences of your choices for a very long time.

For many people, this means that they will have to make many apologies in their future. For others, it means that they will have to live with the permanency of their actions till the end of their days. Consider the ramifications of getting in an alcohol-induced accident and being responsible for killing someone. That decision will not be fondly recalled, nor will the damage that we permanently do to our bodies when we follow foolish trends to alter or mark up our bodies.

Be careful of what you do today because it *will* affect your tomorrows. Live *in* the moment, but live *for* tomorrow and *for* decades to come. Religion is the defining point for many people in this regard. I assure you that your choices will be very different when you do so, and your future will be far, far brighter!

Defining Evil around You

What we *believe* is critical to us, and the way we choose to understand our religion has a heavy impact on our family even if we cannot see it.

The particular religion that we choose is far less important than the way we have chosen to understand that religion. Our understanding is directly connected to our deepest desires. We tend to make choices based upon what *we want* rather than what is true and therefore is good for us. If someone is a troublesome person, will it do us any good to deny that they are a troublesome person? It will not! The truth is that they are troublesome. The sooner we accept that truth, then the sooner we can make proper decisions when dealing with that person. The truth that they are troublesome is not good; what is good is our understanding, our internal admission, and our acceptance of the truth that they are troublesome to us and our families. That is where the good in truth resides, but all too often we fail to release our own arrogance and then sometimes we are the troublesome ones, but we blame others for our own shortcomings.

When you accept something that is not true, then you have placed a wedge between yourself and the Creator, and a wedge between you and joy. Doing so is either evil or it is an incredibly foolish action. And yet, most of us do this at various points throughout our lives. Anything that gets in between us and what is true is an evil thing, even when it is our own self—But this can be *easily* corrected!

If someone is troublesome to us and our family, and they influence us and/or our family to believe something that is not true, then that person is evil to us and our family—period! A person could actually believe, with every fiber of their being that what they say is correct and good, but if they are wrong then what they say has an evil nature about it. If we follow their erred influence, then we are following evil. This influence may lure someone to do something that may be harmful to themselves or others. When we know it is not good, but listen to the bad influence anyway, then we are believing a lie, and a lie cannot be true—Ever! The person who is influencing a family in a negative manner is trouble to that family. The family is better off without that person near their family. Depart from them!

Your Destruction by Divorce

Believing lies is the mother of all problems in our world and doing so leads to yours and your family's destruction. We are doubtful because we like to believe lies. When we believe lies, how can we be anything but a doubtful person? We simply cannot.

Arrogant people will believe lies and have enormous self-doubt from believing those lies, thus, leading to an even greater effort to cover their erred tracks by pretending, even more so, to be confident about their position. They see the self-confidence of those who believe what is true, as if the self-confident people are arrogant. That certain self-confidence is not arrogance, it is *confidence*. Confident people are *certain* because they choose what is true. The cornerstone book *Hot Water* goes in-depth on the topic.

Believing or understanding things wrongly leads us to many bad conclusions for our families, with the divorce statistic discussed earlier being one particular major problem area.

Young people who are in the process of mate selection are being told that they have a fifty percent chance of getting divorced. We are told by these statistics that our marriage is up to the flip of a coin. If that's the case, then we may as well flip a coin *beforehand* and not waste our time courting as we decide to approach our potential mate. Heads: it is eternal, and tails: it doesn't pay to even start! Interesting and ridiculous at the same time, isn't it?

Believing incorrectly-understood statistics influences our perspective. Biblically, we were to have only one spouse. Consider the trouble that it caused Abraham, Jacob, David, and Solomon because they all had children with more than one woman. Their actions had ramifications that still affect us today.

Remember, it is marriage that ends in divorce—not the people. As you may recall from a previous chapter, if you know someone who has been divorced three or four times, then statistically, you likely know several couples who will never divorce—*this point cannot be stressed enough*. If you associate only with people who consider divorce as a possibility in their relationships then it is very likely that nearly everyone you know will eventually get divorced. The opposite holds true as well.

If your family has divorce in it, then odds are that you will know a disproportionate amount of divorced people. It would be good if we could look to "religion" as being a point of stability in marriage, but the divorce rate does not seem much affected by those who tend to practice their religion.

Children desire stability, and they do not want discord or trouble within the perceived stability. A couple who is holding it together "for the sake of the children" is doing more harm to those children than can be imagined. Doing so is living in a lie and is an effort to make it appear to the children that all is well even though it is not. In their own way, the children see through this and come to know the cold relationship of their parents as "normal." Do not take this as an inference to get divorced; rather, take it as a sign that you need to make changes in how you, as a couple, participate in your relationship with each other.

Our children are not stupid. While they may not understand exactly what is happening in the hearts and minds of the parents, they are still seeing the distant interaction between their parents in that relationship. This is extremely damaging to the children, and it teaches them to seek that type of relationship for themselves. It is what they are familiar with, and, to them, *that* equates to "love." This coldness between the parents becomes as if it is a language to the children, and it becomes so deeply rooted in their hearts that they seldom recognize it as bad, if they recognize anything at all.

The lie that "all is well" is not true. Believing that all is well when it is not all well destroys the children's perception of what a good relationship is; thus, they will likely select a person who is not right for them and ultimately end up divorced themselves. This particular language of the heart spreads through the children like a virus, which in turn, creates similar suffering for your grandchildren. In somewhat rare occasions, some children seem to be immune from this and catch, see, and realize their parents' errors and remove those errors from their own lives.

People who are divorced have children who are much more likely to divorce. This is because divorce is familiar to the children. People who have relationships built upon lies and are holding it together for the sake of their children, also will likely see a higher than average divorce rate amongst their children.

When I point out that staying together for the sake of the children is a lie when the marriage is bad and cold, I am *not* indicating that the couple should separate. As discussed in the cornerstone book *Red Hot Marriage*, I believe that if a couple has a lackluster marriage which is cold and unfeeling, then divorce is the very last thing to consider. Any marriage *can* be healed and turned into a *Red Hot Marriage* when *both* people want it to be healed. The secret is in knowing what to do if you are struggling in your marriage and want to regain the joy that you *deserve*. Accepting the notion that in the Bible God made it okay to divorce, is a lie. Just because they were granted permission by Moses due to the hardness of their hearts, did not make it "okay". Do not deceive yourself about that fact.

While divorcing may appear to be better than fighting all the time, divorce destroys more than we like to admit to, and it is against most religious belief systems. Biblically, the people were collectively granted divorce because they refused to reconcile and were complaining to Moses. But divorce did not supersede the basics laid down in the Ten Commandments. Divorce is not a desirable path. Correcting our problems and reconciling is your best choice, and often can even end up creating a better relationship than you had when you and your spouse first met! Divorce is a primary language that far too many children have learned.

What is Enlightenment?

"Enlightenment" is another religion that is typically not thought of as a religion. Individuals are people, and people become mates. Mates have families, and the children of those families are people who are individuals—this circular reality affects us all. The religious choices and philosophies that people are exposed to throughout their lives will affect their lives and their families either for good or for bad.

Another potentially damaging area of religious philosophy is the "enlightenment movement." Since Westerners discovered "Eastern religion" and other means of so-called "enlightenment" we have heard the term enlightenment tossed about freely, but what is "enlightenment"?

To be "enlightened", do we need to sit with legs folded and eyes closed and hum? No, we do not! Depending upon your view of enlightenment, *religion* is an integral part of it, or possibly *religion* is not allowed at all.

The "free thinkers", of centuries past, are said to have been an enlightened group that was an extension of other long past philosophies. The free thinking movement was, and is now, a perversion of the word "free." Some people may have achieved free-thinking enlightenment, but, based upon much of their residual writings, they had beliefs that were largely closed minded. If at any point you have chosen to believe a lie, or are unwilling to hear opposing thought, then you are not free because you are bound by that lie or the stubbornness of refusing to hear new potentially true information. If you can be bound by one lie, then you can be bound by any lie anytime you are given a clever enough argument for you and your family to fall prey to.

There was a movement around the same period of the free-thinkers referred to as the "*Thought* Movement" and it focused on the mind and believed that *thought* produces waves and that these waves are powerful and will send out your mental power to obtain whatever you desire from the Universe. In other words, you can cause something to happen just by thinking it. It is not exactly the same as the telekinetic person attempting to move a pencil on a table, but it is close.

The *thought* movement had many good points about getting your thinking in the right place, which is why it was successful for a time. The movement still exists and likely will continue, but it is not quite as popular as it was in the early nineteen hundreds. The reason that thought-science philosophies work well for certain people, is because they have not been trying to do anything at all. Thought-science encourages action and denies negative thinking. People, who suddenly decide to actually apply themselves, usually achieve a great deal in a short period of time, compared to what they achieved prior to actually applying themselves. The positive thinking principles in the thought movement were stolen from the Bible, from the words of Christ, and from the instructions of the Creator. Then subsequently, the Bible was disregarded by many who adhered to the movement. Aside of any issues of "life hereafter", leading your children down these erred paths can have devastating effects on their lives when they are adults.

To believe that *you* are the power is an error and will bring you to ruin at some point, which is why the *thought* movement cannot seem to keep its hold on its followers for very long. In the meantime, you or your children will begin to fall if you follow these philosophies. Eventually the fraud is exposed. The thought-science movement seems to re-emerge every fifty years or so until it depletes itself. Then it goes into hibernation until a new unsuspecting generation of families comes of age to re-learn its lies that are whitewashed with a touch of truth, only to have many people experience failure, and ultimately reject the movement once again.

Some of the principles of positive thinking and thought-science are sound. Why? The people around us who may have succeeded by following some of these philosophies have somehow filtered out the bad information, and they have adhered to the good information in the philosophies that were taken from the Bible.

The Four Cornerstones of Your Foundation

When you're done reading this book I want you to have grasped a truth so simple and deep that your foundation is truly unshakable! By reading and accepting this family cornerstone you will create a foundation that cannot be knocked down by any lies or false religions. It is my goal to relay the information required for you to get your family placed firmly upon this foundation. But, you must want this for yourself and for your family. If you do not, then it *cannot* happen. Your only requirement is to want it and to be willing to do what it takes to get it done!

Since the success of everything we do depends upon our rock foundation (the earth part) plus the part of the foundation that *we* must build ourselves, there are a couple of things that you will find interesting and of tremendous importance. While *understanding* is the earth-bedrock part of our foundation, we still are each required to prepare it by building a level footing on the bedrock for our family. Failing to do so will cause the structure that is built upon our foundation to be faulty. With regard to *understanding*, the father in a family is intended to be the leveling part of the family foundation.

The word *father* is from the root *petra* (*Solid* or *rock* like in the word petrified.) In the Bible, The Christ gave one of the apostles a new name and called him Peter (Petra) because he said "You are the *rock* and on this rock I will build my Church." There are deeper explanations as to why those words share the same root, but for the purposes of this book just know that *father* and *rock* share the same root. Please research it for yourself if you want to know more.

There are four important cornerstones of a family foundation, and I have written a separate book for each of those cornerstones, bringing the key aspects of each to light. The first cornerstone for a strong family is yourself and understanding yourself; the name of that book is *Hot Water*. How you function and think is of vital importance to a strong family foundation. There is much information within the pages of *Hot Water* that is seldom realized or discussed by most people. The life changing information in *Hot Water* is useful for everyone, and clears away much of the fog that blinds us and causes most of our troubles.

The second cornerstone is your marriage. The name of the book which brings solutions to light for unraveling a difficult marriage is called *Red Hot Marriage*. *Red Hot Marriage* explains the simplistic details that are seldom heard regarding having a joyful and strong marriage. An honest marriage built with a true bond is critical for having a strong family.

The third cornerstone is proper parenting, which is the book you are currently reading, called *Strong Family*. The point of this book you know well by now and will know far better when you're done reading.

The fourth cornerstone is prayer. The book that discusses the subject of prayer is called *Understanding Prayer - Why Our Prayers Don't Work*. Often, we stop praying because we do not get our prayers granted, and we do not get our prayers granted because we do not understand prayer. This, in turn, causes many of us to be led down wrong paths. *Understanding Prayer - Why Our Prayers Don't Work* explains the beautiful innocent simplicity of prayer and how to make it work for you and your family.

These four books addressing the four cornerstones of your family foundation were written in the order just listed. The books have been written to be useful individually and do not need each other, but they are especially powerful when you have them all. If you started this book first, then complete it before reading the others. These books are all written in a linear manner and are best read from cover to cover. Doing it any other way may allow you to overlook critical information. *All* of the information in each book is critically important for those who desire to truly succeed in all aspects of life.

True *enlightenment* will not force you to hum in meditation, or believe some particular thing so that you can get what you want, it will not ask you to harm others, or ask you to find peace through sitting alone by yourself all day long. True enlightenment and practical use of your mind are free gifts that take zero effort and can be done instantly because they are a decision. The reason it takes so many pages to describe something that could be tidily summed up in a phrase is because of the mountains of lies and misinformation given to us by the world. When you read any of the four cornerstones addressing your foundation for a strong healthy family and life, you will quickly see beyond the things that blind most of us.

Right before your eyes you will see life rapidly change for you and your family. You will see your foundation form and you will feel its strength. Understanding all four cornerstones serves to clear away the problems in all other areas of your life as well. I am certain that you will benefit greatly from the truths discussed within their pages.

The core lessons in the cornerstone books are from the words that are found in the Bible that were spoken by the Creator and the Christ. We could assume the question: "Then why read the four cornerstone books?" The best way to understand this is to realize that the Bible has been available for centuries; and while we read it, we are still blinded by the many lies and much misinformation that we hear about it—people, marriages, and families *still* fail. We fail because of inaccurate interpretation caused by not understanding the sometimes mysterious passages in the Bible. Reading the four cornerstone books takes the information that is critical to having a strong family, self, marriage, and life, and assembles it in a concise manner in order to help people in most areas of their lives. Understanding these cornerstones will make reading the Bible far more interesting and useful to you if you should so choose to read it. If you struggle in any of these areas then you will find your days brighter and more beautiful when you *properly* place your cornerstones, regardless of whether or not you have read any books.

Chapter 4

The Way We Understand

Since the *way* we understand things is core to our understanding, *understanding* cannot be stressed enough. You will find that when you understand things in a *true* manner, most apprehension and fears are wiped away, and then you will live a very joy-filled and robust life.

What is "Understanding?"

What exactly is understanding? In its simplest description, understanding is the ability to grasp the truth about something.

Understanding is the rock foundation that everything we do is to be built upon. When we do not understand, we live in confusion, thus causing us to make decisions based upon our confusion. You would think that to understand *understanding* would be a simple thing to teach to others, but it is not.

Understanding what understanding actually is, is amongst the most difficult of concepts to teach to others, even though it is one of the basest and most simple concepts that exists.

The reason that we have a difficult time understanding things is because we believe lies and misinformation—and we love to do so! Once we buy into one lie or wrong information, then everything else we do is built upon that lie. From birth on we are lied to, and the thing that makes it difficult to escape the lies, is that the lies are usually *not* deliberate. Our parents were given incorrect information, just as they gave us incorrect information, and *we* are doing it to our own children. We all learn to believe lies through the education that is the result of the examples we experience in life, examples which are all too often built upon lies and misinformation. Now is the time to change this in *your* family.

I understand that this appears to be a cynical view, but it's true. Please note, I did not say that everything is a lie; I said that we have been trained to *believe* and even embrace lies. This has been going on since the Creation of humans, and has continued ever since, up until today for *you* because you are reading this book and now understand much more clearly.

To "*understand*," you **must** have a desire to want what is best for *everyone*, and you must choose that you will not accept anything less! If you do not have that approach, then you will *never* have the ability to understand anything fully. When we choose understanding, then everything begins to be more exciting!

Do You Know Why You Know What You Know?

The problem with understanding is that people often *think* that they understand because they have chosen to *believe* the lies told to them. Once you have chosen lies, you become blind to things that are not lies and therefore you are incapable of simple deep understanding.

The best way to begin to *understand* is to know *why* you know what you know. You may need to think on that phrase for a bit.

We might think that we understand something, but if we cannot freely explain all of the details that led us to our understanding, then we do not understand it very well.

We have all seen people questioned about something, and then when the questions get beyond their scope of understanding, they become angry, obnoxious, territorial, or they shut down and withdraw all together. Such behavior is clear evidence of their lack of understanding on the subject. A person who truly wants to understand something will embrace those questions and learn from them.

Knowing **why** you know what you know is to *understand* understanding. The critical importance of this cannot be understated. Each of the books mentioned earlier discussing the four cornerstones of a sound foundation all discuss the need to *understand* the details of their respective cornerstone.

You will find a great deal of comfort in knowing *why* you know something. When you achieve this simple, but evasive, state of mind, then your problems will quickly vanish or become insignificant to you. And any future problems become as nothing more than minor inconveniences to you.

Know **why** you know what you "know"

Others Do Not See Things as You Do

Not knowing why you know what you know is why we think others see things as we see things. When we do not know *why* we know what we know, then we are subject to lies and/or misinformation.

If you don't know *why* you believe what you believe, then if someone can persuade you to believe something else with their clever emphatic arguments, you will, in fact, do so. This means that given the right argument, you are susceptible to believing *anything*. If what you are persuaded to believe is not true, then you won't be able to detect incorrect information because you do not know why you believe the things that you do, other than that *who* you chose to respect or see as an "authority" told you the "information" you are choosing to believe. This is the very reason that two "scholars" from the same creed can disagree on their religious doctrine, or two big bang scientists that happen to *not* believe in God can disagree about the method of creation of the Universe. We often think that we know the *why* about a something that we are using as a foundation of our understanding, but we then fail to know the *why* for the **why** part of our initial *why*. Asking why about the *why* is like when a child keeps asking "why?" every time you answer their question. In their innocent nature, they are drilling down to get to the simplistic core of why we do what we do—They want to *understand*! As children, it is natural and instinctive for us to want to understand. If you observe a child, you will likely notice that if something does not make sense to them then they will typically tune out. But if they begin to see how the information can come together, then they become intrigued with the subject. It's no different for us adults.

When we have a wrong understanding that what we believe is true—then we typically have a blind assumption that everyone else will see things in the same way that we see them. In fact, seldom will we ever even think to question the possibility that others might not see something in the same way as we do.

We typically assume that everyone sees something as we do because we have closed off all other possibilities about the topic in our own minds, usually without our own realization. In doing so, we make the unaware assumption that there is only one possible answer and that the proper answer is the one that *we* have chosen to believe. Thus, in our minds, there is only one answer and we blindly assume everyone sees that same answer as we do. This seems good, right? After all, we are *certain* that our way is **the** way.

Well, this might be a good thing, except that often we cannot explain our understanding. In other words, we *do not* know *why* we know what we know.

Blind understanding is by far the most dangerous or risky way to understand anything, and when that understanding is a mere *belief* it sometimes can be deadly! Take, as an example, the various religious groups who have harmed others in the quest to further their own agenda over the past several thousand years. These groups have killed in the name of their belief; yet, *their interpretation* of what they had based their belief upon was often inaccurate in many ways. This means that other people have likely died for those lies and/or errors of interpretation.

So what does all of this have to do with raising children? We think others see things as we do. This is a real problem when raising children because we are blind to the fact that our children might not understand things as we are understanding those same things. This means that we are not explaining things adequately in order for the particular child to properly understand us.

The divide between two people's understandings causes the other person to whom something is being explained, to be able to bring their own thoughts to a completely different conclusion than our thoughts have arrived at. If you happen to be correct, but still do not know why you know what you know, then *you* might come out of it alright, but your children can perceive an utterly different perspective, and thus, go in a very different and potentially bad or dangerous direction in life.

It is important to know that if you know why you know what you know, then you will be able to better and more quickly see that others *are not* understanding something as it was intended to be understood.

> We all have the capacity to **know why we know what we know**, so let's all do it!

When speaking of knowing why we know what we know, we are not speaking of opinion, or your opinion, about the facts, but rather we are speaking of your understanding of the actual truthful facts.

Are You an Original?

Knowing why you know what you know is the primary function of being an original, being unique, or being different. There is a certain entertainment value in listening to people who are being "different" for the sake of being different. The irony is that, in so doing, we are *copying someone* who indirectly suggested to us that we should be "different." To better illustrate this, simply consider the proliferation of permanent body markings and piercings that occurred during the last decade of the twentieth century and at the beginning of the twenty-first century. In being "different," they were copying and thus are not different at all, but rather were cheap imitations of someone else. This sad phenomenon was particularly common in the sports and entertainment industries. And once the followers had marked up their bodies, they all looked the same, with sort of a dark, indiscernible uncomely hue to their skin, which speaks to the importance of long-term thinking discussed in the last section.

Be an original! Don't be a cheap imitation of others. You are a perfect imitation of your Creator and, since your Creator has no bounds, *you* will always be a unique person; but, this is only true when *you* choose to live to be "in the image of your Creator." The cornerstone book *Hot Water* discusses this in-depth and it will be very beneficial for you to understand if you want to build a strong self along with strong children. The big secret to all of the life cornerstone books that are mentioned throughout is that they expose the many lies that we often allow ourselves to believe. Exposing these common but often overlooked lies is what makes the four cornerstone books unique.

It is important to note that lies can be proven to be lies and true things can be proven to be true, but false things can **not** ever be *proven* true, and true things can **not** ever to be *proven* false. It is only when we do not understand, that we become able to be deceived with lies by someone "proving" something true or false when it is not.

If a false thing is proven true in your eyes, then you have believed a lie. If you do this at all, then you have allowed people to repeatedly be able to tell you that false things are true and you will likely believe them nearly every time. I believe in everyone and that all people can rise to this task and complete it perfectly once they have dismissed the lies and those lies' subsequent doubt. When this is accomplished, your full robust creativity will pour forth out of you and you will excel in your life! You will be an original and you will contribute your individual and wonderful gifts to the world. However, until you have embraced *understanding*, you are going to be held hostage by any lies that you have chosen to believe and you will likely be a cheap copy of someone who you unwisely idolize. The moment that the lies are removed from your mind, the beautiful, real, and true you will quickly emerge. Teaching this to your children is important and is most easily done by your example.

When you live a life that is built on believing any lies, you doom yourself, your children, and all subsequent generations of your offspring to the same troubled fate that you currently suffer from. Living in lies makes seeing the light far more difficult for your descendants, unless *you* have made *you* an example of how *not* to live. Yet, even then, your children are likely to follow the errors that made, and still make, your life so difficult. But when you choose to understand, then everything changes and becomes easier to handle. Your days become brighter and the lies become obvious. Your family benefits, you benefit, and the world benefits. Give your descendants a head start so that they do not have to fight the battle unprepared.

How Their Identity is Built

Our children's memories of us and other people's memories of us are all that will be left of us on this Earth after we depart—with or without a God. When we fail in *understanding* and in raising our children, then we have failed our lifetime, which is that duration of time that we breathe on this Earth and are subject to death. The things that will be considered when weighing our work on this Earth, are building children that have a strong foundation, our own intentions, and the way we treated people during our lifetime. If we accept the notion that there is a life after this life, then the end is obvious to us and we know what needs to be done. However, even if we choose to not understand that there is a realm after this life of breath, then let us at least create a legacy of goodness so that people's memories of us are happy, rather than miserable.

Children are people, and their perception of themselves (their *Hot Water*) determines their future. When we know how to build ourselves, then we can begin to truly help others. Grasping the depth of our own *hot water* (*why* we are the way we are) is pivotal in order to be able to *deliberately* pass your understanding on to your children in a way that *they* will understand properly. This book, *Strong Family,* will be of great value to your family, but if *you* are broken inside, it's going to be a much more difficult struggle for you to create a strong family.

Often we are told by the books, teachers, preachers, and speakers of the world that we should build our children's self-esteem by complimenting them and telling them that they are good. This is certainly something that should be done, rather than telling them that they are worthless. Still, with all of this good advice, why then do so many of us struggle in our hearts and minds as we go through life?

Some of the people who have been complimented by their parents throughout their entire life have become arrogant. How could all of that wise advice to always tell our children that they are good, special, and worthy have failed? The advice fails because parents missed the point. Telling our children that they did well may be somewhat better than discouraging them and telling them that they're worthless, but there is something far better, and that is being honest with them and kind to them. If you don't fully grasp this, then use the following example for reference:

If we have a child who is about two years old and they draw a stick figure, roughly representing a person, then it is good to tell them "Very good work!" and praise them for their two year old efforts. Then years later, if they do the same thing when they are ten and we shower them with praise for making the same stick figure, similar in quality to what they did when they were two, then we have lied to them and have failed them.

Telling someone that they did a good job and praising them when they actually did *not* do a good job, is not helpful to them— *honesty* is helpful to them. This does **not** mean that we will tell the ten year old who drew the two-year-old-level stick figure that it is "worthless," but we should show them ways to make the drawing a bit more dimensional, by actually *showing* and *explaining* to them *how* to do so.

If we set an index for our children built upon lies for the sake of false praise to them, then we are setting them up for failure throughout their entire lifetime. This does not do them or yourself any good, except that you might make them feel good for that moment, but they will feel the ill effects of your lie later in their lives.

To make children feel good the rest of their life, be politely honest and *teach* them well. Don't let your children *always* win; instead teach them how to win through their own true passionate efforts and through fair and honest play. Sure, you'll sometimes let your little ones win to teach them that winning is possible, but realize that as they grow and learn, that your praise should be proportional to their understanding and age abilities. Not doing so will prop them up with lies; and living a life built on lies is not a strong foundation. If you yourself have not experienced this problem in your own life growing up, you likely know someone close to you who has. The goal is to teach them so well that someday they exceed *you*, their teacher.

Too Many Rules

To sum up everything said here—**be honest with your children**. We often read books or listen to speakers who have a litany of things that we must do in order to make our lives better. In general these lists are okay, and often the items on the list assist you in your life.

Walking through the checkouts of most grocery stores, we encounter a multitude of magazines, and even books, with "Seven ways to do this" and "Ten ways to do that." All of the items on these lists are, in general, helpful for people, though some things are downright dangerous. But regardless, as indicated in the articles, they are all *rules* that *must* be followed in order to hopefully achieve the end result of "happiness".

I have witnessed many people who have become bogged down in all of these rules, as if there is a set of things that will make us acceptable and therefore happy. When we seek these informational rules, we are asking to be told what to do. People who want to be told what to do tend to require too many rules and will often demand compliance of the many rules from others. All of this is because we do not understand the original and underlying reason for the rules that we seek.

Having too many rules causes confusion and error. For instance, take a look at some of the legislation presented by government officials. I don't think the quantity and complexity of those rules can be adequately described. In fact, it often takes a rulebook and many high-priced lawyers just to describe and interpret the rules, and at that they still argue in the courts about the "meaning" of the rules. Some of these laws can be many hundreds of pages long.

When the Israelites left Egypt they were missing the simple point of personal responsibility, causing them to both need and request additional rules. Over time, they ended up with several hundred rules beyond the Ten Commandments. Ever since then we have been arguing and fighting about those rules, and subsequently writing the debates into legalistic volumes of texts, most of which do little more than interpret the simple and original Ten Commandments.

There is but one rule, and that rule is to always seek the Truth! When you know why you know what you know, then your life will be a tremendously valuable example to your children. *Your* example is what they *will* automatically model their lives after. When you understand this, then you will need to remember fewer rules because most things become obvious to you. When you teach this basic method to your children through your example, then you have taught them more than you could ever imagine!

Chapter 5

Understanding Truth

The previous chapters show obvious bias in favor of the Bible and a God. Understanding the purpose of those chapters is what we must focus on here.

Some of the principles taught by the *Thought Movement* and the *Free Thinkers* are principles that were extracted from the Bible. However, the subject of whether or not "God" exists is a bit different, and we will examine that issue and its connection with your family a couple of chapters from now. I have a firm belief that, in regard to the existence of God, we should be able to state our case without saying, "Because the Bible told me so!" Using the Bible as "proof" for there being a God makes us subservient to our own and other people's sometimes inaccurate interpretation of the Bible. Additionally, as explained in the book series *The Science of God*, when relying solely on the Bible as evidence of God we are subject to the interpretation of those who translated the text throughout the years.

Error in interpretation of the term "truth" is an area of trouble for people when tightly woven cults become a part of their life. Cults focus on the word *truth*, but then distort the word's underlying meaning. The primary importance of understanding truth is to understand the definition of "truth" as what *is*. Not the subject of the "**is**", but rather, the concept of "**is**" itself; this is what true freedom is. It's difficult to express truth because there are no other lower levels or words to describe this fundamental concept. Thus, we end up saying statements that are so utterly simple, like those above, that they almost seem confusing, which is due to the fact that we are more accustomed to obscure and overly complex concepts. But it is simple—Truth is what *is*!

When we allow anyone to redefine *truth* to us, in any manner, then we have lost our freedom. Truth is self-evaluation with utter openness and willingness to face *all* of the facts, and then to fully and honestly consider that information without bias—even if it means that we were previously wrong. This should never be mistaken for thinking that we must tell the entire world *all* of our own mistakes. Our openness and willingness to face all facts, applies to anyone in a particular conversation.

An example of redefining truth is in cult-type groups, where if a leader of a group cannot be scrutinized by its members, then something is probably not true—someone is hiding something. Any discussion without full consideration of *all* points regarding the topic of discussion follows this dishonest pattern. Certainly some things in everyone's life are meant to be private, but if someone follows you for a reason, then those areas of the reasons people follow should be open for re-consideration and further scrutiny.

This is where your ability to understand *understanding* becomes very important. When we are incapable of stating why we believe what we believe, then we have **blind-faith**. Understanding truth is another very simple concept, which at the start would seem to be a simple concept to teach, but it is not. Understanding what *truth* is, is at least as difficult to grasp as it is to get people to understand *understanding*. Truth is a point of light that is so *base* that there is nothing more we can do to simplify it. Truth is about as simple as it gets!

When a liar can get you to doubt truth, then you and your family are susceptible to believing *anything* that the liar wants you to believe. Some of it may have been inadvert, but the free-thinking movement, and the thought movement of recent centuries, sought to undermine truth. A common phrase is "That is *your*

truth." To which I say, there is only one truth; not two, not three—
just one! Anything or anyone telling you otherwise is a lie or a liar.
If you are whipped and crucified then you will bleed! Trying to
believe you can have *your* own version of "truth" that you will not
bleed is a lie. The underlying essence of the words *truth* and *true*
are the same; this point is very important to understand when
speaking of true faith.

Have True Faith

What is true faith? To understand, first we have to define
"*true*", and then we have to define "*faith*." Since we discussed truth
in the last section, here we will ask what "*faith*" is. Faith's root word
is "*fidelity*" or "*trust*." This means that "*true faith*" is *true trust*, but
trust and *true* have the same root as *truth*. *Trust, truth*, and *true*
are different usages of the same concept, and *faith* shares that
concept. We will discuss the dangerous effect that improper faith
has on your family in the next chapter, and reveal the root of so
many family problems. It might seem a bit academic to have a need
to understand these words, but it is much simpler (deeper or more
base), and far more important than mere academics.

Their Freewill

How do you teach your children truth, and still allow them to
make their own decisions with their own freewill? To start with,
you do it through you being their example and model for them for
their lives. Balancing Truth and freewill is a monumental task for
most people.

Your example to your children is, by far, the most impactful
and powerful way your children will ever learn! When a child sees
an inconsistency in you, then they learn that inconsistency as a way
to behave, and they will most certainly repeat your example in their
own lives. As parents, we typically do not want to have our children
make the same mistakes that we made. We often become angry
with them when they make our same mistakes. But many parents
crush the "freewill" of their children in order to stop them from
making those same mistakes. This often happens in a dictatorial

manner with the parents forbidding their children to partake in behavior that results in those mistakes.

In general, there is a level of guidance that children require, but the level of guidance needed is largely determined by *our* actions and examples. The word "*free*" is often perverted; and, in doing so, "*free*" is thought of as being able to think any way we want to think. The only problem is that if you choose to believe a lie, then you are no longer free. With freewill it is no different, freewill works the same; if you do things and act on what is *not* true, then you have lost your freewill—you are held in chains by the lie you have chosen to believe and live by.

If a child is expressing their freewill and they want to defy our instruction, the chance that they are copying our examples is usually quite high.

If we tell our child not to do something because it might harm them, and we then proceed to take part in the harmful activity that we told them not to do, we have shown them to live a lie. We have trapped them in our lie—we are their example! Later on, if they follow our example and we tell them not to do so, then we are being inconsistent—but they are only exercising their own freewill! Right?

Is it really freewill when we teach them to lie through our own inconsistent actions, and then tell them not to live a certain way, which they happen to see *us* living? In doing so, we teach them lies and rob them of their true freewill. The all-too-common *addictive* habits are one small way we do this.

Freewill is **not** doing whatever we want. Freewill is the free right to choose only what is true. When we choose a lie then our choice immediately strips us of our freewill at the very moment we have chosen the lie. At the very instance of our decision of believing a lie we have forfeited our freewill. Placing this burden on our children is humanity's biggest offense. True freewill *cannot* exist without truth.

Don't Pretend to Believe

We'll get further into what true-faith is later, but for now, let's *prepare* to attack the subject. Good people are key to our family's peace, and good families are key to our world's peace. Whether you like it or not, religion plays an enormous role in that.

Your religion, or "*faith*" as it is often called, is examined by your children every second of every day. Many of us have our chosen religion or faith, and we either attend church or we do not. Additionally, we make proclamations, minor or major, about our beliefs. A classic example would be a Christian saying "I would never get an abortion, but I don't want anyone telling me what to do, so I won't tell anyone else what to do."

Our dissection of that statement does not speak for or against abortion, but rather speaks to the contradiction within the statement. Making abortion illegal is **not** forcing anyone in what they can or cannot do. Even if the penalty for abortion was death, the choice is still up to the person *choosing* to get the abortion.

Making someone get an abortion by forcibly taking them to an abortion clinic, or going into the clinic and grabbing the pregnant girl by force and dragging her out against her will before the procedure is started, are both infringements of the girl's freedom. Only scenarios using force to achieve or force to restrain are what will infringe on the girl's rights with regard to abortion. Just because the law of the land says something is or is not legal has no bearing on whether or not someone can or will do it. The difference comes in society's willingness to tolerate such actions.

Pretending to believe something creates a great deal of contradiction in our words and actions. If a girl chooses to remove a live fetus from her womb, that is up to her. But you choosing the position that *you* would never get one, yet do not want to tell *her* what to do because you don't want *her* to tell *you* what to do, is living in contradiction. This contradiction is made evident by the way you vote for your elected officials. If you are against abortion personally, but then go on to vote for elected officials who you suspect will place abortion-supporting judges on the Supreme Court, then you are being inconsistent in your life. The same would be true if the situation were entirely reversed.

It is important not to get hung up on the subject of the example here. What we are discussing is not abortion, but rather, the inconsistent nature of our thinking regarding the subject. There is an important point about abortion to be made here and it is that abortion is a minority belief, meaning that there are more people that are opposed to it than support it. But, abortion persists because too many of us have bought into the "I don't want anyone telling me what to do, so I won't tell anyone else what to do" sentiment. It is each our own choice how we will conduct life, but here you must ask yourself: If someone was going to irreparably harm you, then would you want someone with the power to step in and stop the person from harming you to do so, even if, by law, it was okay for them to harm you?

To have a baby or to have an abortion is the business of the persons involved. Even if all elements of the entire scenario was reversed the thinking is still contradictory. Abortion harms and therefore is an offense to those who it harms. Asking all of the citizens of a nation to condone abortion is a distortion of what is good. Having an abortion is the *choice* of each woman whether or not it is legal. To force the rest of the people to legally agree and pay for any part of the sexual errors of others is essentially a form of terrorism due to the fact that if we refuse to pay taxes, because we disagree with legalized abortion, we will be terrorized by our own government through fines and/or being imprisoned.

When we display these subtle contradictions to our children what can we expect? Should we expect them to be able to make quick and solid decisions? No, not likely. If we teach them to waiver, then waiver they shall. Removing legislation that makes abortions legal does not dictate what the other person can or cannot do. Unless we are forcibly stopping someone from doing so, we have not infringed on their "right" to choose. Our *actions* and *words* should match if we want to have our children receive the right message(s) from us. This is not about the route you choose, but rather it's about the consistency with which you approach a particular subject. Often, we go overboard and move from rejecting an idea of those who hold opposing views, and we jump into hatred of *them* rather than hatred of their *views*—hating them is *not* our goal. We can utterly reject an idea and still *not* hate those who hold fast to the foolish idea that we reject and abhor.

Our religion works the same way: Many will say that they believe in God and they will even go to Church, but then all other actions in their lives run contrary to that. This inconsistency is seen and duly noted by our children, and then emulated by them.

Be consistent and be honest! We may not be perfect, but we can at least try to correct our own errors and inconsistencies when we spot them so that we can move closer to truth. Doing so creates a more joyful you and a more joyful family!

Truth is Good Character

Good character is something that we look for in people but have a difficult time finding. Too many of us are wrapped up in our own contradictions to be able to offer good character to our children and others. If you are a business owner who has tried to hire employees, then you likely will be familiar with the character problem often found, or lacking, in some employees.

What is good character? Many will look at it as dependability when the person always shows up for work on time and gets their work done promptly. However, is that really good character? I would call that *dependable*. Dependability is a desirable quality to have and exhibit.

The term "character" is not a term that is very specific, so its meaning is subject to the perspective of others, unlike truth whose meaning is constant. Truth is a very specific term and allows no alteration, it is one thing and one thing only; this is undeniably true, though, some will try to assign other meanings to the term **Truth**. The term *character*, on the other hand, can more easily have a handful of variations in definition.

When you have truth, you automatically have character as we typically define the word *character*, but when you have character, as we typically define it, you do not necessarily have truth. Being true in everything that you do is the singular pivotal point that will make having a strong family and guiding them in the right direction nearly effortless.

The Importance of Order

Order in your family is critical for a strong family. Your goal within all of the words written here in this chapter, and throughout the entire book, must be to understand what truth **is**. This free thing that we call *truth* is not tangible; meaning, truth is something that we cannot touch. We often have a difficult time grasping truth and how to determine it. This **Truth** of which we have been speaking will bring about a tremendous amount of order in your life. It will clear your mind and the minds of everyone in your family once it is understood and fully embraced.

The order that truth brings about in you and in your family's life is unparalleled in beauty, but this is something that you will need to experience first-hand in order to fully grasp it. Once you experience truth you will never go back to where you once were, nor will you want to.

The importance of the resulting order that truth will bring into everything you do cannot be understated. People who are successful have a certain type of order in their lives. Then other people work to achieve a similar appearance of order and experience success with it, but their problem is that they do not control their own lives. However, *you will* be in control of your own life once you have grasped what we are discussing here.

Order is a concept that is often difficult for people to grasp because many have not experienced it the way they should have. Anything out of order will not function as it is designed to function. This applies to ourselves, our families, and our checkbooks.

There is typically order in numbers such as, two plus two equals four. If your life is in *disorder*, then two plus two can appear to equal five to you. For many of us, this seems good; in other words, "If I cheat and lie then I will have more, so I will keep telling myself that two and two is five." While we all understand this simplistic math example to be an illogical, untrue, and a ridiculous perspective, our ability to discern order becomes far more hazy when it is not something that we can see as clearly as we see basic math.

Order can be many things, but in truth it is all one. Law and order, the order of rule in numbers, and even the organizational methods used in your kitchen cabinets are all the same. All of these share a method of index or rule. Imagine the chaos that would ensue in our world if two and two suddenly became five, or changed randomly. Our economy would look much more the way many of our garages, attics, and basements look—chaotic.

Order is dependable. Order can be relied upon. The Universe is highly ordered. Interestingly, the physicists refer to this order as the "laws" of physics. As an example: If gravity did not behave similarly in all cases, then getting to the moon would likely never have occurred.

Similarly, a checkbook with errors will often cause problems, resulting in you not being able to buy something you want. Having disorder in your checkbook is the same as believing two and two equals five. (Depositing two-hundred dollars and then another two-hundred dollars will *never* equal five-hundred dollars in your check book.) Leaving *empty* containers in your fridge or cupboards will have a similar deceptive effect on your household food inventory.

There is *nothing* that this basic model of order cannot be applied to.

> Where there is chaos,
> order does *not* exist.
>
> All chaos will eventually be
> painfully forced back into order.

What is true *is* in order, and what *is not* true is out of order and is chaotic. Chaos can only be created by our free will and it will eventually be brought into submission, usually with much pain to us.

We could debate about what "chaos" means regarding our checkbook example, but that would be futile. Because, while it is true that you may have neat and *orderly* penmanship when writing in your checkbook, your numbers may still be out of *order*.

Where there is chaos, there is no order; thus, neat looking numbers might have good order in their form, but the error in the value of those numbers is chaos in the mathematics. It is up to you what you want to call it, *rule* or *truth*, but to deny that order is the basis of good, traps you in a dangerous cycle of trouble, causing you to repeat the same errors over and over that you have been experiencing for so long that cause you and those around you so much pain. This same concept applies to *everything* that you do!

Dependability in the Absence of Truth

Truth without Order does not exist for any part of life or existence. If your checkbook numbers are not ordered in their math, then it is impossible to depend upon them for anything near accurate.

We often scoff at a one cent error, but are frightened with a one hundred dollar error that is not in our favor that we have made in our checkbook. To a computer programmer, those errors are the same. An error is an error. In programming, if it is off a penny, then it may as well be off a million dollars because it means that the programmer has made an error that will not be acceptable to the users of the program.

Imagine how difficult it would be if your checking account balances did not add up as the numbers are expected to. If you did your addition properly, but the bank's balance was in error due to a programming problem, you would get in contact with your bank promptly, and the responsible programmer would quickly feel the pains of his or her oversight of the problem.

The programmer could be the nicest person in the world and could be trying really hard to do a great job, but *trying* to do a great job will not make an error go away. Only *correcting* the source problem will remove the error. Even if the programmer person shows up for work twenty-five minutes early every day and works diligently all day long and stays late, if *their attitude* is that the error is of little consequence, then, will that help your account balance problems? I assure you that it will not.

Character of dependability without truth has little value. Yet people are still *perceived* to have "character" even when they have little or no true character. This inaccurate perception occurs only because they reliably show up for work. In our world, character flaws are typically hidden by money or prestige. The example just given illustrates how the illusion of good character permits people of little character to be allowed their own self-delusion of actually having character.

Sadly, those who interact with people of little character often embrace that illusion and imagine that the person has character. If the programmer is a kind person who goes about wearing expensive designer clothes and driving expensive cars, then people will often perceive this person as "a person of character." Little do they know that *he* or *she* was the person responsible for the pain they felt from the computer generated errors in their own bank account that caused them to be charged hefty overdraft fees.

Truth matters, and character matters! Without the character that truth brings, you *will* lack "character."

Importance of Accountability

If a programmer has no accountability, then they wouldn't have any need to correct their errors. When a person has no character that is exactly what happens.

Accountability is very important for your children to understand, and *you* are the one to teach accountability to them. Programmers are among the most accurate people you will meet— if they are *true* programmers. Very good programmers will not allow errors in their work. Programming is a good example to use to show how the order of another person's life and work can dramatically, and *remotely*, affect *your* life. Teaching accountability is nearly impossible without order. If all of us have no order in our lives, then what exactly is it that we are to be accountable for? Parents who are not enforcing accountability in the family and in their own lives can *expect* many problems with their children as the children grow and mature.

A simple and quick lesson for accountability is teenage children and sex. If you have not taught your child, or if you fail to do so, with regard to the accountability of premarital sex, then your children will have little thought of it and will likely proceed to recklessly partake in premarital sex. This lack of order will likely cause them great difficulty and will likely result in an undesired pregnancy and often leads to disease, abortion, a single mother, or an unhappy marriage, and even death—and possibly all of the mentioned effects. Some people do make it through and live happily-ever-after, however, those who do make it had a good relationship beforehand, and very likely, at least one, or possibly both spouses, had reasonably well adjusted families.

If young adults truly understood *accountability* while dating, then there would be far less sex occurring on dates. This would greatly reduce unexpected and/or unwanted pregnancies and would result in a tremendous reduction in the abortion and divorce rates.

Accountability works similarly to the numbers in your checkbook. If you allow errors in your addition, then you are likely to have problems when making purchases. If a person is not accountable for their actions, eventually their errors will catch up with them. With young adults and sex, the result is undesired pregnancies, and with your checkbook, it is a rejected payment. When we allow disorder, we are rejecting what is true and the result is chaos! The chaos is the corrective order of truth and you will feel the pain of that correction.

Bringing truth into your life will always bring accountability into your life, and accountability will bring more order, and order will bring more peace.

Be prepared for people who have been benefiting from your lack of order up until this point, because often they will fight against your choice of seeking only truth. They will do this until they finally realize that your mind is firmly set, and that your life is different now, where **you** control your life rather than **them** controlling your life. It is probable that they will lash out in a jealous rage because they are no longer able to affect you and control you in the same way they had in the past. Truth has the effect, for people who reject truth by believing lies and/or misinformation, of causing them to react maliciously.

Your Life's Map

Your life's map is not complete, and it will not be complete until long after your death. Everything in your past, and even your parents' past, is all a part of this map. With regard to the four cornerstone books, your life's map could be considered a visual of your *Hot Water.* Your *Hot Water* is everything that made you who you are, and most importantly, it is your own perception of that.

Few people understand their life's map, or even take the time to reflect upon it, if they even realize that it exists at all. Your life's map includes everything that you have done and thought. It also includes *your perception* of everything that your parents have done.

Understanding that you have a life-map in your head is an important point to grasp. Think of it like a map you might use to travel with. If you do not realize the map is there then you will not look for it.

A map does not tell you what to do; rather, it is much like a ruler or a measuring stick. A map is an index that shows your current position relative to your past and to your possible future positions.

Know Where You Have Been

Your life's map has your entire past on it; you must know and understand this truth in order to move ahead smoothly in your life. Once you understand that your map exists within your head, then you're more clearly able to understand everywhere that you have traveled on that map, and, whether those things or places in life were good or bad for you. Knowing where you have been allows for reflection and its subsequent comparison against where you are today.

Comparison of your past experiences is critical in your life. If we do not use comparison we will experience a great deal of trouble in our lives. Our sight uses comparison with variations of light. Our bodies use comparison with regard to hot and cold. Our minds use comparison with regard to our past life experiences of pain versus joy. Those old or past experiences are your life's map and they should be compared to your current life experiences.

It is good to not dwell on bad experiences because they will certainly distract your future, but forgetting them all together is like being lost and then throwing away your roadmap—***Know*** where you have been and avoid re-entering the bad areas!

Knowing where you have been shows you where you were, thus allowing you to know where you currently are.

Know Where You Are

If you ignore your past errors then you cannot know or understand where you have been, and you will wander aimlessly as you move forward. However, when you acknowledge your past errors and know where you have been, then you will have a good index of where you currently are in relationship to where you have been. This is critical in order for you to know where you are going. Without knowing where you are, you are likely to repeat your past errors by going back to where you have been. To better illustrate this, consider the following example:

Knowing where you are can only be done when you have created the map showing where you have been. One could think of it in terms of a large blank sheet of paper. And where you currently are is a dot in the center of the paper with drawings showing where you have been. Without your past on that paper you will not understand where you currently are in relation to your life. Knowing where you have been is the printing on parts of the paper, and the printing of your past is your index to understanding where you are—it is your map. Once you have established where you have been, which started with a dot on a *blank* paper when you were born, you can know where you are now.

If you are unable to determine where you are on your map, then it is highly likely that your perception of your past is wrong or missing. To add to this principle, you should also understand that just outside of the borders of your own map are your parents' maps. Your parents had the same sort of blank paper at their own birth. Their paper will connect to your paper as did their parents' paper connect to theirs. As your map is drawn you will begin to connect your map to theirs and you will begin to understand where they have been on their maps as well. Their map is a part of your familiar life (your *hot water*), and you need to understand this in order to have some indication of where you have come from so that you can avoid their errors.

Facing your life in a truthful way shows you where you are on your life's map. Believing things that are not true will cloud your perception of your location on your map *if* you can find yourself at all. Not facing your past in an honest manner can be thought of in terms of traveling through Mexico with only a map of Spain to look at. Clearly, a map of Spain will be of little use when traveling through Mexico. If your current location is in Mexico, then your current position could not be shown on the map of Spain that you have in your hands. Your current location would be on a map of Mexico, which you *do not* have in your possession. You will not know where you are and you will not know where you are headed when you are using the wrong map. Make sure that you are honest about *your own* life's map, and that you have the map for **your own** life in *your own* mind.

Often we use other people's maps to navigate through our own life with regard to our own life's map. While that can be helpful to steer clear of cliffs and can even be useful to know approximately where something is, it is your own life's map that matters most to you and will best guide you to your most successful and joyous life.

Knowing where you are in life is the only thing that truly matters in your life regarding moving forward. Many of us wrongly see this in a competitive nature and are always looking at the maps of others, trying to beat them or be greater than them. This is not good or useful to you or your family. As a family, knowing where you are is your index to where you are going, which is an important key to a joyful family life.

Where Are You Going?

To know where you are going, you must be honest with yourself and your family, which means to be *truthful* with yourself and your family. Make sure that your past is clearly laid out, and that you know exactly where you have been and exactly where you currently are. Do not try to *be* other people or be like other people. Being like other people and using their map only makes you an imitation of them and their family.

We must all be true to ourselves and each look at our own life's map and locate where we were and where we are now. Then, and only then, can we have a joyful future in knowing where we are going. Without doing so, your *happiness* is left only to chance—it is a roll of the dice!

The root word of *happiness* is *hap* and it means by *chance*, where on the other hand when we have *true joy* it is a deliberate and intentional state. People who experience true joy understand where they have been, they know where they are, and they understand where they want to go.

Please do not misunderstand this: Merely having your life's map laid out in your mind and knowing where you are does *not* guarantee your future joy. However, without doing so, you are guaranteed that joy in your life and family will be fleeting, at best. Your past is written on your life's map, and what you do today is the pen that is creating your map. But you get to imagine, plan, and sketch out the blank page before you in any way you desire. Plan your future map well so that whenever you look back you do so without regrets.

The joy in your family is based on a constantly honest life. Not having an accurate map, whether unintentional or deliberate, is not a *true* map. When your life's map is not true you *will* experience undesired and unneeded strife.

Those who want joy in their family life need to have an accurate perception of their *past*—which is their life's map. We must understand where on that map we currently are; only then will we be able to accurately choose where we want to go, and more importantly, *actually get there*.

For our purposes here, your *past* means from any current moment of life, backward, to include all of your existence. It also includes the effects that the past existence of your friends and family had on your life, including those who are now gone. So, if your past and your family's past are not accurately perceived by you and your family, then your trip into the future will most certainly be unpredictable and include undesired results, causing *you* to unnecessarily repeat the errors of your parents and their parents. Utilize the mistakes of others as lessons for yourself of things to detour around and avoid while you are alive, which is one of the key points of the Bible.

If your parents made many mistakes, you *are not* required to repeat those errors! In fact, if you choose to repeat their errors, then you have to admit that you are being rather foolish if you are aware that they made the errors.

When you use any map that is not your own you will be aiming for Mexico with a map for Spain and end up on the cold dark continent of Antarctica. Your map *will* connect with other people's maps, but it is *your own* map that you must focus on. Understanding that there are connections between your own map and other people's maps allows you to better understand and focus on your own map. It's okay to look for detours due to damaged and dangerous roads on other people's maps, but *their* way home is not *your* way home. Honesty and/or truth in your perception is your key! It is a choice—a choice that only *you* can make.

What Does It Mean to Forgive?

Truth *is*—what *is*. To sum up the big picture of this book, if we claim something to be so, that is actually **not** so, then it is a lie! Thus, we are a lie along with it. We can easily change this by questioning all of the things that don't make sense to us. But as adults, we have the same problem that young children do; when something doesn't make sense to us, we tune out. So when society, or our elders and authorities, tell us things that are incorrect or are outright lies, we either follow in their footsteps or we tune out and don't want to deal with it. When we do this, we never get down to the truth of the matter, causing us to become believers of lies, or worse, we become complacent.

Forgiveness goes hand-in-hand with truth. The meaning of the word *forgive*, or **fore-give**, is to pre-give or to give in advance. When we forgive someone, including ourself, then we have, in advance, released the person of their offenses. We are so accustomed to the lies on which we build our lives that we have become blind to those lies. We have become accustomed to the problems that those lies bring to us, to our family, and to our lives.

Releasing a person of their offenses is an issue of trust. As mentioned earlier, trust, true, and truth are all the same. This means that once the person who has been offended has decided to release the offender of their offense, then that forgiveness is no longer up to the person who is actually doing the forgiving; rather, the completion of the forgiveness cycle is now up to the offender.

If someone has offended you, then they have offended your trust in them and they have, therefore, violated you. If that person comes to you with a true confession, offering an apology, then you will recognize the truth in their confession and the truth in their apology, and you *will* accept the apology if you have *truly* forgiven them.

But, in truth, they were *already* forgiven by you; so then, the choice to be forgiven was always within *them*. It is technically impossible to fully "forgive" someone if they have not come upon the realization of their own errors and offenses against others. The forgiver is only waiting for the violator to realize the error and confess it to them with sincere apology and then *no longer violate*. The forgiveness part was already done by the forgiver, in advance; and in most cases, well before the offenses ever took place.

Often, we miss this following point completely: to better illustrate, let us assume that a person in your life has repeatedly offended you and you have become bitter towards them. Then one day something happens to this person and they finally come to the realization that they have been offending you and are very sorry for doing so. They then come to you with a tearful and heartfelt apology, and subsequently cease any further offenses against you. After their full and proper confession and apology, if you will *not* ever trust them after they have clearly stopped offending you, then you have *not* forgiven them.

Alternately, *when you **have** forgiven* someone and hope that they will change their ways, then you will be waiting with eager anticipation for them to change and you will be filled with joy when that true apologetic confession and change occurs in them—you will embrace their change and welcome it!

We do not need to confess all of our errors or mistakes to everyone, but we do need to confess those things that we have done to those who we have harmed or wrongfully offended. In doing so, we show them that we now understand that we have wrongfully violated them, and we are explaining to them that we have come upon the realization of exactly what we did wrong; and further, that we will no longer offend them. Confessing, ceasing, and correcting errors or violations allows the forgiveness transaction to be completed.

When it is our own self that we are confessing to, then *everything* must be confessed to ourself when it is remembered. This process can take years as each error is eventually recalled by us or revealed to us. Our offenses against others are an even greater violation against our own self than they are against those who we have violated.

Forgiveness has two sides: One side is that forgiveness is done *in advance and in hope and in anticipation* of true awareness occurring within the heart and mind of the violating person about their own behavior—the violator who will at some point realize that they have been offending others. Forgiveness is up to each of one us to do.

The other side is up to the offending person in the scenario. If a violating person refuses to change their ways, then they have chosen to *not* be forgiven. At some point our patience will become worn thin and we will eventually ask the repeat offender to depart from us, but this does not mean that we haven't forgiven them. We must dispel the notion that we resent or have not forgiven a person who chooses to continue to violate other people or ourselves.

If someone in your life chooses to be unforgivable and they strip you of the ability to forgive them by their continuous violations against you, then it's okay to distance yourself from that person. Not only is it okay, but it is wise with regard to protecting your husband or wife and children. Biblically, we were told to depart from evil. It is an incorrect notion that we are all supposed to simply accept other people's bad behavior by being "tolerant" of the behavior. This ridiculous notion goes against almost everything we are instructed about in the Bible and is usually promoted by the people or person practicing the offending behavior. Recall how The Christ overturned the money changers' tables in the Temple. And when The Christ was hanging on the cross, one person being crucified with him mocked him, but the other asked for forgiveness and was subsequently told he would meet The Christ in paradise.

Exposing your children to someone who repeatedly offends but refuses to change, damages your children irreparably unless you and your family embrace truth. That exposure to negative behavior sets a very bad example for your children. There are many ill effects on your family when you allow such a relationship to continue. If you feel that this is unforgiving then you need only ask yourself one question: will you allow that person—the offender—back into your life if they have *proven* that they have truly changed?

If you will not ever allow them back into your life, then you have *not* forgiven them. But if they prove their change by their future actions, and you *are willing* to accept them back into your life when that change occurs, then *you have forgiven them.*

Understand that just because you have finally seen the light about your offending ways, does not mean that those who you have hurt and offended will want to be around you. They can have forgiven you, but they are not required to socialize with you.

When a person violates you they have broken trust with you. They have shown themselves to be false and not true. It is the violation of truth, which we have been discussing, that we do not like—it is an offense to us. A good friend who betrays you has violated truth between you and them, provided that you are in truth yourself.

The two-ended action of truth, forgiveness, and repentance of error, applies to you whether you are the offend**er** or the offend**ed**. Both sides also apply to you yourself. In other words, *you* must forgive yourself for the violations you have committed against others *and* against yourself.

We all have to remember that forgiveness has two elements: first, *in advance before they violate you,* you have to forgive someone for their errors. And second, the person who erred must realize and admit that they did wrong and then cease from continuing in that error. When that's done, the transaction of forgiveness only needs the acceptance of the apology, which is often shown by us accepting the forgiven person and allowing them in or near our life.

Most of us have a problem when it comes to forgiving *ourselves.* If we cannot forgive ourselves it is unlikely that we will ever admit to, see, or realize our own errors and offenses against ourselves.

When we live in truth, then we have no lies in us, but if we live our life and our family's life built upon what is not true, then we will offend our own self. If we are not living by what is true, then we will generally be unforgiving. This puts us in a dangerous position personally, because when we lie, we offend ourself and often close our eyes to our self-offenses, giving us the appearance that we are doing no wrong, or that we have forgiven ourself for our errors.

When we build our lives on lies, we find it difficult to forgive, and then we offend even more. When we do this to ourselves, we become trapped in our lack of truth. When someone is living their life built or founded on things that are not true, it will produce bitterness in that person. This is why truth is so utterly important in your life and in your family's life. Truth is all that you need, the rest follows on its own.

If you do not have a life built on truth, then you will not be able to forgive, and you will not be forgivable. This applies to others as well as to yourself; but with yourself, it causes a real personal problem for you. The bitterness that resides within our own hearts due to our lack of truth causes us to be competitive and jealous, or better stated, covetous!

You cannot *forgive* without embracing truth, and you cannot *be forgiven* without embracing truth. Lying to yourself and believing something, that is actually a lie, to be true, will not make it true. Truth is true, it is what *is*!

Truth is often associated with God; however, when speaking of truth we need not even discuss the issue of the existence of the Creator—the truth about this reveals itself to you when you accept truth. The beautiful simplicity of truth is all that is needed in order to know such things. Truth proves itself to be truth, and that creates our index to see that untrue things are untrue.

Do not be deceived if someone is using the word "truth" when what they are using it for is not true. Weigh their ideas in your own mind on the balance scale of truth.

To expose a liar or a person who is not accurate, we merely need to look at their methods. A liar will deceive and steal in order to further their lie by attacking the root of someone's understanding, and then they will call that root their own.

When the word truth is tossed around and mixed with lies it deceives many of us. When this happens, we feel that something is amiss and tend to believe the lie because they stole the root of truth from us. It is then perverted by adding lies, and calling it their own. All lies and misinformation work this same way, and the balance scale of truth is the only thing that can prove truth and make the lie apparent to you. This is fundamental to *everything* in life, including the way in which you teach your family. Truth is a concept so basic that it is its own judge. I cannot judge it, and you cannot judge it— Truth can only judge itself. Truth is self-correcting and always exposes lies or things that are not true.

True forgiveness requires truth, and without truth you cannot forgive or be forgiven. Without truth, your life and your family's life *will* experience much strife and pain. As stated earlier, we have become so accustomed to the lies on which we build our lives that we have become blind to those lies and we have become accustomed to the problems that those lies bring to us. This occurs to a point where we mostly do not recognize truth.

Promoting Yours and Your Children's Creativity

Truth promotes creativity. When we live a life built on things that are not true, then we become competitive in order to build ourselves up. This is because we believe that we are of lower value. This ushers in competition and arrogance that then distracts us from our true creativity and inhibits our ability to realize that this is happening. When we are competitive, we are trying to be like, or be better than, someone else. Being better than someone usually involves you trying to do what they do, better than they do it—in essence you are copying them. It's okay to do the things others do, but to simply copy them and then to attempt to excel beyond them so that you believe that are above them traps you in self-arrogance. This causes us to lose our true uniqueness and steals away our own true creativity. We lose this creativity when we believe things that are not true, and doing so inhibits your family and your children.

Forcing your children to believe in God is not going to make them creative, nor is teaching them that there is no god. Over the centuries, various people have tried to prove that there is no Creator and have built some seemingly compelling cases regarding such. Their arguments do not prove their theories true, nor does the Bible prove the Creator true. Truth is the only thing that can prove either case to be true or to be incorrect; and truth is the only thing that can prove the Bible accurate or inaccurate.

What is, *is*—and what is not, *is not*. Believing anything but that, is simply *not*, therefore it is wrong and does not exist. Understanding truth is a choice. This is difficult for many of us to grasp because our lives have been built upon a foundation that is anything but true. For some time now, science has "proven" that "there is no god" and that "we have descended from apes or primates;" but, has this been fully weighed on the scale of *Truth*?

Too often we want to know the truth *about* something, but in all of that is discussed here we are referring to truth itself and not the subject of the truth. For example: If someone says something "that is not true", the *truth* we speak of here is not referring to whether *what* they said was true or not; but rather, we are referring to the *concept* of truth itself—the *is* part. When we fail to grasp what truth is we render ourselves incapable of discerning what is true.

Chapter 6

The Faith of a Child

What is true—is true. Truth is so simple and base that it cannot be refined any further; yet, we must teach truth to our children. Since so few of us were taught the method of seeking truth, a rare few of us are able to properly teach the method of truth to our children. We generally, "Tell it like it is" with regard to our children, and we tell them "There is a God, and He made us all and the whole world" and we might add "and don't argue with me because *that's just how it is!*"

If Mommy and Daddy tell the little children that there is a God, then those children will generally accept that and will not question it unless they are given reason to doubt. "*The Faith of a Child* is an admirable thing, or so it would seem. After all, The Christ said "Unless you have received the kingdom like these children," referring to the faith of the children—but, do *we* really understand this "faith?"

Do You Have Blind Faith?

Blind faith is both foolish and dangerous! Does this make The Christ's statement about having faith like a child wrong? Think about that question for a moment.

First, let's look at *blind* faith: Is *blind* faith bad or good? If I say to you that there is a God, and He made the Sun and the Moon and you accept that because *I said so,* then you have blind faith.

From a very early age, many of us have been told that God exists and is mysterious and we cannot understand God, and therefore we must accept God as presented. In other words, this is how it is "because *I said so*," or, in this case, because "the Bible told me so."

But, what if the Bible is wrong? Or, the more likely scenario, what if *our understanding* of the Bible is wrong? Then what of our blind faith?

Blind faith is the scourge of mankind! Blind faith has created all of the religions in the form which they now exist. If these religions, and those of us who practice them, were true throughout, then they and their doctrine would never change—*ever!* And all religions would agree. But, since change within religion is frequent and there is contention between doctrinal interpretation of the various religions, we can understand that our understanding of "religion" is not based upon absolute truth.

While the Bible may or may not be wrong, it is true that most major religions are widely based upon the Old Testament of the Bible. Often we are told that the Bible is just "stories", and because *we* do not use due diligence in processing this idea when we are told that it is just stories, we lose our ability to know and believe that it is accurate information. Families fail, not because of lack of religion, but rather, from lack of the Creator. Being able to know that the Bible is a compilation of accurate historical accounts is very important to a strong family. It is not so much the details within the book, but rather our lack of certainty that there is a Creator—a lack of certainty which is caused by our misunderstanding of the book.

Let us understand the Bible, first as an account of history, rather than the "inerrant word of God." Certainly the "Word" of God is inerrant, but is the Bible the actual "Word" of God? Some things in the Bible are difficult to prove true or to prove false, but many tangible things mentioned in the Bible are still standing today as remnants of the historical accounts listed in the Bible. Because things in life often change, many of the places' names in the Bible have been altered to an unrecognizable state—*unless* you understand what to look for. Many places mentioned in the Bible have also been conquered by invaders who have laid claim to the area and changed the area or city name since the Biblical accounts were written. Over the centuries this may have occurred several times to any one particular area.

The changes in names and borders make some of the Bible's proof cloudy to most people and even most "scholars" in our contemporary times. Translations of the Bible are somewhat phonetic, thus, due to dialect we have lost the essence of some of the names. So even if the place still existed we would not necessarily recognize it by name. Yet there are many things in the Bible that can still be clearly seen today. Since archeology has become so popular in relatively recent times, there is a regular progression of ancient artifacts being found that support the historical accounts that are listed in the Bible. To deny this is to deny that what they find is truly before your eyes. This does not make the Bible true in the sense that the Bible is the origin of these findings. After all, the Bible could have been written long afterwards and included all of these places, things, and the accounts of events.

But let's look a bit further: Are there other historical documents that would testify to the Bible's account of events? The answer to that is most definitely yes! While we cannot say that every event in the Bible is also documented by other sources, there certainly are similar documents from other peoples whom the Bible mentions, that give their accounts of similar or parallel historical events. But this does not prove the Bible true in *all* accounts. Evidence of the Bible's historical accuracy is greatly aided by people attempting to disprove it, as well as by archeologists with hope of verifying its historical accounts. There is much buried evidence supporting the Bible being unearthed on a fairly regular basis.

Taking the position that the Bible is a bunch of "stories" that are only fabrications is choosing to be deliberately ignorant. Many of the historical accounts in the Bible are as provable as accounts of Napoleon or Washington. We have no actual photographs of those people and the paintings may not be accurate. We could dig up their graves and find their decayed bodies; but then, can we prove that those bodies are actually Napoleon or Washington? Or that the people depicted in the paintings are them? The answer is no. Unless *you* actually witnessed their death, burial, and exhumation you would not be able to know for certain. At some point we must accept written accounts of history, but with questions being allowed to be asked.

Understanding that the Bible is a good historical account of events is a wise thing to do, but understanding this particular point is up to you alone. Since history is not always recorded accurately, we can make the assumption that there could be errors in the Bible, or that the interpreter's or translator's understanding could be in error. But just because the accounts are possibly imperfect, does not mean that the Bible is altogether wrong. There would be a great deal less bickering in our world if this simple fact was understood by everyone. It's actually good that some people try to disprove the Bible because it tends to keep the rest of the people in check by challenging their sometimes erred conclusions of the meaning of what is written in the Bible. If something cannot stand the test of scrutiny then we must question its validity.

Blind faith to accept the Bible as it has been **presented to you** is both foolish and dangerous. Why do I say this? Because few people have actually ever read the Bible from cover to cover, yet most people who *believe*, accept what we are told about it. This means that our perception of the Bible is through the eyes of someone else. This *blind faith* approach to this particular book, the Bible, is the cause of much doubt and many lies. Read it for yourself and then draw *your own* conclusions based upon the text *you* read and upon the archeological findings that have been accruing on a regular basis—findings that support the historical accounts listed within the text. Do your best to not be the type of person who *thinks* that they "have read the Bible" when they never even completed reading Genesis—and please take note that "children's Bibles" do not count for adults in this regard.

Prepare to Be Led Astray

If you live in danger by accepting blind faith, then your children will have that same blind faith also, causing them to be led astray along with you. Getting back to what The Christ said about having faith like a child, we must understand what was meant in that statement.

To understand the meaning of "faith like a child" we must understand that to have faith is to be true, but it was not the "faith" that was being brought to attention in the statement "unless you have received the kingdom like these children." What The Christ was bringing attention to was the *manner* of the faith. It is the strength or level of faith that is important in the statement. The meaning of the statement is that you must not doubt—***at all***!

The reason that we doubt is because we were trained to live our lives built upon lies. Since a great number of us have our lives built upon lies, we experience disappointment on a regular basis. This disappointment results in our doubting of things that we have been told are true but are really not true; this has been occurring for a very long time. When someone lies to us and we believe their lies, then we are immediately trapped in our doubt because we only vaguely can see the error. We can't realize or see this error clearly because we have chosen to accept the lies.

Due to our own believing of lies, we doubt, and then we become trapped and find it difficult to believe anything at all. The Christ's statement "Unless you have received the kingdom like these little ones" does not indicate that we should believe everything that we are told. It means that ***when*** we know the truth, then we should not doubt the truth—yet we doubt the truth all the time!

It seems that we have a tendency to be more willing to believe a lie that falsely claims it will help us, than we are willing to believe the truth about a situation. When you know the truth and do not doubt, then you will be at peace and no one will be able to lead you astray. If you teach this truth to your children, no one will be able to lead them astray either.

The reason that the debate of evolution versus Creation exists today, is that everyone has an agenda and they will do anything and create or believe any lie to further their own agenda; this includes both evolutionists *and* creationists.

Merely saying "My geological column *proves* the age of the Earth," or saying "My Bible says it is so", is not enough evidence to accurately make the claims that each side of that argument makes. If we interpret the "geological column" or the Bible *incorrectly*, then we are wrong. If the rest of us follow other people's speculations based only upon *their* interpretations, then we too will often be wrong.

The only things that we need to doubt are things that are not true. Doubting something that is true is both foolish and a waste of our time, but it is okay to check and verify. Looking for proof does not constitute doubt. In fact, looking for proof is quite the opposite; doing so means you are certain enough that you know you will find evidence of that truth. If you're an honest person, you won't taint your findings with geological or religious blind faith or ignorance of other facts.

Being led astray, with regard to evolution, has had an enormous impact on our faith due to our blind faith. If someone can destroy the credibility of the Bible in your eyes, then it is far easier for them to offer you a replacement set of explanations that will cause contradictions within your thinking and reasoning. Any contradiction that you allow to remain in your thinking and reasoning becomes habitual and negatively affects your family. Contradictions need to be filtered out using the method of *truth*.

Anticipation

Anticipation is one of the handfuls of joys that we have in life; but without truth, our anticipation is mostly tainted by our acceptance of what is not true. Thus, we have negative anticipation from accepting what is not true, which is the root of unhappiness, commonly resulting in suspicion, depression, and indecision. Too often we anticipate bad things, rather than good things.

There is a point where each person must make a decision. Accepting that you are Created as truth, and accepting the *truth* that you were Created for, *immediately* wipes away almost all negative anticipation in your life. You might still need to deal with a few of the un-pleasantries that your past errors have brought to you, but doing so becomes effortless once you have embraced truth. When we do not understand why we are here, and then go on to accept lies or other wrong information, we then end up making our decisions based upon that incorrect information. This typically does not end well—and it *will* affect your family.

Alternately, positive anticipation comes from reward, and in general this is good. We often have anticipation of promises, but when those promises are not kept we become disappointed. And in the case of promises, it means that someone was not true to their promise. It is generally not the fact that the promise was not kept; but rather, it is the fact that a particular person who we were working with violated *our expectation* of *them*.

Little of what we do has anything to do with the inanimate objects that we utilize. Our whole existence is based on our interaction with other *human beings* who *can* choose. It is not the lie that we are bothered by, rather it is the fact that a *particular person* lied to *us*. This is why we often tolerate lies in business, because we had not yet developed a deep trust in the person or company who violated us. While it is still a concern and is wrong, business lies generally do not affect us in a deeply personal way. However, the situation is quite different with family and close friends because we chose to trust them in a very deep and personal way. Trust is something that we can rely on, where with a business we have not yet built that level of personal trust so their business advertising lies are of little consequence to us.

Having *blind* faith allows us to believe in something only to find out later that it is not true. I call this "*The Santa Claus Effect*".

What is The Santa Claus Effect?

I suspect that you are already clued in as to where this section is going. When we tell children about Santa Claus and that this fat and jolly person comes and delivers toys to all of the good little girls and boys all over the world, we are setting children up for "*The Santa Claus Effect*".

It is called "*The Santa Claus Effect*" because it is a very common tradition that touches a sizeable portion of the population of the world, and because Santa Claus is an excellent, simple, and obvious example of what we do to, both, our own selves and to our children.

For the people in all of the societies where this tradition is common, we boldly tell our children that a jolly fat man comes and brings gifts from his workshop that is built in an extremely cold place on the Earth that has only water and ice beneath it. Our children, being born in truth, do not suspect that the two people who they love, admire, and trust more than anyone in the entire world would actually lie to them.

Young children are inherently honest; and thus, they will blurt things out that they are thinking—and often it's much to Mommy's and Daddy's displeasure. They say things like "Mommy, why did you say she has a big butt?"

Understanding *The Santa Claus Effect* helps you to understand where your children are coming from and how much damage you can do when you practice the Santa Claus hoax in other parts of their lives.

We will discuss the serious issues arising because of the Santa Claus Effect more in-depth later; but for now, understand that our children generally believe what we tell and show them regardless of whether or not it is true. And regardless of whether or not we *intended* to show or tell them what they have actually seen or heard from us, they still see and hear it.

The Dangers of Not Understanding

Since we discussed *understanding* quite a bit, and the importance of doing so, it is my duty to point out the dangers if you as a parent do not understand *The Santa Claus Effect.*

If you are a parent who plays the Santa Claus game for your children in other areas of life, then it will cost both you and them dearly in the long run. Anything that is not truth is a lie—big lies, little white lies, and everything in between, they are all lies and all result in the same outcome—personal chaos.

Somewhere in your life, there will be a price to pay for promoting things that are not true. The cost to you may vary, and often it may be only a small cost, but you *can* be confident that there *is* a cost to you and to your children when you deceive them.

When someone lies to us we begin to lose our trust in them and everything they say. Let us not confuse this with someone deliberately trying to trip us up to cause us to misstep, thus causing us to not be able to keep our word. In the case of someone deliberately trying to trip us up, typically we are fighting their offense against us. However, when we choose to believe the lies of others, then *we* trip *ourselves* up.

Our true intent is what is going to matter in the end. In fact, when someone is true in all other areas of their life, but falls short in one area, we will typically keep trusting them repeatedly. We do this because we feel a trust in them; thus, we are more tolerant of those times when they let us down. But, given enough repetitions of their erred behavior, eventually we learn that we cannot trust them any longer.

Similarly, when you use The Santa Claus tactics on your children in other areas of their life, they eventually will not *entirely* trust you *or* what you tell them. Their lack of trust for you is good in this case, because you are, in fact, lying to them. When this practice becomes normal in your life, it hurts you later on when you are actually trying to tell them the *truth* about something else. This occurs because they have become cynical due to *The Santa Claus Effect.*

Do You Create Cynicism?

When we repeatedly lie to our children we cause them to be *cynical.* Look up the root for *cynical* on your own; but in general, *cynicism* is not a good thing.

Cynics like to blame others where no blame is due. When you lie to your children, no matter how small the lie, you are building a cynic brick by brick and lie by lie. Eventually this will catch up with you and with your children.

When we lie to our children we give them sound reason to blame *us* for *their* shortcomings—and we deserve it! When we are honest and kind to our children, then *their* chosen behavior is on *their* own shoulders when they reach the age of being able to reason. But because we are all born to trust—their perception of their lying parents skews their perception of what is true; from this they learn to blame where no blame is due.

It is important to separate blame from—exposing lies by telling the truth. Exposing lies can appear as blame, but it's not blame. We don't need to specifically expose lies; we only need to speak the truth and the lies become obvious in light of truth.

When the truth is known and accepted, then the lie will become apparent and quickly fail because it becomes exposed when it tries to stand against truth. Any lie that tries to stand against truth *will* be defeated. When we say things that are in truth, then that comparison exposes the lies, causing the person who is doing the lying to attack whoever presented the truth. In an effort to hide their own errors, the person who is lying typically unjustly blames or accuses the person speaking the truth. We see this often during unjust political protests.

A lie is like paint or whitewash, it covers what is really underneath—it conceals! The words *conceal*, *hide*, and *hell* all have a similar meaning and root. When you live in lies, then, in many ways, you have bound yourself and you are experiencing hell. Blaming others for our own errors or hiding those errors has deep, lasting, negative effects on our family and, specifically, on our children. Our children become like us! Truth or lies—it's your choice.

It's Not Just Santa Claus

The Santa Claus Effect touches many parts of our lives. If we use the Santa Claus tactics in one area of our life, then the likelihood that we use it in other parts of our life is very high.

Most parents lie to their children in a multitude of ways. Our deliberate lies are obvious and we know that we are doing so when we are doing it. Living a lie by doing things, such as working at a *permanent* job that you hate, is similar to *The Santa Claus Effect*, but with a dissatisfying job you are not speaking the lie—you are living it. When we do this sort of thing, we are slowly teaching our children that it's okay to live this way. They will likely repeat our error and live a mundane, dissatisfying, and often troubled life, and they won't know why.

To sum up *The Santa Claus Effect* with regard to "the faith of a child": We destroy the truth that our children were born with and we teach them to believe lies through our outright actions and our outright deceptions; this causes them to doubt *us* because we have betrayed them. When they doubt us, then they will doubt everything that we have told them. This occurs when any contrary proposal comes their way, provided that it seems logical to their well-conditioned, *Santa-Claus-Effect* affected minds.

Chapter 7

Celebrating Joy

Joy is an important part of having a great family; without joy we live dismal, lackluster lives that will only have random moments of happiness. When this is the case, it means that we are not in control of our situation, and, as a result, the happiness that occurs in our lives is purely by chance. Joy is the long-term result of truth, and anything else that is not a result of truth and appears joyful is the result of chance. Chanced joy, technically, is *happiness.* Anger, cynicism, and frustration are all a result from the same source—they all come from non-truth.

For most people, the majority of what makes us feel good that we experience in our lives is *happiness,* rather than *joy.* Joy is deliberate and comes *after* you have established your life in truth. Joy is something that should be celebrated, and it is something that you should take a great deal of pleasure in when experiencing it. The joy of truth is our fundamental purpose here in this life, and it is what we were designed for.

It's important to understand that joy is the result of truth; and also remember that anger, which is caused by frustration, is the result of non-truth—or lack of truth. Even if the non-truth that surrounds you is someone else's offense against you, it still causes *you* problems when you allow it in your life.

When we become angry, we tend to get *very* angry and we celebrate that anger through yelling and screaming. We typically cut a person down to show them that we are angry by not allowing them to rationalize or justify their behavior. Because of the way humanity embraces things that are not true, we deserve anger, and we unwittingly work for anger for that very reason.

When it comes to joy, often we **do not** celebrate it, partly due to our cynicism, partly due to our training, and partly due to other people's dissatisfaction towards *our* joy.

Oh, If We Only Could be as Joyful as We are Angry...

Think about this: when we get angry and we show our anger, we are telling the person that we're mad and upset about something that they did. This is often accompanied by our shouting and screaming at them or the situation. When we do this, we are celebrating our frustration and anger. In this way, we give life to it when we show our frustration to everyone.

Did you ever experience someone asking, "What the hell are you so happy about?" while you're walking around with a smile on your face? When you're angry, very few people will want to get near you or speak to you; this allows your anger to thrive. While on the other hand, joy is often mocked. Anger tends to get more respect than joy does, which is a very sad case indeed! Joy should be celebrated with the same, or *greater* intensity with which anger is typically celebrated, but for some reason we often feel that we need to get drunk or high to express ourself in a jovial way. Yet for many of us, someone only needs to momentarily make us mad in order for us to show our ferocious anger.

If we could all be as joyful as we are angry—Wow, what a world we would live in! If that were the case, then we all would be kind and helpful to others, and through that kindness we would all be celebrating joy, instead of harming others while celebrating our anger by shouting and making angry hand gestures at them.

Joy is a wonderful thing! When your family has embraced truth, and you begin to see joy entering your family life from truth that you have embraced, then celebrate your joy with the same level of intensity that you normally use to celebrate your anger. Get in the habit of doing so with a clear mind.

Beware of Your Negatives

Truth is the single *universal* thing in life. Scientists have sought to understand a unified theory—Truth *is* that theory.

Truth explains everything, even lies. Without truth, nothing can be! Negative thoughts are a violation of truth and will eradicate truth from your life. Negative thoughts are essentially doubt. In other words, when we have negative thoughts, we have made ourselves susceptible to lies.

If we know that some particular unpleasant thing is going to happen, then it is true that it will happen and is likely due to our previous choices of following lies. Living a life based on what is true allows you to know, that as soon as you address the errors from your past and do whatever is reasonably possible to make the needed corrections, then the error is in the past and you no longer will need to anticipate the troubles caused by your past error. When you make errors, be quick to correct them; and when doing so, look beyond the correction period to when the problem is resolved, rather than dwelling on the uncomfortable often required correction period that usually comes first.

All too often, we focus on the period of time where we are correcting our mistakes. In doing so, we also focus on the pain that we typically feel during the correction process. But what is the pain that we feel? Is it not the humiliation, actually the shame experienced from being put back into a position of being in truth where we belong?

When we base our lives on things that are not true, we then build ourselves up to be something that we are not, and by doing so we become arrogant. Then, in that arrogance, and with the whitewash of our arrogance, we further try to hide our doubt that we created in ourselves through believing lies in the first place. This cycle feeds on itself and causes many of us to spiral into a negative way of thinking by always placing focus on the pain that we must endure while attempting to correct our previous errors.

Negative thoughts will destroy you and your family. Negative thoughts make people feel worthless. The only time you are worthless is when you believe lies. The only escape from believing lies is to weigh *everything* on the scale of truth. Focus on the certainty that truth is the proper way, and focus on the positive that comes *after* the pain that must be endured during the correction process of *your* past errors. This stops the out-of-control downward spiral that sometimes results in depression that people experience when avoiding dealing with their actual problems.

We have been taught, and we have taught our children, to think negatively through living by what is not true and then subsequently believing lies and finally we live by those lies. Not many people escape this. The only question is, how intense is the negativity?

Strengths and Weaknesses

We often think negatively to the point of destruction of ourselves and our children. Through this, we teach our children to focus on their own *negative* aspects. We need to teach our children to *not* accept lies, while at the same time teaching them truth. Sadly, we often go beyond that and press our children to do things that are not natural to them. Every human is born with their own natural talents, but because we are taught lies, our talents are seldom accessed by us or seen by us or by the world. Too often we are falsely taught that if we do not attend college then we are "failures." Believing this lie brings about the weak foundation of lies of which we have been speaking. This does not make attending college wrong, but it does mean that doing something that is not in your natural inclination or desire is not using *your* natural talents as those talents are designed and meant to be used.

Earlier we spoke of computer programmers. A good programmer often does not need school because they will learn the needed information regardless, given the progressive accessibility of information in any modern times. School may help them, but the logic that is natural in a good programmer, is *natural* in them, and natural programmers will use that logic very well. Where, on the other hand, for someone who is not natural in the sort of logic needed for programming, they will struggle just to do work that often ends up being poorly done because it is not their natural affinity.

If someone does not possess that natural sort of logic, then typically nothing will make them a good programmer. If someone chooses programming as an occupation and they do not have that natural inclination of logic, they will be like a mere monkey, repeating things as they are told causing the final outcome of the work to be left wanting. Their true natural creativity will be buried for the sake of more money which is often wasted away anyway, which is all truly sad.

We certainly want to teach our children the basics in life, like fundamental math, reading, and such; but trying to make them into something that they are not, just to please us or for the sake of more money and prestige, is a tremendous error.

Let your children flip burgers for a while, maybe they will end up running a chain of restaurants or maybe they simply truly enjoy flipping burgers; There is nothing wrong with doing so. *Forcing* them to endure years of college that they don't want to attend, is both expensive and foolish. If you feel that your children are not responsible enough, and that they must attend college to be a qualified cog of humanity, then apparently you have failed to teach them how to be a responsible human being and how to exhibit their natural given talents and how to seek truth.

When raising children, this general approach to life is often the cause of children dropping out of school because their natural talents and their hopes and dreams are not being addressed, recognized, or utilized. If their natural talents, hopes, and dreams have been crushed, and they believe what they have been told, then life will hold a very difficult path for them, often causing them to choose a rebellious path or altogether give up. Modern culture has been increasingly teaching children to be what they are not.

When people come to this realization, they typically feel like failures because they failed their children. To this I say that it is partly because your parents probably did the same to you. Our problem as a society is that we keep crying about our problems, but then fail to correct those problems. Realizing that this is a societal problem that is handed down from parent to child can at least relieve some of our own guilt burden in this regard. But once we become aware of this, *we* must work to correct the problem and stop passing it on to the next generation. It is our responsibility to do so.

Children should only attend college for the primary purpose of learning more details about things that *they* are passionate about and will enhance *their* natural talents. The world would be a far more beautiful place if we all were to utilize *our own* gifts, rather than the gifts of others. When mentioning this, it is in regard to the children's natural talents, not the false sense of desires that advertising and societal pressure places on them.

Of course, we must teach our children the basics of life even if they are not naturally adept at those basics. Beyond that, let their natural talents blossom by teaching them to live life in a true manner. Celebrate their natural talents with Joy and understanding. Make sure that your children's natural talents are *theirs*. Do not confuse their natural talents with other people's talents or with the negative influences of our world. And don't succumb to other people's perception of who *your* children should be or what they should do, unless that person happens to be referring to your child's actual natural talents. A child whose foundation is built upon truth will have natural talents that increase the world and make it a better place, even if it is "just" selling burgers while feeding thousands, or "just" being a Mom and building awesome children! As a parent, it is your duty to encourage, but not force, your children to pursue their natural gifts. What we often fail to realize is that their "natural gifts" might appear to us to have a very narrow use, but when we open our minds we can see the vast diversity that any natural gift can actually be utilized for. A child who can rattle off a list of sports statistics is probably not best suited to be a sports caster, but rather they are someone who can use their skill of recalling details in *any* job they do where they will excel because of that gift.

Do You Focus on the Positive?

Placing focus on the positive by teaching children to live life in a true manner accelerates them and gets them nearer to those who can truly assist their actual dreams. Pressing them into a lackluster existence will blow up in their face, and in the long run, doing so will cause a great deal of dissatisfaction and frustration in their lives.

Over the years I have watched many people go away to college only to party and get mediocre grades, so that they can get a job that they don't like, just because they have a degree for something that they are mediocre, or even horrible, at. Then, they must subsequently repay the massive college loans for many years to come, which is often for an education for a job that, in the end, they will only have for a few years, *if* they use the education *at all*. Often graduates are unable to find a job in the chosen field that they were educated for, so instead they are forced to take another job doing something else they hate just to pay the school loan(s)—Oh the drudgery! Drag your tail out of bed and force yourself to drive to work only to come home to complain about the people at work and about a job you hate. This is tragic, because, not only are we unhappy when living this way, but we also have taken a job position from a person who could actually enjoy it and is more capable and deserving of the position. If this is only a stepping-stone towards your real goal then it is not a bad thing, temporarily. But sadly, society has adapted to this sort of worker and has become accustomed to hiring such. Is this really what you want for your own life and for your children? Would it not be better for us all to seek out that which we love, and then pursue it with passion?

College is alright to attend provided that you have the proper understanding of what is occurring. You must realize that colleges are businesses, plain and simple, and they play into our children's weaknesses just as any other business advertising their products or services does. However, many colleges are far worse in their hypocrisy because they are supposed to be teaching truth. But instead, they pretend they have all of the answers and that you are only worthy if you have graduated from their school. They will gladly take your hard earned cash without the slightest hesitation while they teach your child arrogance as they teach them far too many useless classes that they cannot use for anything other than teaching others the same misinformation when they become teachers because that is the only thing that the information can be used for. Not all schools take this impractical approach, but far too many do. And further, they don't want to risk their reputation so they like to only take the highest achieving students while they leave the lower grade students behind—this is pure unadulterated arrogance and hypocrisy.

You, your children, and the rest of the world will be far better served when you focus on your children's natural skills. It is a parent's mission to understand in what ways their children can use the natural skills and gifts born to them to make the world a better place, and subsequently, consistently improve themselves; thus, enriching their life by doing so with something they are passionate for that is natural to them. What we miss is that *all* people have natural talents. The problem is that when we see the true child prodigy who needed no formal training we believe them to be rare, and indeed they often are rare. Then we insist that they take lessons to further their natural talents. But what we fail to see is the fact that there are many wonderful things to be naturally talented at. When we open our eyes to the truths about children, we are able to guide them and recognize their natural talents. Maybe it is only to be "just" a Mommy, but if that is a particular woman's gift, then that gift should not be suppressed. In fact, women who have that natural gift are the women that I want to see bring more children into the world. The world will be a better place wherever Mothers love what they do. When done well, motherhood is the *most important* and best job ever!

Put your focus on your *children's natural* abilities; those talents are there for a reason! There is nothing wrong with being a plumber, a banker, a stock broker, or even just flipping burgers or mowing lawns—it's all the same if *they* enjoy and can reap the benefits of it.

Teach your children how to manage their money and they will need to make far less of it for the same quality of life that a higher paying job can offer them. This gives them the freedom to do whatever good thing they want to do for a living, and will result in them enjoying their life more abundantly all of their years.

People only work about forty years (which is sad), so spending four to ten years in school while running up unjustified tuition bills that they will be paying off for decades sets us back a great deal and it places an unneeded and unwanted financial burden on everyone involved. The money that we could have earned during that time doing something we actually like to do makes the offset even greater. Often, the chosen education is not even used in the job we end up taking.

A child, who is taught to save and work, can earn enough to buy a starter home for cash in the same time they would have been in college running up those hefty unwanted tuition bills. Can you imagine being twenty-three and owning a home outright, and not having to work at a job you hate in order to pay for a mortgage you can't afford and for the education for the job you don't like for the next 15 to 30 years? If you are going to go to college it should be for something that you love, and it should be done in order to learn more about the gift that you have.

Teach your children what is true so that they can make those decisions for themselves. Teach them to properly manage their money so they can keep out of the slavery of debt. Focus on *their* natural skills and talents, and embrace and nurture those skills and talents. Expect that those natural interests may change as they age. Focusing your children and feeding their natural skills teaches them the valuable skill of focusing on—the joy of doing what they love— to a higher degree of quality, which will be used all throughout their lives! Much of our joy comes from utilizing the natural gifts that were bestowed upon each one of us that make the world a better place. This is one of the answers to the mysteries to prosperity. Sure, it's okay to have other jobs as you work your way to your goals, but encourage them to have goals towards *their* natural good talents, and teach them to work in that general direction and eventually they will achieve it.

Some people might mistake this section to mean that you should stand firm and not work unless you are doing your passion or that you should skip college, but this is not so. If you have expenses, then you *must* earn to pay those expenses. So I am *not* referring to holding out until you get your way. What this section is getting at is that your goal should always be your passion. And work, that you possibly do not like, that you do only to pay your bills should be thought of as a temporary solution that is a stepping-stone towards where you desire to be. College should be to learn more about a field of study for which someone has a passion rather than a weak crutch toward some towards some utopian fantasy.

Praying Properly

A very important part of having a strong foundation in your family is properly understanding prayer. Without this understanding, the direction in your life will follow a very confusing and uncertain path. The cornerstone book *Understanding Prayer* explains prayer in depth; but briefly: celebrating joy is important, but most of us do not celebrate joy; instead, we celebrate fear and anger, and then we proceed to beg God to correct our errors and to remove the resulting pain caused by our following something that is less than true. Our prayers are lackluster at best, but we can sure make some noise at a sporting event or when we are angry. Why do we *not* celebrate joy or pray with that same intensity?

The typical person's prayers are left wanting as a result of our lack of truth. First, we have the issue of doubting the existence of the Creator to whom we are praying. Then we tend to only pray to *get* something, and that *something* for which we are praying is usually built upon a lie. Basically, we say "Hey God, give me money please!" while we stay and work at a job that we hate, and that we chose of our own freewill. Imagine that your child asks for something from you: "Hey! Mom and Dad, buy me some overpriced clothing that I don't really care about and only want because the other kids have it, because I want to copy them so that I can feel cool like I think they are." That is exactly what we are doing when we pray for something that is not true. If something is not true, then it cannot truly be ours and we are essentially stealing it if we take it without asking.

There are references stated in the Bible about "casting lots" (rolling dice) for decision making. I am not referring the soldiers casting lots for the Christ's robe, there are other such references. Flip a coin to make your decisions if you will, but don't believe it to be Divine providence. You may pray for something and when something comes your way, you might mistake it as an answer to your prayers, even though it was not. In the unlikely event that the Creator would ever produce something for you that you asked for that appears to support something that is not true, then realize that the situation is a test of your own making. And in accepting that which is not true, you will have failed the test. Be cautious not to assign an ungodly result to a prayer request. To do so is a grievous error and is in violation of Truth.

Few people understand prayer and how to get what they want through prayer. The simple secret is to stop living in a manner that is not true. When you do that and ask for that which is true, good, and beneficial to your life being lived in a true way, then and only then, will your prayers be successful. For those who have actually achieved that in their lives, the next step is to focus on your intensity. The Creator is more likely to answer an angry forceful prayer, than a lackluster, boring, somewhat happy prayer.

Pray with true intensity! If your child comes to you and asks for something in a manner that gives you the perception that they are not excited or sincere about it, then, are you going to want to spend the money on something that they do not care about? Do they deserve something that they won't care about? Or, if they are *pretending* to be excited about what they ask for, will you not detect their fraud?

Live a life built on what is true and then pray for what is true with true intensity. Then, as discussed in the cornerstone book *Understanding Prayer*, when what you ask for is good, you will find all the right elements coming your way in order for that prayer to come to fruition. Pray with intense and true Joy!

Your Joy versus Your Happiness

We discussed joy and happiness a bit earlier. Anger and frustration are the result of following what is *not* true, but even in following what is not true, sporadic *happiness* will occur in your life. Happiness is often a forced result in life; when it is not forced then it is pure chance. The difference between chanced and forced happiness, versus Joy, is *intent*—Joy is deliberate, but it is not forced—Joy is natural!

Often, we try to buy happiness, which is usually done with money that is borrowed and subsequently repaid by working at a lackluster job that we really don't like; a job that we have taken from someone who would actually love it and excel at it far better than us. Where with joy, you will live based upon what is true. When all of that which is not true is removed from your life, you will be in a near constant state of joy. You will not need to rely on money to bring you fleeting satisfaction. Money will only serve to enhance your joy *when* you live life based upon what is true. The effects of truth on your family will be profound. Living in a truthful manner teaches your children to do the same, thus freeing them from making the mistake of building a life based upon things that are not true.

Remember that the very essence of the words *happiness, happen,* or *hap* all have the underlying meaning of—by *chance.* This means that something good came your way by chance and it is not easily or dependably repeatable. But Joy is deliberate and intentional! Joy is not forced. Joy comes only through the specific action of building your life upon only that which is true—it's that simple!

Understanding your origins and grasping who and what you are is the beginning of your personal joy, and it will spread throughout your entire family. Too often, we get drawn into senseless theological debates about our origins only because we do not have any good answers like those found in the book series *The Science of God.* Our lack of understanding in this regard causes us to doubt what is true and it steals away our joy. Don't let it happen to *your* family. Cast away blind faith and have full and robust understanding wherever you can, especially with regard to your origins. Live in truth, and celebrate your joy in prayer! Joy is derived from truth that is within yourself and in the relationships you allow around you. Have **True** faith.

Chapter 8

Evolution versus Creation,
Does it Really Matter to Your Family?

The four cornerstones of life are important, and they have been under attack since the very beginning of humanity. Our *not understanding* the necessity of a good foundation is a serious problem for most families. The cornerstone of family has been greatly undermined by the evolution versus Creation debate.

The human-evolution belief system has infiltrated so deeply into culture that we barely notice how often we reference it. Our blind faith belief of evolution has clouded our view of the obvious brilliance of our children. We tend to look at younger children, and often treat them, as if they have the mentality of animals. We dismiss their genius as if they have erred, and when they call us out on our lies and wrong doing, we reprimand them or tell them to "be quiet!" The mental conflict of evolution versus Creation starts with incorrect thinking.

There has been an illusion for many years that simply going to church on a regular basis was the key to having a great family. However, since the divorce rate and other family troubles of church-goers rivals that of non-church goers, it is evident that great families are obviously not created by attending church. While there are many good upstanding church-goers, there are also far too many unkind, cruel, and arrogant people who are regular church-goers. Additionally, the children of church-going families have nearly the same amounts and types of problems. We are left to conclude that attending church has little bearing on a good foundation for your family.

Church attendance fluctuates from generation to generation, but regardless of attendance levels, what is being preached in the churches is often based upon blind faith alone. This blind faith has devastated religion. So long as the blind faith was not challenged there was no threat to the Church or its believers or church attendance levels.

During the era covered in the Old Testament of the Bible, churches—as we think of them today—were not yet developed, and people were somewhat on their own regarding their religion. As the story goes, Noah and his family climbed aboard the ark and they were the only link left to the origins of mankind. After the flood, Noah's children had children, and within a few generations of children being born they had already forgotten the lessons that were taught to them by Noah and the flood. Once again, humanity foolishly began to worship and serve powerless wood, metal, and stone carvings as if any one of those idols were a god that could actually do anything to serve them. We humans quickly gravitate towards what is *not* true; but why?

It is because, too often, we like to and we want to believe lies! The reason that our affinity for believing lies gets more complicated is because we each have different reasons for doing so. Though, in general, it is because human nature is selfish. Why is it that we, even in current times, have an evil and foolish inclination for not believing in a singular Creator, yet we will subject ourselves to something that is obviously in error? What power is there in a crystal or statue that someone would serve it and pray to it, or even bow to it and ask or expect favors of it, as in a lucky rabbit's foot, or a lucky shirt?

In the sixteenth century, the free thinking-movement re-emerged and ushered in a tremendous amount of doubt as to whether or not a supreme Creator exists. Some of this doubt was well-deserved because many people would believe anything they were told by the Church leaders with regard to religion. Their dangerous blind faith led them to being manipulated by the clergy for status, power, and financial gain. When some of the free-thinkers began to question the clergy's perspective, it opened the door for tremendous speculation and doubt.

The Church insisted that the Bible stated things as *they* (the Church leaders) interpreted them. Some of these interpretations did not agree with new scientific discoveries. Since the Church had a history of denying, and being very slow to accept newer and more accurate information, this new movement went on a rampage to prove their points opposing the Church's opinion. Some came up with some fairly absurd speculations that were beyond reasonable, while others were accurate.

When the concept of evolution came along, the proponents were able to lay down an argument that was satisfactory enough to conquer the lack of understanding that the Church and its congregation had about the origins of mankind. This does not prove those theories to be true, but the arguments offered by the proponents of evolution were more compelling than the arguments offered by those who subscribed to the other people's interpretation of the Bible's account of Creation. This was due to the simple fact that many Creation believers had misread the information and had been standing on blatant misunderstanding, which comes from misinterpretation of the simple text in the Bible.

Evolution, and its counterpart the Big Bang origin of the Universe, would have us accept that humans have descended from the same branch of life as monkeys or apes did, and that the Universe spontaneously occurred with a "big bang." Then, out of pure chance, all that we see around us occurred via the details in those two theories.

Accept these theories if you choose; no one can make these decisions for you. Even if we believe they are forcing something on us, it is still our own choice of what we truly choose to believe internally. If you're going to accept evolution as true, then at least be consistent.

Picking and choosing information, whether scientific or religious, so as to create the illusion of consistency, so that we can believe something that we *want* to believe, is *not* a foundation built on what is true, and it will not build a strong family.

Give Infants the Credit that They Deserve

Our often ignorant human nature is enough in itself to have us overlook the brilliance of an infant; but additionally, the acceptance of the human evolution theory has increased our ignorance many times over in this regard. Too many parents have a notion that babies are "stupid" or that "they don't know." This inaccurate thinking is further fed by the theory of evolution's flawed structure of thinking. As parents, we must stop believing any notion that babies are "stupid" and have no ability to understand things. They may not have the capacity to grasp a concept in the same way, or at the same speed, that adults do, but they do grasp those concepts whether or not we choose to realize it, and they learn at a rate that boggles the mind when you stop to grasp what they learn.

Infants begin learning in the womb, but for the sake of discussion let us assume that learning begins only *after* the birth of the child. Within days of being born a baby has learned how to get Mommy's or Daddy's attention, and leverages that ability within a week or so in order to be picked up and held at baby's will. This does not seem like something a null person would do. Infants learn at an incredibly high rate, and likely, far faster than adults do. The difference is that the infant needs to figure out some very primary functions—spatial, eye, body, and hand coordination for instance. We look at these tasks as some sort of inherent natural thing that we just do, but they are not. Babies *learn where* their hands and face are by their movement and by their own observation of those movements. By the time babies are a year old, they can crawl and say some words; many children even walk by that time, and some may even utter short sentences.

Most of us give little thought to the amount of information-processing that it takes any human just to move our hands to our mouth in an accurate manner. This is even far more complicated when it comes to actually having enough balance to walk. The calculations that our brain and body do just to walk are astounding beyond our comprehension. To add to this complexity, we must consider the additional ability of a young child to walk on almost any texture or surface at relatively fast speeds making spontaneous adjustments as they go while never having experienced that surface before. Babies are amazing, and they take in more useful information in one day than we are willing to comprehend. Most Artificial Intelligence (AI) and automation programmers who have had children while being involved in programming, can attest to the deep abilities of the baby human mind, because to try to program any one small motion or reasoning function is typically a formidable task.

Give Your Children the Credit They Deserve

Similarly, children that have moved from baby status to toddler status are also very capable and intelligent. The erred notion that human evolution is real has tainted our minds, leading us to believe many things that are not true about humans, and especially about human children. Children are brilliant! But this is typically overlooked by us often ignorant adults. Some children might appear to learn more slowly than others, but they usually excel in another area unnoticed by us adults. Additionally, some children might excel in other ways, but just a bit later than is typical of other children of a similar age.

When we parents tap into what the child excels at, then we can nurture that gift in the child. But do not make the mistake of thinking that this is what they will always be interested in. Children are children, and they are learning daily. There is much that they have not yet seen, and they may very well see something that suits them better within years, months, or even weeks of their last point of interest in any particular subject. Children are incredible learners, they explore *when allowed*, and they will generally absorb whatever surrounds them—Good or Bad.

Forcing a child to do anything that is not natural to them, and that they do not have a desire for, is like forcing *you* to eat something you do not have a taste for. You like what you like to eat for reasons of your own, and so it is with your children: they will like what they like for reasons of their own. Please separate this from the very common practice of saying that we don't like something when never having actually tried it.

It is the parent's job to guide their children to live life based upon what is true, rather than in a manner that violates their nature of life. Anytime we violate what something is designed for, we have breached what is true and have then violated its design. Using a hammer to pound in a screw is no different than forcing a child to follow a path that *you* want; such as, *forcing* them to become a four-year-old beauty queen when they want no part of it. But this is not to say that some little girls do not want this for themselves. Too many parents fail to understand that guiding their children to use their natural abilities for the betterment of everyone is essential.

When children become more independent, they will experiment with life and do things that might not make much sense to us. Your job here is twofold: First, it is good to find out what's going on in their little heads; and second, you must guide and show them how to reason through their future actions. Children are very smart and have the capacity to learn a great deal more than we give them credit for. Yet, we must still be cautious not to take them too far beyond their years when teaching them. Humans have always been this way and all evidence points to that conclusion. Choosing to believe that you and your children are the product of evolution takes away your ability to realize the true brilliance of a human being.

Your Children Get Bored

When children become overactive, they are typically over-tired, hungry, hopped up on sugar, or more often than not, they are bored. Occupying the brilliant mind of a child can be a difficult task if you are aiming at the wrong target and if you think we evolved. If your child has no interest in something, then it is likely that their lack of interest is either due to it being more than they can currently handle or it is less than they need, and therefore, it bores the daylights out of them! Something that bores a child will *not* keep their attention. When we believe that people have evolved and that we stemmed from animals, then we tend to miss the brilliance of children by believing them to be somewhat animal-like. You need not observe long to see that an animal nature is more often taught *to* children, rather than being taught *out of* them.

If you have a bored child, then try teaching them something of value like a creative way to understand how to choose what is true; this is something that only humans seem to be able to do with any efficiency. Not doing so teaches children the habit of not being able to focus, causing *you* subsequent misery when they start being antagonistic due to their boredom with life. This leads to much displeasure for your family, and it is completely unnecessary.

Parents sometimes foolishly sit their children down in front of the TV as a means to occupy them. In general, this is *not* a particularly good idea. But if you are going to choose that route, at least have the good sense to sit them down to watch something that teaches them good lessons in life. Also, teach them how to detect what is true and what is false. If you foolishly choose mindless TV viewing for your children, it should, at the very least, be something that will help teach them to *live by* that which is true. View the programming yourself *before* you sit them down to watch it. Not knowing what is in a program is as good as consenting to the program's worst message—**Know** what your children watch!

Give People the Credit They Deserve

Whether an infant, a toddler, or an older child, they are people, and they are at least as smart as you are, though their intelligence may be shown in different ways. People are people no matter what their age or mental condition. Buying into the lie that, at any age, someone is not smart is an insult to humanity.

When someone is an "idiot" it is likely that they have been trained by their parents to be so. Even most people who are considered "slow" or "retarded" (mentally handicapped) have a place where they can excel when allowed to do so. It is the assumption that people are stupid, that is stupid.

All of us have minds that are incredibly powerful, and the problems often come in our *brain*, rather than with our mind. Our brain is the interface to our mind—to us. Some brains malfunction and disrupt the fluent ability for our mind to express itself in what we think of as a "normal" manner.

When we make the assumption that we have evolved from the process of natural selection through a lower primate or as a relative of a lower primate, then the value of our mind is reduced considerably in our own minds. If someone's brain is in peril and does not function as expected, then they are often thought of as worthless, or as "freaks" that have no abilities.

It seems that the trend of condemning people whose brains function differently has reversed somewhat. People are beginning to realize that those of us whose brains are not functioning as what is thought to be "normal," also have something wonderful to contribute to the world.

Your Children Grow Quickly

Your children learn quickly and abundantly, and they also grow up quickly. They did not evolve and they are not branched from or anywhere near primates. Do not put off until tomorrow what you can do today! Your children will be gone from your home within about twenty years from their birth, and you will find that those years flew by when you get to the end of those years.

Teach your children good and true lessons while they are young and are learning their primary communication skills. We will discuss these primary languages more deeply later. But, for now, it is important to understand the incredible body machine that you and your spouse have created and placed a new soul into at conception.

Human bodies have amazing abilities that are being continually discovered over thousands of years. The deeper we look during our ongoing quest to understand the human, the more amazing details we find. No other creatures do this. This was even more of an amazing journey starting around the beginning of the twenty-first century, where computers and electromagnetic sensing allowed live views of the inside of the body and brain *without* cutting the body open. And electron microscopes allow doctors, scientists, and researchers to see things at magnifications down to the atomic level. All of our research and attempts to understand the body, brain, and the mind, only seem to bring about more mystery with every new and deeper level of understanding we achieve with modern technology.

Your children are incredible and they grow up quickly! Do not blow your opportunity to build great people. These people will be in your life for the rest of your life. And if you fail them you will suffer the consequences of your own lack of diligence—so let's do it right.

What is Artificial Intelligence (AI)?

At some point you will likely be confronted with the topic and questions regarding artificial intelligence compared to human intelligence. Equip yourself with understanding before you are faced with such topics.

To better understand the importance and depth of our human abilities, and why it's important to know about this for building a strong family, we will explore the idea of *intelligence*. Our bodies are incredible machines that are very specific and precise. Our ability to be able to explain how our bodies work does not prove or disprove evolution, but it does give us a clue as to the intricacy with which our bodies are formed and function.

The most evasive aspect of humanity is our intellect, or our ability to gather and use information. "Artificial intelligence" is something that has been sought since the dawn of the computer. The speculation as to the level of achievable artificial intelligence has wavered over the years, but the capability seems to increase on a regular basis. In fact, what was done shortly after the start of the twenty-first century would have had those who dreamt about artificial intelligence in the mid-nineteen hundreds, believing that computers where smarter than people.

The discussion of whether a computer is smarter or more intelligent than a human depends upon your definition of "intelligent" or "smart." Since those terms are somewhat ambiguous, it will be left to the beholder unless we chose to designate boundaries for the definition of the term "intelligence." But even then, to state that a computer is "artificially intelligent" still begs the question in the minds of most of us: Is it human? Can it replace the human essences we all possess? Consider an infant. Can a computer offer anything that a child offers? Obviously not, computers are tools and will only ever be tools.

Artificial Intelligence, by loose definition, means: human-made gatherer. What is being gathered is information or trivia, and it is done by a machine built by humans. It is easily possible, that by this definition, a computer has more "intelligence" than humans. This is because a computer can store as much trivia as we choose to provide storage for and access to. The information is then stored in the database and/or on a storage device for nearly instant retrieval. However, in the end, it is still only a tool that *we* use to aid our work, unless you are gullible enough to believe otherwise.

When you have chosen to believe that we have created something greater than its creator, then you have deliberately chosen a slippery slope to be deceived.

This should not take away from the utilitarian purpose of artificial intelligence. We should use it, and use it well. "Artificial intelligence" can be used for the good of mankind. But sadly, "the *good* of mankind" is a loose term that is subject to every individual's interpretation; thus, making the word "good" potentially dangerous to us all, depending, of course, upon the mind that is defining it.

The stigma that the term *artificial intelligence* (AI) has is that of potentially being superior to humans. While AI may surpass any particular person's ability to retain and retrieve trivia—it is not human. There are many other seemingly insignificant technical human factors to consider that are typically not addressed when thinking in terms of artificial intelligence. What makes us human is an evasive question for most of us.

The wide embrace of the theory of evolution has diminished acceptance of the existence of a Creator from the minds of many people. The proper understanding of the Creator will greatly aid you in building your strong family. Getting a firm grasp on the *complexity* that our bodies are built with, versus the relatively simplistic functionality of any computer, will better help you to properly understand the Creator. Evolution places our only real value in our brain and steals away the fundamental concept of a Creator, making everything about *us* and only about us. Don't allow the notion of artificial intelligence to cause you to doubt your Created nature and the Creator. Such doubt is a trap that many fall into when subjects such as AI are discussed, ultimately ending with them abandoning good sound reasoning for the deception of artificial "intelligence." When we abandoned the Creator, we ultimately abandoned our family and ourselves.

The Evolution of Your Brain

Another area where we can learn a great deal about the magnitude and complexity of our Creation, and where we can get a better understanding of the Creator, is by considering the human brain. The human brain is the most amazing device on Earth, right next to the largely unexplainable heart. While we know a great deal about these two organs, we still do not *understand* them anywhere near completely. We are able to explain elements of how the brain works, but we do not truly understand it.

Understanding that we use our intellect to do our lab experiments is very important in order to expose the whitewashed contradictions perpetrated as truth by "science" for the sake of funding. Sadly, the science world has, in many ways, become more foolish and selfish than some people in the Church ever were in the past.

It seems to be that the human mantra "I am going to do what I want to do **and so are you!**" was, in the past, done by some leaders in the Church—but now science is guilty of the same sin—only more intensely.

Our brain is a beautiful thing and we should welcome the exploration of it, but just because we believe we can explain it does not mean that it evolved *or* that it was Created. Understanding how our brain functions simply means that it is.

We seek knowledge and believe that this knowledge will bring us success. Often it brings success of money *when* we have learned how to utilize the knowledge, but then we often choose to manipulate the knowledge for our own personal gain regardless of truth. This causes us trouble because our true goal of finding truth is ignored, and is mistaken for the prestige that typically accompanies understanding, which is, in turn, typically confused with the prestige of money. Do not teach your children to be duped by status and riches.

Do You Buy Into the "Age of Enlightenment"?

When considering the evolution versus creation debate there is a wrong notion that if you are "religious" then you are not enlightened, and if you believe in the complete model of evolution then you are enlightened.

The importance of truth, with regard to a strong family, cannot be stressed enough. The problem that we face is the distortion of what *truth* is. In the seventeenth century, a trend developed that we hinted to earlier, a trend called "Enlightenment." The term *Enlightenment* refers to our ability to seek the truth. Some great truths have been exposed through this movement; but sadly, as our human nature would have it, "I am going to do what I want to do, **and so are you!**" or better stated "I am going to *think* what I want to *think*, **and so are you!**" generally prevails, both in life and while we teach our children. They tried to fight this during the Enlightenment Age of Reason, but once again, our own humanity had defeated many of us.

In truth, you cannot be considered to be "enlightened" when you have any agenda that is not of pure truth. The enlightenment movement grew out of a new freedom. The new freedom was the freedom from that which held them in bondage—which typically they believed to be the Church of that time.

Some of the leaders of the enlightenment movement believed in a Creator, but they had difficulty mentally separating the Church organization from the Creator. This presented problems in their desire to be able to accurately communicate their vision, which, in turn, caused the people who were listening to and interpreting those words and goals to misunderstand much of the true intent of the original messages.

This new mental freedom fueled the discussion about the possibility that the Church was wrong—they doubted the existence of a Creator. The advent of the theory of evolution was occurring during the same time as the enlightenment movement was going on, and they fed on each other.

Separate those who **wrote**, from those who **read** the writings. What was written is not necessarily what was understood by the readers. This movement sought truth but in many ways failed because too many of its proponents had an agenda of trying to prove some particular point. They were blinded by their own brand of enlightenment and thought that they were seeking the truth while they pushed their agenda. Yet, while a few may have achieved enlightenment, many had a "truth" of their own. They had a truth which they were going to prove, even if they had to *force* the truth to agree with their own erred ideas. The only way to force truth is to lie and deceive—but then it is no longer truth. Truth stands on its own. Truth does not need you or me, and truth will endure forever!

Once we begin to doubt the existence of the Creator, our view of the fossils that we find becomes distorted. This has built a complex tale woven deep into the hearts of many people, serving to bring about more doubt regarding the existence of the Creator. Without the proper understanding about the Creator, your foundation for your family will be built upon lies, and you will have no power to overcome internal problems when they come your way. The only way to have the strong foundation that your family deserves is through utter truth—this is the only true *enlightenment*!

Your True Enlightenment

True enlightenment requires that you weigh *everything* that comes into question, in a *fair* manner, on the balance of truth. Embracing single trunk evolution, where all species came from the same trunk or primordial soup, without proof is as ridiculous as accepting the Church's medieval account of the movements of the Universe.

Just because someone claims that they have found a human skeleton and claims it to be from a given era does not mean that it is actually from that era. We should take their *findings* into account in our world and in our life assessments; but, their *conclusions*, are an entirely different story!

The father of evolution accurately observed many things—but, his *conclusions* were only *speculation*. Ever since then, people have been blindly following his erred conclusions as if they were witnessed first-hand by us all. Obviously we were not physically here before we were born, and not only did we *not* witness his conclusions being made, but we were also *not* there at the speculative time about which he made conclusions regarding when life may, or may not, have begun.

The actual theory of evolution was started a minimum of forty years before the "father of evolution", Darwin, was even born. This means that we credit the wrong person for the erred theory. Investigate this for yourself if you doubt this information. If we don't get this part right, then, can we expect that o*ur interpretation* of the findings and conclusions are correct?

To be "enlightened" you cannot blindly accept evolution as true. If you believe that the "geological record" as presented is consistent, then you have your eyes and mind closed to the subject, and you need to re-examine the origin and the measurements of that index. True enlightenment is nothing more than to embrace what is true, to abide in it, and to share it with others. All of these same rules apply to the discussion of Creation as well. When we fail, with regard to the honesty and openness of our research-approach, it causes our minds to follow irrational lines of reasoning.

There is no need to meditate, hum, or believe that "science" is the truth, in order to be "enlightened." Truth is the truth, and it will always prevail in the end. That is what *true* "enlightenment" is. When we blindly embrace, in our hearts and minds, the human evolution belief system that arose out of the enlightenment era, our erred belief will have a negative impact on our families. We discussed truth at some length a few chapters back. It is my hope that you have grasped truth in your heart and mind, so that you can teach it to your children, and in doing so avoid teaching them the inaccuracies conveyed in *any* flawed theories that you or they may encounter as they grow up. They will be challenged on this topic during life, especially if they attend public school or college. Their entire life value system will be, in some way, affected by the evolution versus Creation debate. Prepare them well for life if you want them to follow the straight path of truth.

Chapter 9

Abortion versus Life
It Matters to Your Family!

Since this book is about families, I would be remiss in my work if we did not discuss abortion. Without children there is no family. Even if you choose to call *two* people a family, which by definition is true, in a single generation's time that "family" will cease to exist if no offspring comes out of the family.

Sure, you can adopt or bring someone who is hurting under your wing and call *them* family. But, if we abort *every* baby, then, within a lifetime, all of mankind will cease and there will be no families, anywhere! I would **not** recommend an abortion for anyone for many reasons, but the two biggest reasons to not do it are one's own personal regret plus the harm to another individual (the child in the womb.) Adhering to erred theories such as human evolution, greatly devalues our view of humanity, allowing us to readily accept abortion as an okay view with little or no feeling of guilt.

Whether it is legal or not, abortion is a choice, and it will always remain so.

Being in contradiction in your own heart regarding abortion, causes problems in your family in deep and subtle ways that are typically never recognized as connected to this kind of thinking. If you are inconsistent in regard to this subject, then you are almost certainly inconsistent in many other areas of your life. Our inconsistent nature is inadvertently taught to our children. The only way abortion **will not** be a choice is if we tether the mother to a bed until the baby is born so that she cannot terminate the pregnancy. I personally have heard no accounts of this.

When Does Life Begin?

Purposely stopping innocent human life is considered murder anywhere in the world, so the key point to be made, in order to allow the termination of life as something other than murder, is to define or redefine "life." If we are able to define life as *beginning at birth*, then, in our societal-eyes, abortion is okay at any point during the pregnancy prior to birth.

Calling the baby a "fetus" makes it easier for our minds to believe that it is not considered "life" during the time before birth. The "fetus" has been referred to as "a blob of cells." These "blobs of cells," which we call a fetus, are so far advanced from where science is, to a point where the fetus is almost of inconceivable complexity to us, that our disregard is laughable. Science is nowhere near fully understanding cells. We cannot even create a single functioning cell from scratch by copying what is already Created using chemicals and elements we already have at our disposal. And even if we do ever achieve such a monumental task, in the end, we have still copied what has already been designed, and we have used elements that have already been Created.

The reason this is being pointed out is that the scientific community, by their own words, is trying to *create* what the scientific community refers to as "*life.*"

The science community is seeking to know how "*life*" began, where with abortion, we call a fetus a "blob of cells" as if somehow the "blob" is not alive. There is no consistency in this rationale when both perspectives are held by the same persons.

We cannot go into court and have scientists testify before the entire world that the thriving, dividing "blob of cells" in a womb is not *life*, and then go to work and try to create "*life*" in a laboratory flask or petri dish in a monumental quest to create *one single cell* and claim that "*we* have *created* life!", especially while using federal tax monies to fund the research. This is disingenuous, outright fraud, inconsistent, and arrogant. Similarly, when we spend billions to send missions to other planets in effort to find, "evidence of life" we are also being dishonest in relation to abortion and the living "blob of cells." And when there is even the slightest indicator in the mind of a single researcher of any vague hope that a finding might show that "life" may have existed or been found on the distant planet, it's national news. And yet we abort robust thriving obvious well-formed human life thousands of times every single day. This is terribly dishonest and absolutely contradictory behavior.

Culturally, we humans are able to conveniently disconnect two tightly bound things within the thoughts in our heads. These tightly bound concepts, which belong together, are unraveled in our minds in order to achieve our own personal, and typically selfish, agenda. We allow ourselves to take a single thought and assign two different definitions to it for the same purpose.

A two-part example of agenda-driven fraud is the following: First, apparently, a *cell*, in "a blob of *cells*," which we call a fetus, has less value than a cell that is being sought in vain effort to "*create* life" in laboratories or that we seek on other planets. If the laboratory cell has "life," or making a "living" cell is the quest, then we *must* use the term "life" equally when discussing functional living cells of a fetus that was created due to normal human intercourse.

The second part of the example is that in court, with the testimony of "scientists", *life* is defined in a very arbitrary manner. We fail to come to an agreement as to when "life" begins in the womb, but in the laboratory, apparently "life" begins while *attempting* to create a single cell from scratch even though the cell is not complete, functional, **or alive**. And when seeking "life" on other planets, we don't even have the opportunity to physically handle the supposed evidence of life in our hands because it is all done remotely. Much of the laboratory research to create cells and the cost for planetary missions is directly or indirectly funded by public government funds; that is to say, the people's money—our money.

There is only one truth, and what you choose to believe defines you and your integrity. That choice is up to you and you alone! You and you alone will be accountable for your choice of following what is true or what is not true. We each are accountable for our own thoughts and the choices that we make and have made due to those thoughts. Our choices affect our families.

Arguments for Abortion

The arguments for abortion are light at best: First, a person must place their own desires before the welfare of the "blob of [*living*] cells." Next, we must redefine "life," and then extract the "blob of cells". But, before doing so, hardships must be discussed of the potential mother and how the potential child may have a rough time in life, and therefore it is better that we terminate the fetus and end the mother's torment and the future anticipated peril of the child. We cannot show any picture of the procedure that shows the "blob of cells", because that will upset and outrage people, and it could change the mind of the carrier of the fetus, which would be unacceptable to those who support this cause. Abortion must hide much in order to flourish. If you want to promote the "right to choose," then you must hide as much information as possible. Do not show or tell the explicit details of the procedures to the world and, especially, not to the pregnant mother; and make sure to tell the mother that the fetus feels nothing. Let us be clear here: A "Mother" is any woman who has *ever* been pregnant.

Also, you must: Support the definitions of life that best suit your specific whim at any particular time. Be demanding and shout to get your point across. Do not allow other discussion or points of view to be expressed. Suppress anything that does not agree with your end goal. Avoid the truth about your agenda at all costs. Do not allow true comparisons, because those comparisons might hurt the mother's feelings. Failing to do any of the above mentioned manipulations will result in failure to accomplish abortion on a large scale.

Arguments For Life

Abortion has little defense if you actually want to be consistent and honest. If you care nothing for consistency or truth in your life, then abortion is of little consequence in your heart or mind. Your choice of consistency and truth in regard to abortion will impact your children in many ways if you have chosen to have children or if you should so choose to have children in the future.

When using the scale of truth to weigh our actions, we need to be consistent with regard to the words *life, cell,* and *fetus.*

If we're going to say that we are trying to create a "living" cell in the laboratory, then we should have the same scientific index and criterion in the court system. The same is true for finding "life" on other planets. The word "cell" should carry a value in the womb, at least, as important as it does in the laboratory, since it is the cells in the womb that we are ultimately trying to copy in the laboratory. Finally, the word "fetus," in its native language, means: "the act of bearing young, offspring, fruitful, etc..." If the population was being true in its assessment of the available information, then our societal perception of "life" would be very different with regard to abortion.

Life is life. If it is not true, then it is *not.* And that would make the "live" thing dead. We cannot make an argument for life beyond that it **is**. When it **is** no longer, then it is not, and does not exist.

Life needs no support or defense in order to sustain it, life only needs to be true. The "right-to-life" movement makes the mistake of thinking that they need to defend their position or beliefs. They need not defend what is true, they only need to stand to protect the infants who are still in the womb. But, that which is not true attempts to defend itself against what is true, but in the long term it cannot. If it cannot stand on its own without our deliberate ignorance and lies, then it is an obvious lie. In the end, what is not true will defeat itself while trying to destroy what it can destroy on its way down to its own self-destruction.

If we go about saying *true* things about humanity, life, and abortion, then we will be seen as attacking abortion. This is so even though we have not specifically spoken out against abortion. This is because any lie cannot stand in the face of truth. The lie must attempt to hide or look away from the truth in order to be perpetuated—there is no other way. Ask the following questions to those who support abortion and you will likely agitate them:

If the courts rule that a fetus is a part of the mother's body and therefore can be aborted because the mother can "do what she wants with her own body," then how is it that the fetus' DNA is different? How is it that half of all fetus' do not share the same gender as the mother? How is it that the eye color can be different? How is it that the hair color can be different? How is it that the blood types can be different? How is it that, in many interracial marriages, the skin can be an entirely different color than that of the mother? How is it that the heart beats at a different rate? How is it that the fetus has a brain of its own? How is it that the mother does not feel the pain inflicted on the fetus during an abortion? How is it that the fetus does not feel the pain of the mother? How is it that the fetus moves independently of the mother? How is it that the fetus can be a 'fetus' one moment, and then the next moment survive on its own as a "baby", especially when born prematurely in the third trimester? All of these questions and many more lead us to only one truth; which is, the fetus is **not** a "part" of the mother.

Another argument often used by those who support abortion is that the mother can claim that the fetus is *dependent upon her* for life. Outside of forced insemination, whether it is intimate or in the laboratory, sex (intercourse) is a *choice* with the *known possibility* and outcome of pregnancy. To make the point clearer: Participation in intercourse carries with it the possibility of pregnancy.

Enjoying the pleasures of intercourse without accepting pregnancy when it occurs, is like enjoying a meal at a restaurant, and when done you shove your finger down your throat to vomit up the meal onto the table, and then ignore the consequence of cleaning up your own mess by walking out without paying for it all.

Or liken enjoying the pleasures of intercourse without accepting pregnancy to signing a contract to have your kitchen remodeled, and then when the work is complete you cook one meal, tear the kitchen out, and stop payment on the check to the contractor, and say "Tough, I didn't realize that signing that contract would make a new kitchen in my home."

If a female has been taught that there is absolutely no possibility of pregnancy from participating in intercourse, then her parents and society have failed her terribly! The same applies the male. To be clear: Anytime any male sperm gets near a vagina, the possibility exists that a single living sperm cell will find its way to a female's waiting egg. While the chances are remote if the sperm is not deposited directly into the vagina, the possibility of pregnancy *does* exist. Further, it is believed that a sperm cell can live for several days inside of a woman's body, thus, increasing her chance of pregnancy. These are good things to teach to your children as they come of age.

If people understood the simple truth of needing to teach children proper intimacy, then pregnancy amongst teens would be greatly reduced, if not eliminated altogether. Information that is not true, or is inaccurate, has been keeping the populous in the dark with regard to pregnancy resulting from sexual activity.

"Abortion" is deliberately stopping innocent life. We can call it "a blob of cells" or a "fetus" to ease our conscience but life is life, it either is or it is not. Let's at least be honest enough to say "I am going to do what I want to and kill my blob of fetus cells even if it is life." This way you will not be accountable for *other people's* abortions or for spreading things that are not true that will cause others to be swayed by your inaccurate information. Deceiving others **will put _their_ blood on _your_ hands!** As parents, we often fail to give our children the correct messages. This is especially true when we support abortion by not rejecting it.

It is quite disingenuous for the abortion movement to have complained that abortion was illegal in the past and that women were going to get them anyway in back alleys and other locations with questionable sanitary conditions causing "risk to the woman's life" saying "It is for the safety of the woman"; where in the early twenty-first century many states wanted to force the abortion clinics that were then "legal" to adopt the same sanitary conditions and equipment that all hospitals and other honest medical establishments must abide by and use. This caused outrage amongst the abortion crowd and caused the closure of a sizeable percentage of the clinics in some states. It was seen as an attack on abortion rather than a protection of the women. You can't have it both ways and still appear credible. At some point the lack of truth in a position, such as abortion, will make it evident to society that the entire premise is built on lies, destruction, fear, arrogance, and selfishness. If the people want to force the abortion clinics to abide by similar medical standards that other medical establishments are required to abide by, then it will clearly be advantageous for "*the health and safety of the women*." You can spot the liars by seeing who argues against *the safety of the women* regarding better standards for abortion clinics. If a clinic shuts down because of such a logical regulation, then we have to wonder why?

Your Sexual Conquests

With regard to abortion, I would like you to entertain this thought: Many abortions are done in secret. Why?

Is it not to hide or conceal a truth? In cases of rape, a woman may choose an abortion and may want it done in secret in order to hide the fact that she was raped, but in the end, what she is hiding is her pregnancy of the life within her that reveals the *unfair and unjust* attack against her. In the vast majority of cases, abortion is **not** the result of rape, so what truth is the abortion trying to hide? Is it not the **Life** that was brought about by abusing a privilege—a privilege that is best utilized during a fully committed relationship? Additionally, since the inception of legal abortions, abortion has become a convenience and is done in a very brazen manner. This way of thinking was brought about by a free and open sex movement during the later nineteen hundreds. But make no mistake in this regard: women have been aborting their children through various methods for a long time before the late nineteen hundreds, and it is murder nonetheless.

Are you proud of your sexual conquests? Do you encourage your children to repeat the reckless behavior of *your* youth? Glamorizing sex outside of fully committed relationships is reckless and foolish way to teach your children. We should not be opposed to telling our children, who are of a proper age, that intimate relations are very enjoyable between a man and a woman. However, we should include within that discussion, the details of pregnancy, the reasons that pregnancy occurs, and the truth of why sex is best utilized in a fully committed lifelong relationship.

While we, as parents, may have made mistakes due to our own not understanding things well enough to avoid error, there is no reason that we should not use these difficult lessons to our family's advantage. When the situation calls for it, teach your children with the experience you have gained from your own errors.

What did You Teach Your Children About Sex and Intimacy?

In teaching children about sex and intimacy, it is wise to get them to understand exactly what a 'fully committed" relationship is. "Fully committed" does not specifically refer to marriage; though, marriage is the common result of true commitment. Many marriages are missing commitment in almost the same way that many uncommitted relationships are. Being married does not constitute commitment, but true commitment generally does include marriage.

A fully committed relationship is one where *what is true* prevails. It will be a relationship built on honesty. The **only** reason relationships fail is because they lack what is true. This leads to violation and subsequent disappointment, resulting in frustration, and then anger, and finally resentment. Then the relationship loses trust; and a relationship without trust will *not* succeed.

Our task then, becomes to understand what trust is. The trust we are referring to here is not so much about intimate fidelity, but rather it is the trust of—not having the other person violate you *in any way*.

Teaching our children this very important lesson keeps their value of intimate relations high, and thus, they will be less likely to waste their virginity in a foolish and unproductive manner.

Allowing the school systems to be the educators of intimacy of our own children cheapens their understanding. Doing so gives someone else, with potentially entirely different values, the power of instructing *your own* children in intimacy. If you do not understand these things, then it is best that you learn them and understand them, and then instruct your own children in this regard. If you are utterly certain that the person instructing your children shares your exact same values, then allowing them to teach your children is fine. But, if you know that their values agree with your values, then you already must know about the details of intimacy; and so, you as parents would be best served to share that information with your children on your own at the appropriate times.

Abortion is clearly a disregard of life. Allowing your children to learn that abortion is okay and that it should be the mothers' choice, and that the fetus is merely a "blob of cells", is deceitful. Allowing such teachings to be taught to your children without restriction or explanation is a violation of their understanding of truth, and, in this case, it is you who has allowed them to believe the lies. This cheapens life in their eyes, and it cheapens *them* because *they* could have just as easily been the product of an abortion and thrown away in a waste basket.

Ask yourself, what value does it teach someone if their life is so meaningless that it is okay if Mommy does not want them and decides to rip them out of her body limb by limb before they are born, and then throws them in the trash, or worse, their parts are sold for experimentation for a profit?

Your position on abortion *does* matter to your children, and what you teach them, and what others teach them about abortion matters to them. Abortion is counterproductive to life, to family, and to humanity, and it matters to your family.

Chapter 10

Health and Truth

Typically, when parents are bringing their children up, a book about *family* is often aimed at disciplining *young* children. While that is an important part of a strong family, *Strong Family* is written for families with children of *all* ages, including ourselves, so it's not only about raising children. When your children are your age they will still be *your* children. For your own good and for their own good it is best to have a firm grasp of reality regarding health so that you can weed out the lies that come your way. The connections between health and truth are vast but subtle. Since the dawn of man, science (the questioning by mankind) has continually been *only beginning* to understand the connection between health and truth. It seems that the more we figure out, then the more we realize that we do not understand.

In reviewing history, we find that most societies felt that they had things figured out, only to come to destruction financially, socially, politically, and in health. This is likely to be repeated with any current society, provided that—*what is not*—gets whitewashed with lies and called *true*.

Our use of statistical analysis and its interpretation is greatly perverted by our own interpretation of the statistics and by our interpretation of society—this includes statistical health data. Based upon our skewed sense of statistical analysis, it appears that every disease is the *fastest rising* disease, or the leading *cause* of some health issue.

Over the years, we are slowly relearning that truth is an enormous factor in our health, though, it is not stated in such terms. Your family's health is affected by many things. When someone in your family suffers from ill health, it can be a heavy burden on your family. Your odds of having a healthy joyful family increase greatly when you address *all* aspects of health.

Eating Well

The old adage, "you are what you eat" has an obvious nature about it. Most people understand that eating well is good, and that eating bad things or poisonous things will harm you.

There are basics of eating that we all have a natural inclination for. We need water or water-based liquids and nutrition in fats, carbohydrates, and proteins, plus essential vital nutrients. Most of these are naturally sought by people through particular cravings, even though we may not realize that this is occurring in us.

Eating naturally occurring items that are grown with care have some of the best food value and will bring your health to the best it can be through means of food. But that is obviously not good enough because there are plenty of "health conscious" eaters who die at far younger than average ages or are of ill health. Why is this?

Do You Fall for the Health Lies?

There are a multitude of quality resources available with regard to eating well, so we won't dwell on that here. However, we will look at something that has far more of an effect on us and our families, yet is so subtle that we seldom realize its impact—it is *truth* and *lies*.

By now you should have grasped the *truth* and *lies* theme in this book. So as to not miss anything, we will cover all of the basics of its effects, with your family's *mind*-health being a very important element.

It has long been understood that when we are in deep concern, or intense worry, that it negatively affects our health. Few people would choose to be so blind as to challenge the obvious nature of this observation. What is not known is the *amount* or level of the affect that worry and certain methods of thinking actually have on our bodies.

In the beginning of the twenty-first century there was a great deal of research and analysis done on the human brain and its effects on the body. In line with our *in*accurate reading of statistics, we are similarly inaccurate with our reading the results of magnetic imaging and the dissection of healthy and unhealthy brains, their functions, and their condition—it is the basic cause-and-effect battle. In other words, which is the cause, versus, which is the effect?

To have a joyful strong family you must become a long-term planner. Think of your children in their old age; Do you want them of strong mind until the day they die, or do you want them to lose their senses and be unhealthy in their old age and die lonely in an unfeeling eldercare facility?

The cause-and-effect battle with the analysis of our mind health, brain health, and body health is similar to the assumption that because we *understand* something, then that is the cause.

An example would be: Because our brain is showing unusual activity and *from* that activity we have become depressed, versus our brain showing unusual activity *because* we have chosen to be depressed. In other words, which is the cause and which is the effect? Is our brain's activity from the depression or is the depression from our brain's activity?

All too often, the assumption is that, because our brain is showing peculiar and potentially unhealthy activity in a particular region, the activity is the cause of a given problem. This assumption has brought about an onslaught of medications that promised to cure the ailing brain and eradicate the problem behavior. Such a narrow view of our brains, and subsequently our bodies and our actions, inhibits true growth in the understanding of humans, humanity, and our bodies. Some of the deception is for financial gain, but most is from our own ignorance (**ignor-**ance is to ignore.)

Besides the inaccuracies and outright lies of society that we must weed out in order to get the truth, we also need to do the same with family. Society and the medical establishment often tell us that we have genetic predisposition to certain ailments and disease that has been passed down to us from our parents. But is this true? I am not saying that nothing is passed down genetically, but I am saying that very little if any disease is passed down genetically. The family disease lie is a very easy lie to fall for because it appears so apparent. In some ways the disease is passed down within the family, but not in the way we typically understand it to be transferred. We must be more careful in our analysis of exactly what it is that is being passed down from our parents. The family disease lie tells us that because our parents had a certain cancer or disease, then we are genetically predisposed to getting that same cancer or disease. But I propose something different: It is not a "mutated gene" that is passed down; but rather, it is our subtle mental and physical habits that are passed down that we get from our parents—it's *mutated thought.* Since the way we think and the way we eat have such tremendous impact on our health, it is logical to realize that it is our *habits* that we inherit from our parents. And it is these inherited habits that are often the cause of most of our ailments and health troubles.

I have not yet met a single soul whose health did not benefit from them changing their *eating **and** thinking* habits for the better.

Your Brain Activity

Regarding mind-body versus body-mind (the basic cause versus effect battle), as of the writing of these words, the scientific evidence of—which is the cause, and which is the effect—is inconclusive. But, the evidence for the correlation between your behavior and what is happening in the brain is very compelling, clearly indicating that there is a connection between the two regardless of which is the cause and which is the effect. It is up to you to test this in yourself and in your family. The truth will reside in your own clear-minded observation of your results.

Here is something that you can be confident in: Embracing what is true brings only good to your family. You have nothing to lose and everything to gain in choosing to live by what is true.

However, when embracing living by only what is true, you might feel a temporary let-down while eradicating the bad things and bad people from your family that you incorrectly believe you have become dependent upon. But, in doing so you will be building a foundation for your family that is beautiful and is *not* subject to future erosion.

Our bodies are machines of unparalleled beauty and complexity. These machines thrive on the way we each perceive life, and on the choices that we make, and in the way in which we use our brains. Our "mind" is an obscure term that is separate from our brain.

Some people believe that our mind and brain are one in the same, while others liken the *mind* more to, or as—the soul. The battle is in the semantics of the word *mind*, but in general, when "*mind* " is discussed we are referring to our individual nature—It is the part that makes you, **you**.

Artificial intelligence can produce amazing results, but seems to fail at the ability to converse and create as a human can create. This is where the *mind* comes in; the mind is what differentiates. So then, does our brain control our mind, or does our mind control our brain?

Making the assumption that, because our brain appeared a certain way in a scan image we will behave a certain way comes up short of true understanding. It is because we behave a certain way that our brains show various activities; this was made apparent in the research during the early twenty-first century, but was largely ignored by many in the medical and scientific communities.

Much of the testing during the era was done via live imaging. Brains of individuals who exhibited certain behaviors were imaged, and common patterns emerged in these peoples' recorded brain images while they partook in various physical and mental exercises. The conclusion was accurate in making an association between the thought-behavior and the patterns observed in the brain, but the medical-scientific error often was in the conclusion that the brain condition caused the thinking behavior, rather than the thinking causing the brain image patterns.

The reason we can, instead, deduce that the cause was actually the thinking behavior caused the pattern rather than the other way around is because, in other tests, the test subjects were being imaged and were instructed to undertake given mental tasks, which when carried out showed a predictable result on the subjects' brain scans. When they implemented the mental actions of those tasks, then their brain's image would display semi-predictable brain region patterns in the result.

In other words, the way we think makes the pattern, rather than the pattern causing the way we think.

It is true that, which of these is the cause and which is the effect can still be debated. However, we must at least fully consider that the activity we see in the brain's image may be, and likely is, the result of a person's mental behavior and thinking, rather than the cause of it.

Our *thinking* being the cause of the way our brains appear is the likely reality, as opposed to the brain's condition causing our behavior. In truth, the most likely explanation is, and will prove to be, that anomalies of the brain start with our thinking and our mind. It is our thinking and our mind that affects our brain and its activity patterns, and subsequently our physical actions. Yet, we cannot ignore the reciprocal effect of this. If you allow yourself to feel "down," it will certainly set up patterns in your brain, and those patterns will chemically add to your "down" mood. In a similar way, the opposite is true for Joy! Meaning: if you feel "up" you will likely feel even more "up" by feeling up because of the positive chemistry then output by your body.

What Goes in Your Ears, Goes in Your Body

From a scientific *and* naturalist perspective, the effects of words on the body are undeniable. Since our bodies are chemical machines, everything that occurs within them is a chemical action or reaction. This means that when you, or more importantly, your children, hear something, then those sounds affect their inner ear functions and those functions send instantaneous physical and chemical reactions through the ear and the connecting nerves, producing the reactions in the brain and causing the part that is *them* to perceive the words sensed by the ears.

Your children's perception of your words causes a reaction of an emotion, including the largely overlooked emotion of indifference. All emotions alter our children's biochemistry and cause them to act or speak in a certain way and display the connected emotion. When this happens it is permanently and irreversibly affecting their bodies. This point is not up for debate, though we can debate its *level* of importance or effect on the body. The same situation applies to any way in which we receive information or sensory perceptions with any of our body's senses.

When you say words to your children, or communicate with them, then in general that communication is becoming an actual real part of their physical body. Their disposition will be affected by your words, and it will subsequently affect their health. Speak bad words to them and you will create bad chemical chain reactions in their bodies causing their health to begin to compromise. Or, speak wonderful joyful words of love and encouragement to them and create in them good healthy biochemistry. It's your choice. Do not mistake this as saying that you cannot get angry with a child for their poor behavior. If you allow a child to behave in a poor or bad manner, it is equally as damaging as unfair words used towards them. Always discipline when discipline is due.

When we speak truth to our children they will absorb that truth and it becomes a part of their physical body via their body's chemistry. Conversely, when we teach them things that are not true, then that also will become a part of their body's chemistry. When we are not discerning, and allow our children to live life without weighing everything on the scale of truth, then we have chosen to allow them to believe lies. Thinking or believing things that are not true *will* affect their body's chemistry.

Choosing to believe that we evolved from a single cell is no different than believing a brick house evolved from a single brick just because the house is made of bricks. Believing a simple rock that appears chipped away to a point to be a direct and intentional design for use as a spearhead by ancient humans seems so easy for people to believe; but believing that a highly complex but tiny cell occurred as a result of *deliberate intention* is a stretch for many of us. Our thinking in this way is inconsistent, it is not? In reality, is it not more likely for a rock to simply get chipped to a point through erosion or in a cataclysmic catastrophe, than for the complexity of even the simplest cell to form through the chance effects of natural selection?

This sort of evolution belief inhibits you from being able to consider the following: *We* were Created for Truth! Violating our purpose for bearing truth, paints over the facts about the effects that the violations against us have on our bodies when we believe things that are not true.

When our mind is in conflict, then our bodies suffer greatly. Did you ever have an argument with someone who was very close or dear to you? How did you feel? Do you think that living that way will increase or decrease your lifespan and health? Do you think it affects your body? Did you feel your heart race? Did you get shaky or tremble from fear or anger? Did you think about it afterwards?

As you can see by your answers to these questions, it is blatantly obvious that what is in our mind has tremendous effect on our bodies.

Only when you have chosen to believe that we are Created with purpose by a Creator, will you be able to begin to fully understand the negative effects on you, of living a life embracing what is not true.

A Scientific Conclusion

While medical science will never, and should never *absolutely conclude*, science is more and more finding that our genes are more affected by the way we think, than is the way we think affected by our genes and chemistry. This observation of the data is difficult to refute when looking at the data with open eyes *without* ignoring the obvious.

Your Children and Medication Abuses

Our bodies are amazing and complex chemical machines, the brain being the control center through which—*that which is you*—controls the body vessel.

The body machine is designed to receive communication from its environment and respond accordingly. This is in order to learn, share, and to protect and preserve itself. When our brain, or more importantly, our children's brains, are subjected to things that are bad, or contrary to what is good and true, then those little brains will respond accordingly by putting out various corresponding chemistry that is sometimes harmful to their little bodies.

The response often is displayed in the form of frustration and anger, or withdrawal. When their life is contrary to their natural desire, then they *will* act out. When this is repeated often enough, then parents sometimes bring the child into the doctor for analysis. Then the tests typically indicate that the child has any one of a litany of behavioral diseases or disorders. This is nothing new and in some form has been going on for a very long time. Medication is then often prescribed for the child and the medication chemicals typically become a substitute for the chemicals that should normally have occurred if the child was living a life built upon a foundation of *understanding* and *truth*.

The medication chemicals can cause irreparable damage if they are abused and used too long, thus causing the body to shut down or inhibit its ability to produce the original chemicals because the brain no longer senses a need of those chemicals due to their artificial substitution. This is similar to what would happen to your muscles through atrophy if you did not use them and instead hired someone to do *everything* for you.

Using medication in this way is clearly drug abuse. And the doctors, teachers, and even parents are the drug pushers. If our brains are having something else produce the chemicals for us, then the brain has no need to change anything or even to try to change anything. The likely result of long-term usage of substitution chemicals for this purpose creates a dependency. This dependency will destroy the *purpose* and the *will* of those who are subjected to those chemicals or medications. Further, it allows us to ignore the true source of the real problem in the person's life.

Changing Your Reality

The enlightenment movement spoken of earlier has a belief that you can change your reality as if it is somehow different from everyone else's reality. But you live in a world with the rest of us, and your reality is our reality, and our reality is yours. Though, your circumstances are your own and *are* alterable by you.

You cannot change your reality, but you can change your circumstances by the way you think—and *that* is very important to understand and to teach to your children! Your reality is real and it is what **is**. Your reality is true, and whether it is good or bad, it is still true. You may have built your foundation on untrue things, and reality reflects the truth about your situation or condition. Reality is what **is** and we are all in it together!

Do not try to make two plus two equal five, because that is a waste of time and will never happen. It is not a reality. But you can change your circumstances by rejecting lies and not accepting things that are untrue. Teach your children this skill and teach them to live by this, and then it is likely that both their mental and physical health will be increased, and their lives will be enriched and lengthened for decades of Love, Joy, and Peace!

Chapter 11

Is it Really In Your Genes?

The topic of genetic disease goes hand in hand with the mind/brain and body topic that we just covered. Blaming all of our health and mental woes on genetics will not ever make our health or behavioral problems vanish. We will not say here that some peculiar disease developing in a part of our bodies cannot be genetic, but let's explore the topic a bit and get a real sense of the genetics issue.

Are there people who have ADHD or Autism or other such behavioral "diseases"? The answer is yes and no. Initially, these types of disease names are created to describe peculiar strong tendencies to behave in certain ways. However, many of these labels have become the scapegoat for our own parental failures. This is not true for every child diagnosed with such diseases, but it is true for far too many children who have been improperly labeled as such.

Blaming Genetics Won't Make Your Problems Go Away

One prominent area of genetic blame is that of obesity. People say, "My parents were fat and therefore I am too." Believing this will keep you overweight for as long as you choose to believe it. There is only one way to lose weight; and that is to use or burn more calories than your body absorbs.

The deception of genetic predisposition to obesity is easy to spot and is only believed by those of us who do not want to change our eating habits and/or our activity levels. This topic is even more difficult when we're discussing certain kinds of disease, such as cancer and heart disease or mental illness.

Both cancer and heart disease are often thought to be genetically transferred. However, there are subtle effects of life that are commonly ignored in the equation. Where do these subtle effects occur? Subtle *family habits* of course.

Family habits have an impact on our health. First the obvious, such as similar eating habits within the family. In many homes, the mother makes meals based upon the desires of the father, and then the children become very familiar with those eating habits and adopt those habits as their own lifelong eating habits. This means that if problems occur due to eating habits of the parents, then problems will likely follow the children due to the children's subtle eating habits that are adopted from the parents.

The effects of our eating habits on our health are obvious, but the very subtle effect our mind has on our body is not so clear to us.

Family mentality most certainly occurs, and this is obvious because children often have views similar to the parents' views. This means that if the parents have poor life-views, then the children are likely to have similar by poor life-views. As we discussed earlier, our environment, which includes the words we hear, the things we see, or any other form of perception, is, without question, processed by our brain and thus affects our body.

If your family mentality is very negative, or in constant strife, or if you are in constant doubt in your heart, then all of that is being taught to your children. Whether or not you realize it, this is all becoming a part of them and their bodies for the better or for the worse.

Since what is true is good, and what is not true is *not* good, it is reasonable to assume that what is *not* true is therefore bad for you and will ultimately harm your body. If you think in a negative manner, then you are harming yourself, and you are teaching your children to do the same.

Blaming Genetics is Like...

Blaming genetics is like putting *your* work on someone else's desk and expecting that it will get done. Your boss will ask, "Where is your work and why isn't it done?" Then pointing at your parent you will answer "On his desk." Then your boss will say, "Why is *your* work on someone else's desk?" If you are honest you will say, "I was hoping that they would do it for me so that I wouldn't have to deal with it." When we blame genetics for everything, we are performing this same action and are hoping that placing the blame somewhere else will somehow excuse us, or that it will get someone else to solve our problem for us, but it won't.

The possibility of DNA alterations occurring from the way that we think or the way we use our mind is not precisely scientifically quantifiable, yet, but is highly probable. Mind, thought, and soul cannot be measured in a scientific manner. Their value is strictly based upon true or false. If you are not in truth, then you are in a lie and you will suffer the health consequences of your own mental choices. This is true even if you are unaware that you are doing so. This cannot be denied without being wrong or believing a lie. It is such a simple truth that it is seldom noticed by us; and thus, it is ignored. Meaning, you likely have been blinded by the errors in society's conventional thinking.

What is Disease

Disease is another nasty label that, when broken down, means *dis*, *un*, or *not*, and the *ease* part, in this case, means *comfort*. "Disease" means *not-comfortable*. The labels of most diseases are often either the name of a person who had the disease, a doctor who outlined a common pattern of the disease, or the label that is a description or an abbreviation of the symptoms or its chemical name. It's sad to watch people embrace diseases with such fervor, it's as if *we actually want to complain* to brag about our disease; or worse, we want to brag about our child's disease. We often hear people boldly proclaim that they or someone else has a particular ailment, as if this is a badge of honor. It becomes an excuse for our lack of desire and ambition to actually make the needed changes in our lives.

Conditions, Diseases, and Disorders

Somewhere there might be hard conclusive scientific definition for conditions, diseases, and disorders, but from a public perspective those terms are ambiguous and commonly freely interchanged. A "condition" reports the state of a disease. In other words: someone's heart is in very bad *condition* from degenerative heart *disease*. Disorders tend to be associated with psychological issues. Regardless of the chosen term, the words *condition, disease,* and *disorder* are ambiguous at best, recalling of course, that the word disease basically means *uncomfortable*. They are all just labels indicating that something is not as it should be.

Hyperactivity

Before the medical community embraced a "disease" or "disorder" as something other than varying discomfort levels, children who were a bit overactive were deemed "hyperactive." This caused parents to use the term *hyperactive* to explain their child's poor and seemingly uncontrollable behavior. Once this trend caught on, a world-wide epidemic of new behavioral diseases was born. These new diseases were perpetuated by money at the expense of our families and children. The sad part is that a large number of parents bought into these untrue perceptions, with vigor, in effort to shirk their parental duties and responsibility for their children's poor behavior.

ADHD

Labels, such as ADHD (Attention Deficit Hyperactivity Disorder), were deeply intrusive conditions/diseases/disorders that took the world by storm in the late nineteen hundreds.

Teachers and parents embraced the ADHD disorder label when they could not control overactive children or children who would not pay attention in class or at home. These children were brought in to the doctor and diagnosed with the disorder. Then medications were prescribed for the child and administered by the parents, teachers, or the school nurse. The medication calmed the children into a mild sedation so that they would remain calm and have better focus. This worked similar to a sedative or sometimes more of a stimulant depending on the situation. But, it didn't stop there; children who were given these drugs frequently needed adjustments in the medication to compensate for them becoming accustomed to the drug; and in many cases, maybe even most cases, additional drugs or medications were given to the children to offset the side effects caused by the initial drugs given.

Some of the side effects were restlessness, tremors, anxiety, nervousness, headaches, dizziness, insomnia, dryness of the mouth, constipation, high blood pressure, and psychosis which can bring about hallucinations, plus many other such side effects including death.

The treatments for the so called ADHD disorder damaged many children far more than the "disorder" itself would have if they had left the child be and simply offered them the proper love, care, and discipline that was lacking in their life.

Autism

The word *autism* is another dangerous and horrible label placed on children that often stigmatizes them throughout childhood and into adulthood. The word "autism" comes from the word *auto* meaning self. We could call the disease *self-ism*. It was named so in order to easily describe or label those who behaved in a manner where the patient behaves in a peculiarly withdrawn way. There are varying degrees of this behavior, but in more recent times, any behavior resembling the description whatsoever, even the mildest behaviors, were often wrongly diagnosed as "autistic".

Sadly, parents and doctors, blinded by their own incorrect beliefs, regarded this as a *disease* instead of embracing it with *understanding*. Their view caused many truly gifted people to be thought of as near retarded (lagging behind), and often they were discarded or hidden away because the parents were embarrassed of the child's uncommon behavior. Understanding a person's unique and beautiful born-in gift can take them from socially being considered a "retard" in some people's eyes, to being a genius to the rest of the world!

The only true so-called "retards" are those who cannot see their way clear to seeing the genius in **all** people. The term "retard", here, has the underlying meaning of being *retarded* or *lagging* behind. If we choose to believe wrongly about people then we surely lag behind others.

There is an awful truth in labeling, and it is that children often become as their parents and elders expect, as is discussed in the cornerstone book *Hot Water*. If your child shows signs of some sort of variation from what you believe is "normal", and you then take them into the doctor for analysis, the doctor may well agree with your suspicion. Typically, when parents buy into everything that a doctor says, they, in some manner, will tell their child the diagnosis. If the doctor's diagnosis is that the child is "retarded", then the parents will often tell the child that they are slow or retarded. Usually, this is done via the parents treating the child as if they *are* retarded or slow.

Sure, there are people who have an obvious and severe handicap to a point where they have difficulty controlling their body movements. But even with those people, we unfairly treat them like they are stupid, when, in truth, we have no idea of how brilliant they actually might be. Just because they do not verbally articulate in a "normal" manner does not mean that they are incapable of learning or expressing brilliance. There is little doubt that there have been many children labeled as "retarded" over the years that would have been considered "normal" as adults. They lagged behind a bit as children, and because of that, "the system" considered them "retards" or "slow" and treated them as such. Then, as a result, they lived as they were expected to and were taught in school in a manner as if they were retarded or slow.

People, especially children, are far more resilient and brilliant than most of us were led to believe. If we teach children that they are "retards" then retards they will be! *All people* deserve the same respect of hope, positive expectation, and Love. Shortchanging a child, as was offensively done by psychologists in the early nineteen hundreds through to the twenty-first century, labeling *them* for *our own* short-sightedness is unfair to them on every level you can think of. To create brilliant children, treat them and interact with them as if they are brilliant! *Expect* them to learn and create. Teach them to learn and create. Give them a chance in life, especially if, for some reason, you wrongly believe that they are "retarded." Short people need to reach further to touch what a taller person can easily touch. When a child appears a bit slower than "normal" they may need to work a bit harder, but that does *not* make them retarded or handicapped, it makes them *different.*

Statistics

As touched on a few chapters back, misreading statistics is the blind spot that many of us have—which is dominantly led by doctors, researchers, politicians, and the media.

We correctly detect that a correlation exists between what we see in the body, brain, and the outward behaviors of those who are labeled with a disease. Science seems to get quite excited when these correlations are finally realized, but the correlations are typically misunderstood and misread.

When you choose to understand the truth, then these correlations are obvious. The difference between truth and something that is *not* true, in the case of disease and statistics is— what the **cause** is, versus what the **effect** is. Understanding which is which will change your view on these and other so called "diseases" that seem to be statistically ever on the rise. Let's give humanity more credit and assume and accept our own responsibility in the matter of raising children.

Know and accept that most behavioral problems in children are induced and fed by our actions as parents.

Dangerous Labels

We discussed labels earlier, but to refresh our memories: Labels are typically descriptions which have lost their meaning in translation or over time.

Name-calling labels serve the purpose of hiding reality as do the other types of labels. We feel powerful when we use labels.

When we call people names it makes us feel good or superior while not needing to explain ourselves.

Even though the name-calling labels may be descriptive and may be potentially true or accurate, they are still mostly nothing more than mere name-calling in order to hide something about our own self. Usually it is our own inability to communicate to a person and our own frustration that we are trying to hide. It's perplexing to hear parents discussing their child's "condition" as if it is somehow something to brag about. Not all people in that position do so, but we see this often where the parents almost seem proud to discuss their child's questionable condition. It's almost as if they are doing it for the attention and the sympathies that they get from the people who they share their woes with.

With conditions and diseases we want to label others who are different or gifted, as autistic or the like, but *gifted* is *gifted!*

Nurture your children's gifts and do not call those gifts a disease. **Your job**, as a parent, is to figure out how to bring those gifts out, and how to make them grow into something wonderful and useful for the child, rather than turning them into poisonous weeds by treating them and labeling them as such.

Labels are convenient and they make **us** feel better, but labels are dangerous to those on whom we apply them. Labeling people becomes dangerous when we fail to understand the labels as they were intended to be understood. Failing to use a label properly allows us to believe that our child "has something" as if it were a virus.

"Disease" labels, especially behavioral ones, are dangerous to your family's well-being. Accepting that your child has a disease of a particular *label* forever inhibits your ability to approach your child in truth and actually solve, or teach *them* to solve, their problem.

Most *diseases* are not true as we typically think of "disease", and believing that they are is a cop-out. It is placing our work on another person's desk and hoping it will get done. It is our attempt for a quick cure for our own problems, shortcomings, and failures. Failing to recognize this will cost you your children and your joy. There are very few children who cannot be cured of these behavioral disease labels through love, truth, proper parenting, and understanding.

Giving children any message that does not build them up is a terrible thing to do to a child. I am not talking about falsely propping them up by telling them they did great when they clearly failed. Rather, I am saying, believe in them and teach them only good things. Children are beautiful and brilliant, smart and energetic, and it is your duty to teach them to be so, and also to let them know that they are beautiful, loving, kind, intelligent, and good!

Chapter 12

Parental Rewards

Don't believe something is true because *I* said so; but rather, believe something because *it* *is* *so*. You will see the rewards very quickly when you understand how to properly embrace truth in this way. Whether your child is diagnosed with a questionable disease, or is going down the wrong path, you will be in charge and will understand what they need from you in order to quickly get them back on track only when you embrace truth. Each moment of realization is another fresh beginning to change your family and to start building sound children. *This* is one of those moments because what you choose to believe about this topic defines you.

Your Children are Little Mirrors

Your children are little mirrors who reflect the image of their parents. This frightens many of us and we tend to ignore this and blame anything other than ourselves, but our children are near perfect reflections of us. This unavoidable and true point is critical for all parents to understand and embrace. The reason that this frightens us is that when our children behave in a way that frustrates us, then we are forced to realize that they are typically copying our own behavior to a great extent. Sometimes children appear very different in their outward actions and logic, but their underlying logic or actions are identical to us parents. To better illustrate this point, sometimes we will even go as far as to say things to our children like, "Just wait until you have children of your own and they act like you're acting." We can deny this all we want and claim that we got stuck with rotten children; but I strongly believe that there are no rotten children, but rather, *we* are rotten parents *until* we choose to change that!

Why are some of us parents "rotten?" It is because we have chosen something other than—the foundation of truth—that we have been discussing in vivid detail. We are corrupted by the things that are not true, which we have chosen to live by. These untrue things are lies and they infect our hearts and minds, and as a result they rot away our ability to accept what is true. To reject what is true is to accept lies. Accepting lies will consistently decay all good things in your life and bring them to ruin.

You Get What You Worked For

The choice of what you accept for a foundation for your family is *your* own choice—it is of *your* own making. And you can be certain that your results will be directly proportional to your choice of foundation.

> You *will* get the pay that is due to you!

If you have chosen to believe that your children have some "disease" and you choose to allow things that are not true into your family, then you will likely also be fairly paid with problems such as doubt, uncertainty, strife, high medical expenses, unhappy children, divorce, and a long list of other such ill rewards.

On the other hand, if you have worked hard and have been a diligent worker in most or all aspects of life, then you will be repaid with a strong family full of joy and beauty. This simple and true statement will not let you down—you can rely upon it! It is a dependable truth; and, with it, you can be certain that you will be repaid according to your works, choices, and decisions.

Aside of the potential afterlife consequences, from an earthly perspective, you will get what you worked for and you will not be shorted in life. Good or bad, we eventually get our due pay.

As a parent, this is critically important because what you work for is reflected in your children. When parents rule with an unreasonable iron fist, or when they fail to firmly guide their children with love, truth, and respect, then the children cannot be expected to show respect towards their parents because respect is partly learned. When a parent gains the full respect of their children, then the parents' disappointment of the children's bad behavior is often enough to detour the children from further bad behavior. When a child responds in a positive way to their parents' disappointment, then it is a truly wonderful thing for the family, because very little punishment is needed, *if* any is needed at all. Be aware that sometimes we parents abuse the disappointment aspect of parenting and use it to manipulate children into doing what we parents want, rather than having the children pursue what are natural gifts within the children's good natural talents and interests.

The Cost of Your Failures

If you fail to embrace these truths, then you *will* pay at some point later in life. It may be tomorrow, or some years in the future, but, rest assured, or in this case *no* rest assured, you *will* pay the price. As stated in the last section, you *will* get your reward—that is certain.

It's interesting that when we follow error we tend to equate it with a *price to pay*. Where, when we follow what is good and we do good, then we tend to think of it as *getting paid* or being *rewarded*. This perception is within each our own minds. Our perception of the "*You will get what you worked for*" statement reveals much to others about our own state of thinking and our state of mind.

Your price for failure is the joy you will **not** see in your family life. You will be constantly chasing your shadow, running in circles in unsuccessful efforts of trying to gain order in your life. The years pass quickly and wasting even one moment's time in such fruitless effort cheats your family out of the Joy that they all deserve. Even people who are mean or ruthless will often succeed in the areas of life where they fully accept and embrace things that are true. This is why *bad* people can succeed, but their success is often at the expense of other people who they have taken from in some manner.

It is said that freedom isn't free. It is also said that soldiers being killed is the price for freedom. *Truth* is the only freedom and you must embrace truth in order to be free. It sounds sort of demanding, doesn't it? I must choose truth or I am not free. That is exactly right! The freedom to choose truth is what so many soldiers have died for. It is your choice to be held in bondage by your own decisions. Following things that are not true locks you into a lie from which there is only one escape! Your only escape is to choose what is true. If you do not choose truth for yourself, then you have chosen a lie.

The high cost of *failure to choose truth* is your family's life, and that is a very high cost indeed! To free yourself from this nasty life-debt, a decision must be made. It is up to you and your family to make the decision to live *only* by what is true.

Your Foundational Keys

Your foundational keys of *Truth* and *Understanding* are the keys to a strong family; and your parental rewards for building and maintaining a strong foundation are strong children, a strong family, and a strong marriage relationship. The joys that you will experience by doing this are many, and your cost is **zero**! Your family *will* thrive when you all choose this way of life.

What You Believe Matters

As a parent, your family will pay a price for your beliefs. Teaching your children the uncertainty of human evolution or the uncertainty of society's inaccurate interpretation of the Bible and Creation costs your family dearly. Be accurate about these things. Research things for yourself instead of just repeating what someone told you. Be consistent in everything that you do, for instance, some parents may be pleased with a pro-abortion view of life, but this inconsistent view is certain to cloud the minds of their children. The only true way to be consistent is to weigh *everything* on the scale of truth. This means that you will hide no facts in effort to make something seem to be what it is not, but rather you will use utter honesty in your own life. We often, hypocritically, hold others to truth, but then we ourselves delight in our own lies.

What you believe and the way you think *will* affect you **and** your children; there is no escape from this fact. When your beliefs are consistent in all areas of your life, then you will be rewarded with children who are focused, content, creative, responsible, respectable, and joyful!

Chapter 13

Building a Child and a Family

Before we get into the finer details of building a family, this chapter gives you an overview so that you can better understand the points made in the following chapters. Everything you have read in this book up to this point was strictly about your family foundation. A foundation is something that is typically not specifically seen or noticed by anyone, and it has many different bricks that seemingly have no connecting thread other than being a part of your foundation but are very important nonetheless. While we typically don't think about or notice the foundation, the foundation is the most important part of any structure. Think of a home; the foundation of a home is typically buried and forgotten, yet, all the while, it is the single most important part of your home, holding it strong and firm, keeping it steadily in place.

The fact that few of us notice a foundation, of anything, is the reason that we often experience problems in our lives. Our failure to notice this is the reason we cannot figure out what makes some families successful, while other families, struggle, and often result in failure in the end.

All too often, our choice of what we believe is built upon the lies and deceptions of others. These deceptions include both the

Church view and the scientific or naturalists views. Both positions have varying views full of accidental, intentional, and ignorant deceptions. These are deceptions that we are left to sort out on our own. Slowly, over time, the complete and full truth will always be revealed. And when it is, it is likely that *everyone* will feel somewhat embarrassed; *some*, more than others. Much of the embarrassment is due to the errors in our own agendas that we are trying to force onto other people.

We struggle because we fail to see the importance of a strong foundation. There is little reason to become angry in a discussion when you stand on the side of truth. It is when we are trying to *unsuccessfully* promote our lies that we become easily frustrated and angry. My intention is to get everyone to open their eyes wide and see it all, and what everything truly is. I do not want anyone to believe what *I* think to be true just because *I said so*. What I want is for everyone to believe something because *you* see that *it is so*. Your family must be built upon this premise in order to be able to withstand the scrutiny of truth.

Two Kinds of People, Which are You?

There are two kinds of people in our world: those who want instructions, and those who want to *understand* the instructions.

Those who want instruction typically do not understand the foundation of the task. They will be competitive and will often be unsuccessful and unhappy with their own results, subsequently letting down those around them and ending in feelings of personal failure about themselves. Those who *understand* the instructions have faced the truths about what the instructions all entail.

Since the first half of this book was about the foundational understanding of truth, we will now focus briefly on the other type of person who desires instructions and does not understand truth.

When we are the type of person who wants instructions, then we are asking to be told what to do. To a certain extent this is needed initially for most tasks while we learn them. But later, it is critical that we have an understanding of the task itself. If we do not, then we will always need to re-read the instructions. This wastes a great deal of our time and effort and causes us to *not* be able to effectively move forward in life.

Society has adapted to, and tightly adheres to, the ill phenomenon of insisting upon being instructed, and we have undertaken to "educate" the youth of the world in this way. This in itself is not a bad thing; in fact, many great things have come about through teaching. The problem is not the fact that we are showing our children, or other people, how to do certain things; the problem comes in when we fail to teach them to fully understand those things that we teach them. We wrongly say "this is the way it must be done" and "if you fail to do it this way then you are wrong" and are thus a failure.

Unfortunately, the schools have become places where children learn that "this is the way it is and you must accept that, and that's all that there is to it!" With each generation of new teachers who have been taught this method of thinking, the problem grows worse.

Some children who have been taught to accept information as stated, without being taught to *understand* the information itself, at some point, will grow up and become teachers. Then when they become teachers, the problem increases its power over themselves and their students. The new teacher, who lacks the ability to understand, will typically not allow a challenge to what they say in the classroom. Thus, forcing the children to believe things as the teacher presents them, rather than learning truth and learning to **dis***cover* on their own.

It is not much of a problem, provided that the teacher is actually correct in their interpretation and presentation of the information to the children. However, when a teacher does not understand the material, then a great opportunity for error arises— it is tragic how often this actually occurs.

When we do not understand something, then we are forced to accept the information as presented and we have forfeited our ability to question or even see things that seem incorrect. We all should be the type of person who seeks to *understand* the instructions rather than to merely *follow* the instructions. It is mostly those who choose to understand the instructions that see great success in their own lives.

The Risky Economics of Two Working Parents

Because we are largely *not* taught the skill of understanding, we fall into traps that waste some of our best days and cause us to throw away our joy—Joy which could otherwise be firmly in our grasp.

Culturally, society has accepted the notion that we must live a certain way, and that if we do not, then we will not be happy.

Two working parents is a very good example of this. If your children are in school, then being at work while they are in school is not much of an issue. However, when we abandon our children, by both parents working or working many extra hours for the sake of a new car or larger house, then we must examine the economics of our choices. Seldom do we purchase our large dollar items with cash. The money is typically borrowed. When we borrow money for a house, depending upon the interest rates, we can end up paying near double for it in the end. With vehicles, the interest is not as much a factor, but when you consider that the moment you drive the vehicle off of the lot that it loses a fair percentage of its value and will lose most of its value within ten years, then you must take serious account of where you place your energy with regard to your family.

When both parents work, they seldom calculate **all** of the costs, such as daycare, extra gas, a vehicle reliable enough for a daily ride to work, work clothing, extra vehicle mileage expenses, increased income tax bracket etc. This list goes on and is dependent upon your situation.

When the extra expenses are balanced against the actual take-home wage, then the balance often tips towards the expenses. Meaning that, it costs some people more for both parents to work than it would for only one parent to work—they actually lose money doing so, which is usually compensated for by borrowing more money.

None of the economics mentioned above are taking into account the stresses on you or your family; nor are these economics considering the effects on your children or the bad lessons that they learn from you doing so. Additionally, it does not consider the financial effects of the medical or psychological care typically resulting from the stresses caused by both parents working and children who have little direction due to the parents working.

Most families with two fulltime working parents, are only gaining a very small amount of extra money from the second income. In most cases, we would be much better off by offsetting our income through being more diligent with our money, or doing some sort of low paying flexible work at home to earn a few extra dollars.

What Working Moms Do Not Want to Hear

We could argue about whether the mother or the father should be the one working, but that is really a family decision. Mothers are often better in nurturing children in the early childhood years, though, many fathers have also proven to be very good at this. Yet, it seems evident that since mothers are the ones giving birth and are built with the ability to breast feed, that those are good indicators that the intention was for mothers to be the dominant caregivers during the early childhood years.

Too many mothers have an incorrect notion that they are inadequate unless they have gone to college and/or have a fulltime job or career. Much of which is because mothers are directly told that they *are* inadequate, or *feel* that they are due to societal pressures when they decide to stay at home to care for and teach their children. When the truth is that there is nothing more important or more noble than to care for and bring up good stable children. Oh what a wonderful world we would live in if that were the case!

Many mothers, once they do have a "successful" job, often feel as if they have missed out on their children's lives. The reason that many working mothers feel this way is because *they have!* Mothers have cast away one of their most precious gifts that they will ever have—*time with their children*; time to teach them things that *are*, and time to love them and be with them.

If you're bothered by this thought, then it is a good indication that something is not right in the way you have chosen to handle your family life. Working mothers: have you examined your motives? Why do you have your job? Is it to better your family, is it to buy things you can do without, or is it for the façade of prestige?

Some mothers are single and left to do it all alone; in many of these cases the mother would prefer to be able to be with her children, but must choose between working for income, starving, or being on government handout programs. Such government programs often destroy the integrity and morale of the mother and the child. Many single mothers would not be alone in this regard had they been taught properly by their parents about the high cost of premature intimacy spoken of in an earlier chapter.

A well-organized family can have both parents working and spending time with their children without placing them in daycare. Your children are with you for a very short time and then, unless you choose to home-school, they are sent off to school.

Typically, well over half of your earnings go to taxes, gas, and other such work-oriented expenses. This means that, for most people, half of the time we spend working goes towards taxes, getting to work, and for the job itself. Of the remaining money, we will buy things that, in general, we don't need, much of which will be gone in less than a year or two. Most of it will be gone in only weeks or even days after we get paid.

We have been led to believe that money is the almighty, and that the more of it we have, then the better off we are. While money is a helpful tool, it is not as important as your time with your children.

Your Time is Almighty
Are You Trustworthy for Your Children?

Money is not almighty, but your time is almighty with regard to your family. You get to choose to save that time up, either in your family account or in your bank account.

This one thing you can be certain of: With each economic collapse, about every five to ten years, people lose a great deal of their "fortunes" and become afraid of what they will do without their money. However, if you put your time and love into building strong children and a strong family, then you will not feel afraid and alone in those difficult times. When your investments dwindle, you will not have to think about how you sacrificed your family for the money that is now mostly lost, gone, and vanished due to bad investments!

Children who are well-taught never turn their backs on their parents. If they do turn against their parents, then one of two things has likely occurred.

One, you failed them in childhood, and in some cases by not raising them yourselves.

And/or two, you were indifferent in raising them and they were drawn and influenced negatively because of your indifference or lack of teaching them what is true.

The older the children are, then the more work and the longer it takes to rebuild their trust in you when it has been lost. Building trust is truly what it is all about. Are you trustworthy for your children? Could your children, in the past, or can they now, trust you as a source of truly *accurate* and *reliable* information? Many of us think, "Well of course! I would give my life for my children." Ah, but do you?

Sadly, many of us are too tied up in the affairs of our day-to-day lives and don't give our lives for anything but our vain desires. Our children expect us, as parents, to teach them what to do and how to live. If we break that trust, then they will not have true respect for us.

Your *time* alive is your *life*. Exchanging it for a pile of money will gain you nothing in the end except for unhappiness. Build your foundation and your family *first*, and *then* worry about your bank account.

"I Raised Professionals, But They are all Divorced"

Many of us have taken a great deal of pride in our careers and have taught our children that to be a "success" they must go to school and focus on their career. Yet, all too often, we hear stories such as, "I raised professionals and they have prestigious jobs and make a lot of money but... they are all divorced and unhappy." Or they have a prestigious degree but *still* live at home.

If having a great career is the answer to happiness, then there would be no family strife in those families where status and money are abundant. There would be no divorce, no drug use, no alcoholism, and no other major behavioral problems—but, this is clearly not the case.

Teaching our children that money and status are the road to happiness is like building a house with no foundation at all, where now the wooden walls are left sitting on the damp soil, causing the structure to, with certainty, begin to quickly rot away. The house **will** collapse; it is not a matter of *if*, it is a matter of **when**. Putting money ahead of your family is an error that is often worse when both parents are working. So where does it all start?

When is it Too Late to Discipline Your Children?

It is *never* too late to discipline children. No matter what their age or yours is, children will always have a certain amount of respect for their parents. The important factor is not their age or your age; the important factor is this: Is what you are trying to tell them undeniably true, or is it something that *you* demand that they do or believe?

Typically, when children turn against their parents it's because they have been betrayed by their parents. This betrayal is usually not deliberate, but it hurts them and is damaging nonetheless. Teaching your children what you heard, or teaching them what you were told to believe—without understanding it yourself—makes you susceptible to being incorrect in what you are teaching them.

This blind faith method of living is why the religions have always had a difficult time keeping their people in the church congregations. If a parent teaches religion to their children and the parents do not *understand* what they are teaching, then those children will most certainly be led in a different direction at some point when other seemingly more plausible theories or circumstances exist. This causes the children to feel as if they have been lied to all of their lives. They feel as if they have been made a fool of.

Children feel foolish because they have nothing solid to base their beliefs upon when they get into school and the teachers tell them of another perspective. Since the children have not been taught how to properly see what is true, they accept the most convincing information that is presented to them *without* asking the proper questions. As long as the argument that they hear sounds good or more logical than what they formerly believed, they will believe it whether it is true or not. Becoming aware that something is inaccurate is a skill that we must teach to our children. If we do not teach them this, then they will not learn it because it is unlikely that anyone else will teach it to them. Instead they will be taken advantage of by lies.

Typically, what occurs is that someone will present your children with a theory of carefully selected and highly biased information. This information *appears* to make more sense than what you taught them, so they tend to believe it. Understanding, *why* something is so, and then teaching them this technique, resists unwanted bad influence on your children.

Often, children attend school and get mocked for the religious perspective that they offer and try to defend while in discourse at school. Not preparing your children for this and asking them to "just believe it," will cost you their respect. The loss of respect of your children causes them to disregard your instruction—even if it is good and accurate.

It's bad enough that we must fight against the skewed and outright wrong perspectives that our children get from others. We need not feed the problem by presenting unreliable information to them ourselves. This is true of children at any age.

When your children are grown, they will likely marry or pair up with someone. There will be outside influences on them from the new in-law family. If those influences are good and build strong children and a strong family, then all is well. However, if those influences are negative, then what and how you taught them will be enormously important to them.

Your children will not always like what they hear, but if it is kind, honest, and true, then they cannot reasonably debate it and will quickly figure out what your advice was meant to stop or avoid. Sometimes they need to try things on their own and will fail to get your message, but *do* deliver that message. In time, they will always figure it out *if* what you told them was true. If it is not true, then it cannot be figured out because it is *wrong*. That is to say, two plus two will never equal five. Something that is not true does not exist. Technically, it cannot *be*, regardless of how hard we try or insist that it is.

What to do With Spoiled Grown Children?

If you have children who are older and are spoiled, or behave badly, then doing what you have always done will produce more of the same result with your children—you will get what you have always gotten.

You may have an adult child in their thirties, forties, or even older who are in constant turmoil in their hearts. If this is the case, then it is highly likely that they will not listen to your counsel. There is a reason for this, and it is almost certainly your own fault.

You will not be able to help your children until you accept that you and/or your spouse failed at parenting while your children were young. However, just because you fell short as a parent while they were young *does not mean* that things are not repairable now.

Your words mean everything to your child. But merely telling a forty-year-old child that they are good, will be of little help and may even backfire and make matters worse by feeding their own self-deceit and ego—self-deceit which you created in them during their youth.

Typically, whenever you see a problem child, you will find a parent who will attack you when you try to explain to them that they, the parent, caused the problem to begin with. When your children behave badly, you claiming that the children were born that way does little good to remove the problem or to make any of your lives better.

Children that are "messed up" are most certainly the result of inadequate parenting—you change and they will change! *You* are their foundation and they will look to you for direction. Young children see through the whitewash of money that we have painted ourselves with. When we live in an untrue manner, hidden by our money or status, then our children recognize that something is wrong. But sadly, as they age they usually follow our example instead of addressing our errors. And because this behavior becomes common to them, it becomes their familiar way. If they approach us on our errors, we typically and foolishly rebuke them.

If you have created children who grew to be troubled older children who drink too much, are involved in drugs, eat too much, or are otherwise emotionally unstable, then start being true now and continue to do so. An apology is all well and good and *should* be done, but it is of little value if your behavior that caused the problem to begin with still persists. If you apologize to your children, but then fail to change, and you continue in the behavior that you apologized for, then you have done yourself a disservice, and they will likely turn further from you than they were before.

To deal with spoiled older children, start with a self-realization that it was most certainly yours and your spouse's fault in the way that you brought them up and in the examples you had set for them—then, change yourself.

The Christ's words, "Remove the plank from your own eye before you try to remove the sliver from your brother's eye" are appropriate here. After you have finally grasped that it was you and your spouse who failed at parenting, tell your children this and apologize to them. Confess what you did and how it came to be, and then explain your realization of the matter and then change yourself permanently.

Proper confession and apology serves to help children to understand that *you* truly understand how you have hurt them and let them down over the years. It also teaches them that it is good to do the same when they err. When the time comes, share this with them when you see them making some of the same mistakes that you made. Tell them that you wanted to let them know so that they do not have to experience the same *unnecessary* troubles and pain as you did. This helps them to regain trust in you and will build a strong relationship between you and them. It will also help you to help them understand things when they are making mistakes of their own design.

Most of us don't want to do this because it cuts into our arrogant existence. If you have propped yourself up with money, and think yourself to be successful because of your money and status, but have children with problems, then you have missed the mark. You will continue to deal with your problems until you figure this out and make the needed adjustments.

True love *cannot* be bought! If you are too arrogant to tell your children how you have failed them, then you probably do not deserve them or their children, nor can you be said to have true love for them. They may be better off with you away from them. If you are afraid to hug your children *and* to tell them you love them, or to show or display your love to them, then your arrogance has gotten the best of you, and again, you do not deserve them and they may be better off away from you until you choose to change. A child has a tough struggle ahead if they are taught this sort of arrogance. Overcoming it can be a long and very difficult task. It's not easy to see beyond what you *think* you *know*.

Sadly, if you die before confessing your errors and explaining the truth to your children, then you have likely locked them into your same doom. Their problems will be difficult to rectify without your keys. And those problems will be passed to their children—*your* grandchildren. This typically continues from generation to generation until someone finally realizes it and says "Not in my family!"—and that is what you are going to say from now on. You will say, "Not in my family!" and mean it!

Now is the time! Reflect on your life and find and admit your errors. This is the only way to time travel. You can reach back into your past and make everything better *when* you are true. You can pull your past forward as life lessons for the benefit of you, your whole family, and for those around you, and create stability in your family and life. The longer you wait then the more difficult the reversal process becomes. Once behavioral habits are formed, and the longer they are formed, the more time and effort it typically takes for us to work them out and remove the bad habits.

In situations of divorce, the case may be even more difficult because you are no longer privy to the information coming *from* your ex-spouse *to* your children. However, you can still do *your* part; doing so will mean a great deal to your children.

If your mate, spouse, or ex-spouse was, or is, most of the problem, it may be so, but that is no excuse for *you* to fail in *your* part. We all fall short, and the sooner we deal with this, then the sooner our life and family life gets better and becomes more joyful.

Arrogance, which is commonly mistaken for pride, has no place in your family or in yourself. It may take some time to accomplish a strong family foundation, but starting now will make the wonderful rewards come all that much sooner for you and for your family.

Chapter 14

Primary Language

Primary language is usually thought to be a child's native language or tongue that they grew up with, for example English, Spanish, French, or any other language they speak from birth. While these are certainly languages, any form of communication is also a language. Language extends far beyond verbal communication, and goes deep into the realm of understanding.

When Does Your Child's Learning Begin?

We touched on this earlier, and for the sake of simplicity we will say learning starts at birth—even though it likely begins as soon as the baby is able to sense anything while yet in the womb. But in truth, *their learning* begins with *your learning*. In a sense their learning started *before* they were born and before they were conceived. This is because what *you* have learned is what you will teach them. However, for our current purposes in this section, *birth* will be our starting point.

Most everything that your children learn is being communicated to them through their senses of sight, sound, touch, taste, and smell. All of these senses are forms of receiving communication; thus, everything that they sense is learning a primary language. Some primary languages like color, numbers, and smells are reliable and easy to see and grasp, but some of the languages being communicated by us to our children are not as readily discernable.

A child sees their parents behaving in a certain way and the child responds as they see fit. This is the area of primary language on which we are going to focus our attention.

Everything that you do in front of your children is being recorded by them as a primary language. In fact, even much of what you do while you are *not* in front of them is displayed in various forms of your behavior at the times when you *are* with them.

Don't be Angry Unnecessarily

When a child is born and sees their brand new parents fighting or arguing, then that child is learning the primary language of fear, anger, and frustration. The subtleties of this are many and they will greatly affect your children over time.

Often, parents come home from work or from dealing with some difficult people and will be frustrated and angry—Anger is frustration fully manifested.

The main reason we get angry or frustrated is because we are having a difficult time communicating something to someone, this includes communicating to have them stop behaving badly toward people. If we are frustrated, then it is our own fault and we need to accept that. Once we have accepted where our frustration is from we need to confront the other person and take decisive action based upon their responses. But we must also check our own motives, accuracy, and truth. Sadly, we often unfairly take our frustration out on those who have nothing to do with the actual source of our problem. When our children learn our irrational behavior they will most certainly repeat it by irrationally attacking those who *do not* deserve the abuse.

Dealing with your anger by kindly but firmly **not** tolerating other people's violations against you is the *only* way to overcome your anger. If you neglect to separate yourself from other people's violating behavior, then you will be their doormat. Don't teach your children how to be angry. The world seems to have that well in hand, and *our* addition to that anger is of no help to our own children. Truth is a great start to remedy this!

Crying

Crying is natural in newborn children. It is a natural way for them to communicate their needs and wants until they are able to speak well enough to tell you, with words, what they need or want. So crying is good—to a point.

When we first have children, and parenting is all so new to us, we are often at a loss and do not know how to read their crying. As parents, when we fail to learn this skill then we run the risk of spoiling our children. I won't go into great detail on this because there are already a multitude of books on the specific subject; however, we will cover the basics.

When an infant child cries, amongst other reasons, they are typically tired, hungry, need to be changed, need to be burped, or are sick. But there is one other key reason, and it is that they want to be held.

Holding your child is a good thing! It makes them feel loved and secure. They feel your breath, body warmth, heartbeat, and hear and feel your very important voice. Your child will build a dependency on you and will quickly learn through experience and experimentation, that crying will result in their problems and desires being addressed.

Please do not misunderstand this, it is good to pick up your infant often, however, as the weeks go by you must gradually ignore their nighttime crying so that they become independent in their sleep-time hours.

It is natural for us as parents to want to check things with our infants when they cry, as is revealed when we care for our newborn children. We must apply our checking things to everything so that we can find what is true, and, through our example, teach our children the same.

It is not how often you hold a child that causes problems with them, it is the *when* you do it and the *why* you do it that the problems arise.

As your child becomes accustomed to being picked up in order to address the child's necessities, they will also learn that they are being picked up when they cry. When a child comes to the blind understanding that crying will bring comfort to them, then they cry just to be held by the person or people who normally comfort them. Comforting a child is good and is natural, and it is as it should be. However, we must use care in the *when* and *why* of picking the child up. If you run to them at **every** peep that they make, even when you know that they are all taken care of and are okay, then you are building a precedent that will be very difficult for you to unravel. The longer the period of time that you build this precedent then the longer it will take to reverse it, and, typically, it will be more difficult to do so.

Loving your children is not just holding and caring for their immediate needs, it is also preparing them for their next stage in life. If you *always* run to them and pick your children up and at their every cry, then you will spoil them and find them to be very demanding when they are older. You will have done it to yourself and you will feel the pain and frustration of dealing with a difficult child for many years to come. The longer you allow this to occur, then the more difficult it becomes to undo. If it is your habit when they are infants then it will likely be your habit as they age.

When children are trying to communicate to us, their thoughts are important to them even when they are infants. And it is entirely possible that the level of importance of what an infant wants to communicate to us, is *to them*, more important than what our very "important" thoughts are to us.

In other words: their thought usage may be more intense than ours—they mean it more than we do. This is because all of their focus is on this one thought; where, with adults, we have many things drawing our attention from our current thought.

This is not being discussed so that we should run to them when they demand so, but rather to actually pay attention to them and their words, which is to say, their crying. We need to analyze their concerns so that we can train them, so that they learn how to *not* over-blow circumstances. If they are the type who have tantrums, then it is likely that we, as parents, have a tendency to panic as well or we have catered to their crying far too much. Panic is a circumstance that has been overblown in the mind of the person who is panicking.

When it comes to newborn infants, parents often fail to address the issues of crying. There are many ways to deal with this problem when a child becomes spoiled in this regard. Choosing the right method for your own family in dealing with this problem is completely up to you, but you must understand that doing nothing will *not* stop the problem.

Additionally, please understand that picking a child up when they are content *is* a very good thing to do. This is because you are picking them up when they are *not* crying; thus, you begin to counteract their understanding that the only way to be picked up is by crying.

New Babies and Siblings

When you have subsequent children, then the problem of your child demanding your attention with crying becomes apparent. It's easy to meet the demands of *one* demanding child, but when you bring a second child into the picture it's not as easy to meet all of the desires of that first child to the same level you had offered to them in the past.

Your second child will require much of your attention when they are an infant, and that attention will be taken away from the first child. If your child has *not* been spoiled with your over-attentiveness, then you can easily include the first child in the care of the new baby and, together, all share in the new baby. But when the first child has been spoiled with your excessive meeting of their crying demands, then they will certainly act out and try to get your attention by crying. This eventually turns into the dreaded temper tantrums.

Children quickly become accustomed to being served by their parents. As the child ages, it is up to the parents to appropriately taper this off to a reasonable point before each subsequent child is born. For your family, dealing with this appropriately is an important part of building a foundation of what is true. Children will test us in this no matter what we do. It is our responses that choose their future.

Allowing children to have attention whenever *they* want it, regardless of the rest of the family's needs, results in them being demanding adults when they are grown. If you are not one yourself, then you likely know someone who is an unreasonably demanding adult.

Jealousy

When we allow our children to become demanding by our submitting to their every whim, then the likelihood that they will be the jealous type is very high. When the other younger children continue to receive the attention of the parents, then the older child often tries to regain that attention. When they fail then they look to the source of their problem—their younger sibling(s). When they figure this out, jealousy is usually the result.

Attempts by the older child to regain the lost attention of their parents *will* occur in some form. Parents who are lucky or did their job well will have that child show extra love to them and attract the parents' attention in that way. But for many of us the child slips into jealousy, with their siblings being the target of that jealousy. This occurs as early in history as the *Cain and Abel* story in the Bible.

When an older child taunts the newest object of their parents' affection, it upsets the parents. This causes the older child to get the desired attention from the parent. Even though this attention is negative attention, it is attention nonetheless. This will become habitual for the child and is carried into their adulthood.

The word *"Jealous"* means to have *zeal* for something, so in that, the child has *zeal* for their parents' attention. But, when they have come to a point where they are seeking more than their share of attention, then they have crossed over into covetousness.

Covetousness is to want to take something that belongs to someone else, and, generally, to want the other person not to have it at all.

The primary language we are discussing here is the root of many of our world's problems and has brought about much bloodshed in the world. This not only applies to older children, but, as is often the case, it can happen in a reverse situation with the younger being more aggressive with regard to jealousy. However, birth order seems to dictate the problem, and so it is more common that the older children are more often aggressive in this way.

Older daughters may not be so affected when the next child is a son because whether or not we realize it and whether or not we admit it, we typically treat daughters differently than sons. Daughters receive a certain type of attention and sons receive a different type of attention. Much of our "cultural biases" in the way we treat girls versus boys has much to do with the nature of girls and boys, with girls tending to be somewhat milder and boys being more energetically aggressive. But jealousy can most certainly occur with daughters as well.

The best way to deal with the problems arising when new babies arrive is to make sure that the other children know and feel that they are loved by you. Just love your other children and show it by spending time with them *and* mentally process the information that they share with you.

Giving gifts does not equate to love! Giving gifts for the wrong reasons will only mask your shortcomings. This is the same effect that money has later in life. Children want and need *your* love, not money or things; those are secondary.

Hate

An extension of the primary language of jealousy, or covetousness, is hate. Hate is an intense hostility towards another. When you have learned to want to take something that rightfully belongs to another, then you are wanting to diminish that other person. This is a hostile intent towards that person. When a child has reached this point, then several things will happen in the heart and mind of the child.

First they come to a point where they want to be better than the others. And since we are all the same with regard to the value of life, they will then try to tear the other person down in effort to make themselves look or feel better. They feel as if they are less than everyone else, which is the reason that they are trying to make themselves better than others to begin with. If they did not feel themselves to be less than others, then they would not be trying to be better than others. This, in turn, will cause them to try even more so to build themselves up by tearing others down.

Once they get in the habit of trying to tear others down, they have bought into the lie that some people are better than others. It is this lie that causes them to be less than they should be. We often see this heinous tactic prominently displayed in political races.

Our senses look around and detect that we are all the same, so to voluntarily adopt the deception that we are better, or worse, than someone else, brings about our own self-doubt, causing us to devalue our own self.

Doubt

Doubt comes from believing lies. Anytime we choose to believe a lie or are duped into believing one, we subconsciously detect many anomalies but will not understand them. All lies are irrational, and because we believe lies, truth seems irrational to us and so we begin to doubt. When we are taught what is true from our youth onward, then seldom will we have much self-doubt, and our certainty will be well-founded.

When parents allow a child to always get their way, then the child is being deceived and allowed to believe something that is not true. What follows is the effect of covetous jealousy that brings about the hate they feel toward those who will not comply with their demands. Their effort to tear down the noncompliant people has a negative effect on themselves. When they believe the lie in their own heart and mind, that they are less than someone else, then they become so of their own accord and often they over-compensate with arrogance. We cannot have true confidence when this is how we function. The lies that we function in force us to doubt, which is because technically you cannot be confident while you are in a lie.

The choice to believe lies degrades a person, and then they become what they have believed. This brings with it a great deal of self-doubt for those children.

Fear

Doubt and fear go hand in hand in most cases. When you have chosen to believe lies, then you have no choice but to doubt just about everything around you—including yourself.

When you doubt, you have trapped yourself in uncertainty and you will experience fear. This problem becomes worse for children when their parents have gone through this same process. Fear produces a type of anxiety or worry.

Earlier in this book we discussed the effects of what we hear and see, and how that can affect our mental and physical health. If you examine this chain of events, then you can begin to see why building a foundation of truth is so vital to the wellbeing of your family.

The damage that occurs to your mind and body due to hate, doubt, and fear becomes very clear and real once we realize the effect our thinking has on our biochemistry, which in turn affects our bodies.

The Paralysis of Fear

Fear paralyzes in two major ways. First, it causes a great amount of indecision. When we are indecisive we do not **do**. We lurk in the shadows waiting for something or someone to force our hand causing us to react, thus we never have need to make the decision on our own because it has been made for us. This allows us to "play it safe" and we can then blame our failures on the thing or person that forced our hand.

The second major way fear paralyzes us is that we react out of fear in an aggressive manner to harm others. This is similar to a cornered animal that is afraid *you* will attack or harm it, so it lashes out at you first *before* you can hurt it. We humans are very efficient at this particular method of displaying fear.

Lashing out because of fear holds us back from where we should be. Our attack on others causes them to resist and depart from us. When lashing out, we damage others and hinder ourselves by rejecting their attempted assistance.

On the other hand, when we build others up, we build ourselves up. This will only serve to create a better world, better friends, and a better family for ourselves. Sadly, some people find our assistance or attempts to build them up as offensive, due to their fear and jealousy, causing them to lash out.

Our fear causes many problems for us, including working carelessly in haste, resulting in untold amounts of trouble for everyone involved.

Working in Haste versus Working Expeditiously

All of our examples as parents are primary languages that are teaching our children how to function in life. If we hurry around then it is almost certain that our children will adopt this primary language. When we fear, then we hurry. Hastily hurrying is inherently counterproductive. Our fears are the cause of haste. At work, this can be in the form of wanting to please the boss. In doing so, we scurry around and demand things from those around us with our unreasonable requests. This frustrates us when others cannot meet these unreasonable demands, and it frustrates them because we ask too much of them.

We also become frustrated when we fail to meet *our own* demands. When we do this, our boss, or our clients and customers will be frustrated when we fall short on our promises that we made to them. Working in haste does indeed make waste, and it angers those around us and causes unneeded strife! Often, we work in haste when we accept the demanding tasks that others burden us with.

But let us not confuse working hastily, with working expeditiously and efficiently. Typically, haste is unproductive and causes error because of its hurried and careless nature, *haste* angers and disappoints family, friends, and coworkers... well... everyone!

But, when we work expeditiously, which is to be prompt and efficient, we take the time to do it right and we get the right people on board in order to achieve the same goal in its proper time—we make sure that we make no mistakes. We do it once and we do it right! It is work that is founded in working in only what is true.

Anytime we are afraid and get caught in the trap of functioning hastily, we deprive our families of our best work, and of our time, because we often end up redoing the things that we hastily worked on.

Arrogance

Another primary language passed onto your children is arrogance. Arrogance is typically present when any of the previously mentioned negative attributes are present. Arrogance is often mistaken for pride, and pride is often mistaken for arrogance.

When we say that someone "has too much pride" we are either wrong in our words, or we are wrong in our assessment of the person. "Too much pride" cannot exist. If it does, then it is *arrogance*. If they have more pride than we feel that they should have, then we probably do not understand *why* they feel proud.

It is those who are arrogant who typically cut down the pride of others. If you have a good family and you are proud of your family, then someone who has a poorly functioning family might attack you by indicating that they feel you have "too much pride" about your family.

If you are balanced and true, then their attack is a very clear sign that they want to bring you down to a level below where *they* feel that they are at—a level which they have chosen of *their* own free will.

Arrogance is to build yourself up to be more than what you truly are. Arrogance is quickly spotted. When you sarcastically refer to others, then you are being arrogant. When you tear innocent people down, then you are being arrogant. When you make yourself out to be better than others, then you are being arrogant. But, let us not confuse this with exposing lies. Arrogant people hide in fear of exposure—by and in the light of truth. When you point out someone's error or lie and *they* believe that you pointing it out harms them, it is **not** an attack on them. In truth, we do not need to point out an error. All we need to do is to speak truth about something. The error will reveal itself when it is compared to truth.

The Original Sin of Arrogance

The term "original sin" is Biblical in nature, though it may not be specifically stated as "original sin" in the Bible. Original sin was due to arrogance. Once doubt came into being, then arrogance was born. Believe what you will about the Bible's story of Adam and Eve, but the principle holds true regardless.

When Eve was told that she could know the difference between good and evil, she *immediately* was in a state of doubt. She had to be feeling that she wanted to be more, better, or advanced from what she was. This means that she felt she could be "better." If she was Created and had done no wrong, then she was perfect as she was. But instead, she doubted that, and then she took it upon herself to do what she was asked *not* to do, she took what was not hers, and in doing so she was arrogant.

Then her mate made the same violation and they both knew it. When their Creator came, they hid to try to cover their shame. At this, the Creator questioned them and they proceeded to dodge the issue and finally passed the blame to the original deceiver.

All of them had to pay the price, and we are still paying the price today. We have adopted their behavior in our own lives, generation upon generation, ever since. The errors of Eve have been passed down to daughters for generations ever since Eve erred. Sadly, by the time we figure this out we have already passed the errors on to our children. The same is true with regard to Adam and his passing his errors on down to his sons and all subsequent generations of sons.

Adam and Eve were humbled. They were put back in their place, which is the ground from which they were taken—"And unto dust will you return." The word *humus* means dirt, and *humus* and the words *human* and *humiliate* are all from the same root which is the following basic scenario: Adam and Eve were humans from the humus and they wanted to be greater, but they were put back into their place and humbled. In their humility they had to accept the cost of their choice, which was death.

They attempted to take that which was not theirs. Similar to borrowing money, taking something which you have not yet earned causes you to have to pay for it later. *There will be a day of reckoning.* It may not come when or how you think, but you can be sure you will pay or be paid according to your choices.

It's interesting how, when we do wrong, we inherently know that we will have to "pay", but when we do good, we inherently expect to *be paid.*

The arrogance that had quickly grown out of their doubt and fear had a heavy price for them to pay. Adam and Eve had joy in the Garden, but were left to struggle outside of the protection of the Garden in the wilderness. This was all because they believed a lie and then followed a lie.

Bitterness

Where there is arrogance, bitterness is close behind. There are two basic kinds of bitterness: deserved and undeserved. Deserved bitterness occurs when someone unjustly violates you, and they continue to repeatedly do so, then you will have a bitter taste towards them and likely remove yourself from their presence. This is similar to what Adam's and Eve's Creator was said to have done with them in the Bible.

The other kind of bitterness is the bitterness that is born through covetous arrogance. This unforgiving nature locks the unjustly bitter person in their own self-imposed prison. They are not able to detect what their trouble and internal pain is from. For those who have chosen arrogance, this often happens when someone tries to correct them. Any correction of them is seen by them as an attack on them. When they feel attacked, they then reciprocate with backbiting and strife. Arrogant people *do not* like to be corrected. Please separate this from those who understand that they are correct and *why* they are correct and will not back down from their well understood position when lies come their way.

Greed

When all is said and done, greed ends in some form by arrogantly taking more than you have earned and more than is your share in life. Often, this is done by cheating, lying, and stealing from others in some form. This could be in a tangible realm, like a business cheating its customers by shorting them, or by stealing someone's idea and taking the credit for it; or in a far less tangible form, by unjustly harming someone's reputation so that you can be above them in the eyes of yourself and others.

Greed is the culmination of this and contains all of the negative elements that we just discussed. When you neglect to deal with your young children in a proper, firm, distinct, and loving manner, then the troubles *will* cascade throughout every level of their entire life and through each of these primary languages during their lifetime.

Further, when you allow other people's greed to alter your good and true ways, then their greed will affect you and even manifest itself in such a way that makes you appear as if you have been or are now being greedy, even though you might *not* have been greedy at all.

How Kind People Sometimes Create Bad Children

It's easy to see how people who are horrible parents and who abuse their children verbally or physically can have children who behave badly. Even if the parents do not harm the child, simply setting bad examples teaches bad habits that can last a lifetime. But how do *sweet* and *kind* people end up with children who misbehave or act tyrannically?

Much the way we have discussed in these last several chapters, children need certainty. They need that rock, and they need understanding. When a really "sweet" parent fails to address the needs of the child that create this type of true order in their life, then the child runs wild and exhibits the negative primary languages we just discussed in these sections.

From a Biblical perspective, consider the children of Adam the first man, Samuel the judge, or David the king, and others. These people who we typically hold in high esteem had failed terribly with their children. The same is true for many contemporary preachers, politicians, and others of respected notoriety.

Properly disciplining your child is the best way you can love them, along with parental affection towards them. It is not always pleasant to have to discipline your children, but you will be pleased with your results in the long run when you do so when it is done properly.

All too often, parents allow their children to tug at their hearts, and then the parents weaken at the tears of the child. Then later, when the child becomes problematic, the parents do not know how to get the child to behave or comply with common human decency. To keep the peace, they bow to the demands of the child, only serving to increase the problem. This troubling method of parenting is all done in effort to appease the child. It is important for parents to understand that this occurs and that there is a point where the parents need to **be the parents**.

Truth

Understanding is the rock foundation that we have been referring to, and truth is connected to it. When children learn the primary languages of understanding and truth, then there is little that they cannot accomplish in life.

When your children have truth, then life will be consistent for them and they will be able to expect a result that they know will occur with certain actions that they choose to take. When this occurs, they learn to hope, to desire, and to set their intent on their goals which in turn become their passion.

Hope

Hope is another word that is often misused, or maybe better stated as misunderstood. When we "*hope*," we are often hoping that bad things won't befall us. Our ability to hope is our ability to desire something—*hope* is our ability to imagine! Without hope nothing could ever really occur for us.

When we *know* something, then it's true and it *can* be relied upon—we know that it is coming. Consider the Sun: We need not hope the sun will rise in the morning, because it will and we know this to be true from repeatedly experiencing it. Even though it may be cloudy, the Sun still rises.

But hope is to be used differently. With hope we are thinking of something which is not yet, and we *hope* it will come to be. When we hope, we are *imagining* something. Without our ability to imagine, there can be no hope, because there would be no object of the hope. Hope is a very desirable primary language and your ability to imagine something good that **is not yet**, is your hope.

When we have no hope, then we will *not* allow ourselves to imagine the possibilities and create things that have never been.

Expectancy

Once we imagine the possibilities, then our *hope* is developed and the next aspect of hope occurs; if you fail to do this then you have lost your hope. This element and next aspect of the primary languages is expectancy. We often mistake hope for expectancy because expectancy is a part of hope. It is separate though because we can also *expect* doom, where hope on the other hand, is to desire good. Expectancy, in the case of doom, would be attributed to fear.

Expectancy with hope is a beautiful thing and is something that you should encourage in your children. Never crush this or subdue this primary language in a child. It is where their passions will be born from—it is their desire.

Seeing the excitement of a child who is in eager anticipation, is always a joy for a parent to experience. But we can crush this when we get them *falsely* excited about things. They become let down and their disappointment quickly follows. Encourage hope, expectancy, and anticipation, but make sure there is something behind it. Regularly telling them that you will do something and then later crushing their anticipation by saying, "No, I changed my mind," will break their trust in you; this is especially true when this scenario occurs very often. If circumstances outside of your control caused the change of plans, then explain to them why, and then substitute what could not occur due to circumstances by giving them your time, love, and understanding, because that is what children really want and need from their parents in the first place.

Love

Love is a term that people cannot seem to fully grasp. We use the term love inaccurately. We claim that we "love" things, but we really do not have much real care of them, though one could argue otherwise.

True love has the requirement of revealing your true self to the ones that you "love". Further, true love also allows the true thoughts of others to be expressed. Your love will invite and accept their true self into you. When you do something wrong and the person you love has the courage to correct you, but you stop them from doing so or attack them as they attempt to explain to you, then you do not love them because you are not receiving their words. You have rejected them! This is a form of hate.

You cannot reject those who you "love" when they try to correct you. Anyone imagining that they can reject wise counsel and still claim to "love" the person offering it, is missing the point of love. Take deep consideration of what is being explained in this chapter about primary languages and love because *love* is perhaps the most abused primary language ever.

We must love people and our children for their truth, rather than for their things, behavior, or apparel. There is this very damaging, and very wrong, understanding that we must somehow "accept people the way they are" in order to love them. This twisted understanding causes many people to wrongly believe that they must accept the poor choices and poor behavior of others. But this is wrong in every possible way.

In truth, if you truly love someone, you will *reject* all of their unacceptable behavior. Rejecting bad behavior is often perceived, by the wrongdoers, as hate towards them. There are certainly hateful people out in the world, but rejecting bad and wrong *behavior* is the only way to truly love people who are doing wrong.

Assuming that the societal perception of Heaven and Hell is correct, then allowing someone to believe that their bad behavior does not matter, could cause them eternal doom. Thus, not rejecting their behavior is a form of hatred and contributes to path to hell for them.

A parent that fails to correct their children is not much of a parent at all. As children age, they will sometimes fight our corrections, but you must still properly point out their errors and teach them proper living. If you fail to do so, they will have no index of what true is. When children become adults they might choose to disregard your correction of them, but correction must be delivered regardless. What they choose to do about it is their own choice and, possibly, is an error. If they reject your wise council in their adulthood then their guilt is on their own shoulders. Correct them in truth, kindness, and love.

Changing Their Ways

We people do not like to change our ways. This is why, often, we don't change our ways until *after* something tragic occurs. Usually a close call with our own death or a loved one dying will get us to at least think about the way we have lived our lives.

If you have failed your children and are unwilling to change yourself, there may still be hope that they'll change when you die. Although, then, you will not be there to enjoy their new direction in life. In many cases, a parent's death without proper apology is of little assistance to the children of that parent, and as mentioned earlier, it can firmly lock your children into *your* poor behavior. This costs them dearly until and unless they see the light of truth, *if* they ever do.

You are the keys for a solid foundation for your children no matter what their age. Take your opportunity *now* to implement those keys and unlock their future!

When "good" parents have children who get off track, then the children have a better chance to change because of the example the parents set in all other areas of life. As wayward children of "good" parents grow older, a greater possibility exists that they will become more like their parents as they age—provided, that is, that the bad behavior did not get too far out of hand to where the children can no longer see any light. Children typically gravitate towards the way they were raised.

If the parents have not changed, and the children do grow out of it, then the probability remains very high that the children will make those same or similar mistakes, and have the same troubles when they have children of their own. Patterns of parental behavior transfer very efficiently from parent to child and have done so since the Creation of Man on Earth.

Focus on Good Examples

When you're teaching your children, you teach by example. Those examples can be the obvious, like when you show them purple and then say "purple" to teach them the color purple, or it can be the less obvious examples, like when they observe the body language that you are exhibiting, which is typically done without intentionally doing so or even realizing that you are doing it at all.

When you begin teaching your children behavioral languages like those discussed in this chapter, then you are best served by focusing your attention, and their attention, on things that are good examples for them.

Think of it this way: If you keep pointing out only the bad things, then they will know what is bad, but they will not recognize good. This generally leaves them with the option of only doing what they know, even if they were told not to do it.

You could think of this in terms of parents who often drink much alcohol in front of their children and then tell them that drinking as much as mommy and daddy do is not good. The likelihood that those children will be heavy drinkers is high even though the parents admitted to the dangers of their own actions.

Focus their attention on things that are good so that they know what to aim for in life, this gives your children direction. Yet, keep in mind that if you do this and you still partake in risky behavior, such as drinking heavily on a regular basis, then they are likely to copy your example, where with positive examples, they can see that they have a choice. For instance, choosing to *not* drink too often will be a positive example to your children.

There are Two Types of Ambitious People

The two basic types of ambitious people are: the passionate, and the attention-stealing. Both are often successful, but the attention-stealing type usually come to ruin at some point.

With the attention-stealing type of person, who has actions born of covetous-jealousy, their eventual arrogance and greed causes them to grandstand or to jump in front of others to steal attention that they themselves have not earned. This type of person is very self-centered and is the root cause of this world's problems.

When attention-grabbing attitude is adopted, then the person will not comply with others, but they will insist that others comply with them. Often their insistence is in a malicious or violent manner.

The other kind is the passionate type of person. Passionate people are constructively creative and have hope and expectancy. They will endure because they have been taught through true things and also that when they hope for something they can expect good things over time. If what they do is true, then they will likely receive those expected things. Wonders, such as inventions, literature, song, food, shelter etc... are typically created by passionate people. It is the passionate people who create most all of the revolutionary wonders we enjoy in this world. They will work night and day to achieve what they know can be done, no matter what negative things other people say—it is their passion!

All of the primary languages mentioned in this chapter are deeply embedded in our culture and deeply affect our families. What most people don't realize is that when we understand the primary languages, then we get to teach the *proper* use of the languages to our own children rather than letting it all up to the world and chance.

Chapter 15

Words Matter to Your Children

In the *Health and Truth* chapter we discussed that what you say to your children *or* in front of your children matters and it affects their lives and health. These life and health effects go far beyond your words. Your voice inflections, your body language, including the slightest most minute of facial expressions, your breathing, the way in which you interact with others, and much more, are all observed by your children.

Mopping the Floor with Your Children

Children are cute little sponges and they will absorb **everything** that you say and do. When you're talking with your spouse or friends or family, your children *are* absorbing it all.

If you go off into another room, and whisper, whisper, whisper, your children are seeing this and they will emulate this behavior. Any "dirt" that you drag into your home will be mopped up and absorbed by your children—of this you can be certain!

Your Influence

During their critical stages of development, your influence on your children is **their** *everything*. All those grunts and groans that you make when you are disappointed, and all of the complaining that you do, will all be absorbed and reproduced by your children.

The things you tell them and teach them are important for sure, but have far less impact than your examples do. All of your actions, expressions, and habits **will** be copied. Even your example of teaching them is, in itself, an example. It is not so much *what* you teach them, though that is important, but rather, it is **that** you teach them that matters regarding your influence on them. This applies whether what you teach them is true or not. It matters to the extent that it will affect them either for good or for bad.

Teaching your children good things, teaches them to teach good things. With this in mind, teach them to teach by example. In addition, when you teach them how to understand what is true, you have given them the gift of true life!

Condemnation is Discouraging

Condemnation is a very judgmental action and is often done arrogantly. When we constantly unjustly condemn people or things, then we teach our children to do the same thing.

Condemnation causes your children to think that they cannot like something or someone. Condemnation becomes a big problem because children are often attracted to what they are restricted from, if for nothing more than out of sheer curiosity. When we judge with condemnation, then arrogance is always a part of our life. Allow your children the ability to choose. This is done by teaching them *understanding*, rather than by teaching them *condemning*.

The *condemnation* form of judgment is confused with the actions of those who have a true foundation. To explain: A person with a sound, strong foundation might say, "That is not true and here is why." Or they will simply reveal the truth and the untrue thing becomes exposed. When we're arrogant, this appears to us as if it is a judgment against our wrongness. This is because with arrogant-judgment we have our own arbitrary set of rules. We deem something bad just because *we* do not like it, or because *we* are not familiar with it.

When you condemn things or people on a regular basis, then you are judging those people or things. When your children see this as their example, it inhibits your children. Children are not stupid, and they often have a clearer vision than we parents do. When children see their parents condemning something, they become afraid to pursue any activity that is similar to the one the parents condemned, for fear of being similarly condemned by their own parents. Sadly, our society often hails foolish things as good and praises them, and then condemns good things and calls them bad. Due to our own fears of being wrongfully condemned, we often wrongly agree with those who express very strong and passionate, but incorrect and unfair, views of others or of a given situation.

If, in the past, your children have been improperly conditioned by your condemnation, it will be more difficult to teach them about good things later on in life because the unfair unjust condemnation will have turned them cynical.

Their cynicism inhibits their desire, and it reduces *their* potential to make *you* truly proud of them when they are adults. Tell your children what is good about the world, and in doing so you will expose the ills of the world without having to specifically point them *all* out. They will ask about bad things and in that case it is best that you yourself understand why something is bad so that you can adequately explain it to them.

The Dangers of Sarcasm

Sarcasm is a most subtle and dangerous means of condemnation. Teaching your children sarcasm is a foolish and idiotic practice. They may get a lot of laughs by being sarcastic, but it almost always is at the expense of others, and usually is at the expense of their own self. While many people chuckle when a mocker does his or her sarcastic work, in reality, most people see the sarcastic mockers themselves as foolish and obnoxious people who are not to be trusted. Most people don't want to be in the company of mockers because they don't trust them because they know that the mockers will mock anyone in order to get the attention they crave so badly. Mockers are the weak people, and they do not like to be mocked or criticized. Their insecurity is made evident as they use their cruel and sarcastic remarks to make themselves feel better. But what they fail to understand is that the more they mock people, the more it is that people don't like them. The only people a mocker has on their side are those who fear being the subject of the mocker's needless attacks.

Sarcastic children brought up in mockery and sarcasm are afraid to express what they truly like for fear of a sarcastic attack back on them. Sarcastic people think that they are funny, until it is *they* who are being mocked, at which point they either retaliate in a rage, or more typically, withdraw into humiliation and shame, rather than self-correcting their behavior.

Teaching the horrible habit of sarcasm to your children leads them to a life lived in fear and regret, unless, on their own, they can manage to figure out what your sarcasm failed to teach them. They may succeed in life, but it is a toss of a coin which way they will go if they don't find truth on their own at some point in life. Our sarcasm and mockery are condemnation and are seldom aimed at our own self. It is not constructive. It is destructive, and it will destroy your children's freedom to excel. This mostly occurs while they are young, due to their fear of your or their siblings' sarcastic attacks. Not to mention the sarcastic attacks that come from others when they are older.

You might think that you're not a sarcastic person because you may not say such things about the people you know, but you must ask yourself if you mock and make sarcastic remarks about personalities on TV for instance. If you sit around mocking and making sarcastic remarks about people on the television, then you're teaching your children that those people are not worthy. So, if you choose to foolishly mock an actor or a singer, for instance, who happens to be very good at their art, then you are teaching your children to be inhibited and to fear opening up to sing. They will likely never excel in life because of the messages that *your* mocking placed in their hearts. You are teaching them fear, arrogance, and cruelty. If you are a mocker, then you are obviously insecure and afraid, and you are teaching your child to be the same. Teaching a life without sarcasm gives your children far better life skills and an ability to ignore any destructive sarcasm that is directed at them when they are older.

Your child might not be sarcastic if this goes on in your home, but they will be inhibited by it nonetheless. This is because you are teaching them, by means of your sarcasm and mockery, that it is *not* okay to do the things that you are sarcastic about. By association, if you are sarcastic about someone and your child wanted to do the same occupation as that person, your sarcasm towards that person inhibits your child from pursuing that occupation, even if your sarcasm was only directed at the person and not their occupation. What is sad about this is that it may be your child's God-given natural talent and affinity that you indirectly assaulted.

Sarcasm is unjustly critical and teaches unjust judgment to your children and to those around you. Sarcasm is ultimately bearing false witness against your neighbor. Sarcasm is typically born of jealous-covetousness, fear, and arrogance. A sarcastic sniper tries to degrade someone by taking well-aimed cheap verbal shots at someone who is true and talented whom they feel threatened by. You can find the fears of a sarcastic person by observing what or who they attack. Their fears are revealed in a very specific way. Once sarcasm becomes a compulsion, it typically becomes very mean and personal, and it is exhibited when the sarcastic sniper is not living up to *their own* potential.

Saying it Louder

When we lose control of a situation that we desperately want to control, then we typically shout. Our perception that our shouting, or loudness, makes us right or justifies us is because our shouting gets mistaken by others as *true* passion and they typically submit to our demands. Generally, the more wrong we feel that we are or the more we feel backed into a corner, then the louder and more forcefully we will shout. If you are wrong then you're wrong.

> Shouting louder
> *won't* make you righter.

Passionate people get excited and speak with enthusiasm! They generally say what they mean and mean what they say. This enthusiastic approach often comes through with elevated sound levels. Another thing that desperate-shouting is mistaken for is when a parent must control a situation and to regain *command*. Parents will shout powerfully to get the attention of the children in order to correct them and the situation in order to bring everything back into order and keep everyone safe.

All too often when people are wrong in their perspective and feel threatened, they imitate this forcefulness and volume and then hope for a result similar to that as a corrective parent or a truly passionate person gets. Sadly, this often works for them, allowing them to continue believing that they are correct and that the others actually agree with them. At times, this false passion wrongly convinces others that the loud person is correct. Though, it is only those who have chosen to *not* follow what is true that are susceptible to the person's incorrect information and belligerence.

Invoking a Curse

Parents often invoke a curse on their children without realizing that they are doing it. When we get angry we shout or say it louder in order to make our point. In our own minds, we feel that the emphasis or strength in the way we say something gives it actual meaning. This holds true with those who hear us as well, in that they perceive that our words have actual meaning because of how intensely we use them. There are certainly times when we must raise our voices at our children to get them to understand the severity of their actions. But when we are angry, cussing (or cursing, which is the same thing) is a part of our dialogue. When we curse, it is the word "curse" that reveals our actual intent. Generally, we don't put much thought into the words we use while cursing during our dialogue.

Cursing is nothing more than to cast a negative stigma onto someone or something by saying statements such as, "this stupid thing is junk." or "you are such an [*expletive*] idiot." These sorts of statements do little to improve the situation or circumstances that we are facing at any particular moment, yet most of us do this to some extent anyway.

Taking this to a new level of our own absurdities, when we become frustrated with someone or something, we resort to using a dialogue that is an outright curse. In our fury of the situation we often utter, "God damn it!" or "You are so God damned [*whatever*]!" When it's an item, then the words are often, "God damn this stupid thing!" If you do not believe in a God then you are truly wasting your breath. If you do not believe, then why ask a god who does not exist, in your eyes, to do anything at all? But even for the dominant portion of society, who *does* believe in a God, why ask God to damn something?

If you believe in God, then this is especially ridiculous. Let's say that you're working on a project and you become frustrated because you cannot accomplish a particular task. In your frustration you utter the words, "God damn this thing!" or simply, "God damn it!" Is this not contrary to the end goal?

When you are working to make something behave in a certain manner so that it can better serve your purpose, and then you go about asking God to damn it, then technically, you are cursing it.

"*Cursing*" is to call a *curse*, or ask to do *harm*. The word "*damn*" means *damage* or *loss*.

If you truly believe in God, then cursing things in this way is a terrible mistake. This is because you are making the request for "*God damage it.*" And then adding to the curse that you are requesting, you are doing it in a deeply passionate or intense manner. This is a prayer—whether you realize it or not, *and* whether you admit it or not.

Regardless of whether or not we believe in God, the contradictory nature of invoking doom upon something or someone that we are trying to make comply with our wishes is a foolish and contradictory thing to do!

We try to get our children to understand our message, but then say things like "God damn it you!" or we work on a project to make or fix something and say "Damn this thing!" When we do this we may as well be asking God to give us a brilliant child and then say, "But deliver them damaged or destroyed!" Or it is like praying and saying, "I want this fixed, but don't allow me to fix this thing!"

Invoking a curse on our children, or anyone, or anything in this way is incredibly contradictory to what we really want from them. Is it any wonder why we struggle so much in life?

They Will See Your Inconsistencies

Children are not stupid. After all, they are *our* children. When we invoke a curse on them, on other people, or on anything that we are cursing, then we are showing our children a most blatant contradiction in our behavior. We are teaching them to completely contradict themselves. This is like correctly making a right turn that will quickly get us to our destination, but during the whole trip we are uttering statements saying we turned the wrong direction and wish someone would force us to go the other way. Any child hearing or witnessing such foolish and contradictory behavior will have no choice but to be confused at our actions. This sort of double-mindedness is futile.

You are your children's example. They *will* see your inconsistencies, and *you* and *they* will pay a steep price in the long run for those inconsistencies.

Our inconsistencies do not end at our cursing people or things; they go far beyond and include nearly everything in our life when we choose to live by things that are *not* true.

In an earlier chapter, we discussed the physical effects of what we sense, and how those sensations actually become a physical part of our own bodies through the chemical reactions that take place in our bodies because of the events or sensations we experience. Our own internal double-minded contradictions are equally as physically altering to our bodies.

The events that we detect with our senses are completed once the chemical-reactions of those senses deliver the messages to our brains. What happens after that is up to our own thinking. It is our thinking that is the problem to our bodies. When the effects of our thinking, our experiences, and our contradictions are acted upon mentally, it affects our bodies in a very profound and chemical manner. This has been repeatedly demonstrated in laboratories throughout the world.

Our inconsistencies physically harm our children because they see and emulate those inconsistencies, thus altering their own thinking and biochemistry. This sort of mental back-and-forth is not helpful to anyone's health and will not teach our children anything useful.

Teach Your Children Respect

Most areas of our inconsistency are less obvious than the very obvious inconsistencies done during our cursing rants. Inconsistency by cursing is completely disrespectful and teaches children to behave similarly. If we do this anywhere in our lives, then the chances that we do it in other places in life are very high.

Patterns do not dictate our lives, but our lives do dictate those patterns. The thoughts and actions that we take part in affect our lives and the lives of our children. It is a fairly consistent occurrence that any disrespect that we show is clearly conveyed to our children. They will repeat our behavior and usually reflect it back at us.

To better understand respect, we need to also consider the word "***dis*-respect."** Respect means to re-look, or re-*spect*acle. When we respect someone or something, then we will look back into the circumstances and information surrounding any particular situation, and then *consider* that information. This might seem insignificant because it is something that we do as a natural habit—it is normal to us.

Disrespect is the opposite. Disrespect fails to look back (to re-look) at the information. We could say that we did look back at the information, but we may not have re-looked at all of the information *and* considered it. Without reviewing the information, properly, we have little right to comment on it in any firm manner.

When we disrespect others we are judging circumstances or actions based on *less-than* all of the information. If someone does not understand something and we call them an idiot, then we are being disrespectful because we are not looking at why they do not understand. And further, we are not helping them to actually understand. This is a form of our arrogance.

When we respect someone, we try to find their area of misunderstanding and make an attempt to share and teach to them our understanding of what we have learned. We make fair and accurate assessments when we respect.

Can we value someone to a negative worth without disrespecting them? Only if *they* have permitted it. But, even then we must be cautious. If we give full and clear evidence, which is provable by that evidence, and the person proceeds to deny that the evidence that sits before them exists, then to make a negative statement about the situation, such as stating that the person is wrong, is not disrespectful.

Teach your children respect and to respect you—husband and wife, father and mother—and everyone else around. You will reap the benefits in your old age. There is no down-side in your children understanding respect.

Honor Your Mother and Father

Teach your children to respect their mother and father by respecting your own mother and father. Your parents may have failed you in life, but you must look back into how they were taught and the examples that they were exposed to as children.

If you condemn your parents in front of your children, then they will learn disrespect. The word *condemn* is actually *con-damn.* When you speak against your parents in a manner that fails to look back and consider everything that caused your feelings about them, including *their* life experiences, then you have disrespected your parents. Where there is disrespect there is no honor—you are *damning* them!

To honor our parents is to hold them as *of value.* But, this is difficult when they have not lived in a way that was of value or if they lived in a way where they harmed us throughout our lives.

Passionately expressing your frustrations will not end well for you later on when your children are older and are in *your* current position. If your parents behaved badly or treated you badly, then you are likely doing much of the same behavior with your children unless you have continuously been eradicating that in your own life behavior. The cornerstone book *Hot Water* discusses, in depth, how we perpetuate our troubles onto the next generation and it teaches how to get beyond those errors so that you do not repeat those errors and imprison your own children, binding them with the same chains of error that bind you.

For very bad situations, you can show respect to your parents by remaining calm and not accepting their wrong thinking. All too often, people think that in order to honor someone that you must allow and accept other people's errors. This is simply not true! If you are seeing these errors at all, then your parents must have taught you some good.

Embrace the good and spread it. This is the best way to show respect towards your parents. Become what they cannot, and do them right via *your* future life choices. This is the best form of respect any child can do for their parent—to not live by the same errors as the parents did. They have already paid an enormous price for their own blind and foolish errors. Do not let their mistakes go to waste. Learn from them and show the wisdom you have gained from their errors, by *not* making those same errors.

Another area of respect regarding parents is when we don't respect our spouse. When this lack of respect is shown in front of the children they will follow this lead. It's common for families to have either the father or the mother making sarcastic comments about their spouse, only to have the children repeat similar comments and attitudes to the victim parent.

Because this foolishly dangerous attitude is sometimes done in an "all in fun" manner, it is seen as light-hearted, but in most cases this light-hearted fun is torturous for the victim parent. Teaching our children this type of disrespect causes them to do this to us (their parents), *and* to their own spouse when they get married. This will, in turn, pass the arrogant behavior on to their children—*your* grandchildren. This can and will go on for generations until someone in the family line says "Enough! Not in my family!" Sadly, it is seldom the case that people catch this and say "Enough! Not in my family!"

Lack of respect can even come back to us from our grandchildren when we are grandparents. To remedy this bad situation, we only need to show respect to our spouse, our children, and to others, and then require our children to respect others; then disrespect will vanish from the family. Your diligence and expediency in this matter are critical for your own future joy!

Getting the Respect of Your Child

Most children will always respect the thoughts of a loving and kind parent. We lose our children when we treat them like their thoughts and opinions do not matter. If we want to create a rebellious child, all that we need to do is to **not** consider their words.

Hearing your child's words is not nearly enough. To "hear" means that you heard it or that your ear sensed it. It seems obvious that "ear" and "hear" share the same origin. When you *hear* something, you have only chemically sensed it with your *ear*; it does not indicate that you **considered** it.

Considering your children's words is what is important. The concept of consideration is similar to that of understanding in that it is one of the most base concepts. If you have not grasped what it means to understand, then you have likely barred yourself understanding the concept of "consider." When your child speaks to you, if you are dismissive of, and do not think about, process, and understand what they have said, then expect them to disregard *you* as well.

"Considering" does not mean that we hear and obey their words, or necessarily even agree with them. Considering simply means that you take the due effort and spend a few moments thinking upon what they just said, processing it, and then returning a good, just, fair, true, and understandable response to them with explanation as to why. Doing so is called *teaching*. Doing this greatly reduces tensions between us parents and our children. There's a second part to this solution: While thinking about what they said helps, it is the logic you use when you reply to them that makes or breaks the deal.

The inconsistencies we spoke of a few sections back are the most damaging in this situation. When your children get reasoning and explanations from you that do not make sense, or that they *must* believe just because *you* said so, it causes them to doubt your answers. This is especially true when outside influences come into the picture with *better sounding* and more attractive sounding reasoning and logic, even if that reasoning and logic are actually wrong.

Anytime our minds are faced with inconsistency, doubt is close at hand. We already discussed the dangers of doubt which you should be well familiar with by now.

Inconsistency is difficult to *re-spect*, even by definition this is so. If information is inconsistent, then it is not possible to look back at it because some part of it is not true, meaning that it is not actually there for review.

If you want your children to respect you, then be respect**able**. Consider *their* words and be able to explain the reasons for *your* words. If you cannot offer an adequate explanation that is testable with truth, then, as a natural response, they will typically look elsewhere for their guidance. If this is the case then they *should* look elsewhere because they will *not* find what is true in you. Also consider that if they need to look elsewhere, then, as is all too common, they might end up looking in the wrong places. Because that is how you taught them with your actions and behavior.

In the cases you're inaccurate it is proper that they do not listen to you and that they seek what is true elsewhere where truth can actually be found. If they do not seek truth elsewhere, then they risk being wrong by listening to *your* inconsistencies. To get, and to keep, the respect of your children, *always* consider their words and teach them consistency by teaching them *only* what is true.

Respecting Elders

Teaching children respect through being respectable is your best solution. Showing respect towards your parents as discussed in the previous examples solves a difficult problem with regard to the examples you set for your children.

Showing kindness and respect for older people reflects well on you. Your children will almost certainly duplicate this behavior with older people and will show the same towards you when you are older.

Respect for your elders is best taught to your children through your examples. History has proven this to be reliably consistent.

Summary of Respect

The skill of respect, or looking back at circumstances, is, in general, critical in life. It can be said, if you do not respect the past, then you do not care for your future. Respect has nothing to do with hearing and obeying.

If an "elder," or older person, is accepting foolish notions and trying to force those notions on to you, then it would be equally as foolish to accept the folly of such behavior. Respect is shown through kindness and through what is true, and then kindly teaching that to others, especially, when they are wrong.

This brings us back to what *true* is. When you have grasped "true", then all of the rest of what we have discussed becomes natural in you. Respect is the key to all decency and kindness on Earth. Our ability to ponder our past and consider it, in order to choose our future, is a key to a joyful life.

Chapter 16

Teaching Your Children to Believe Lies

Throughout most of this book we have been referring to what is "true," or, more to the point, *what truth is*. Truth is a skill that we are born with but lose as we are taught the ways of the world.

To regain the skill of truth, truth needs to be re-taught to us. Only this time, we must teach it to ourselves. When we fail to teach our children what is true, then we are teaching them to believe lies through our failure to teach them truth. Even if we were to try to teach them nothing, we leave them susceptible to believing lies; which is far worse than our teaching nothing—Instead teach them truth.

Respect and consideration are the two most important aspects of you teaching your children *truth* through your examples.

Harmony Between Mom and Dad and Your Marital Lies

The respect that you and your spouse show towards each other is another critical aspect in the quest for a strong family.

There is an obvious and unspoken understanding of the bond of a husband and wife. This bond is observed by everyone, especially by the children of that union. Societal messages and observational evidence support the idea of the need for harmony between parents.

The natural expectation of harmony between parents exists whether we like it or not, and whether we agree with this view or not. Your children will be watching the interaction between their parents every moment they are aware of anything concerning both of you. When this natural expectation of harmony is violated in the minds of the children it has drastic effects on them.

Parents who have been struggling to "keep it together" and are considering divorce, have locked themselves in an inescapable trap due to their own arrogances. If you stay together for the sake of the children, then you are lying to them. And no matter how minute, the tension *will* impact the children. If, instead, you choose to divorce, then often the separation devastates the children. Struggling in this way is a lose-lose situation. When you live this way, your children's chances of repeating the same abhorrent behavior and eventually divorcing are extremely high. This occurs because you have taught them that cold uncaring relationships are the way life is to be lived—It becomes "normal" to them.

There is a noteworthy mistake in the statistical and analytical information regarding divorce. It is thought that divorce damages the child, but it is not the divorce or the separation that harms them. The division of the parents is certainly painful for a child, likely near to the death of a parent and probably worse depending upon the age of a child and the circumstances of the parents' relationship. The real problem is not the divorce; rather, the problem is the *behavior* of the parents that causes the divorce in the first place. The behavior that culminates in divorce is *betrayal*, which is violation. If you are interested in understanding more about repairing a marriage, the cornerstone book *Red Hot Marriage* exposes the violations and problems so that they can be stopped and harmony can be restored in the family. Harmony between parents is critical in a family and it greatly affects the children produced from that union.

Living in conflict and flirting with divorce is witnessed by your children and there is nothing that can hide it! No matter how hard anyone tries, they *are* being exposed. If you do a good job pretending that everything is okay, then you are lying to your children. Does this mean that you should fight in front of your children? Probably not.

However, you had best politely point out your violations of each other—*to* each other—and then stop violating one another. This is best done sooner, rather than later.

Divorce devastates children and increases the likelihood that they will repeat your behavior. The divorce rate is something near to four times greater in children from families of divorce, than it is in children from families where the parents do not divorce.

Divorce has nothing to do with the divorce rate numbers. The divorces are only how we quantify the breakdown of a family and marriage relationship. *Red Hot Marriage* breaks down the details of the problems that cause divorce; but for quick reference, divorce is caused by broken expectation, resulting in violation; and typically, this behavior is repeated over and over. A refusal by either person to correct their own bad behavior, tragically, often ends in separation or divorce.

When we live outside of what is true, then we are bound to what is *not* true. When we live this way we make many errors. In various ways we try to hide our doubt and our errors caused by our following lies. When we do this we become violators—this result cannot be avoided. The behavior can be called *lies*, and if the violations happen in our families, then our children see this and learn from it, and typically they copy the behavior. This teaches them to believe lies because they are living with, and in, the lie of their parents' cold relationship.

Don't Accidentally Teach Them Fear

Believing lies, or what is not true, is the root of doubt; and doubt is the root of fear. Sometimes, lies are a means to cover our tracks or paint over and whitewash our errors. We paint over our lies out of our fear of being exposed.

Once we have bought in to the idea of painting over our lies in order to hide them, then we perpetuate even more lies through the same behavior. Trying to make ourselves out to be more than we have chosen to be *is arrogance*. Taking part in any of these behaviors teaches our children fear. It is difficult to exhibit any one of these behaviors without being subject to all of them.

We do not need to be the type of person who hides in the corner in order to be considered afraid. For instance, we may arrogantly, or even confidently, "strut our stuff at work," but then when we are required to sing in public or dance at a wedding we refuse because we are afraid. Later, when our senses have been dulled enough from alcohol to make us feel that we are courageous enough to dance or sing, we will do so, which is also a form of fear. It seems that the more "cool" someone is, then the more likely it is that they will refuse to step forward, unless they consume courage through drugs or alcohol. This is an obvious and very common way we accidentally teach our children fear. If you think on this a bit, you quickly see many other ways most of us negatively teach our children by accident.

What You Teach With Your Job

One of the other areas we teach fear is with how we handle our job. What we teach with our job does not stop at fear. It goes far beyond that. Your job can be a great teaching example for your children *if* you like your job.

Our children hear our conversations through the walls and at the table. Aside of the issues of mutual human respect, when we complain that we hate our job, or a person at work, we are, by example, teaching our children to accept a job that is going to make them miserable. A part of the message to them in this is *fear*. After all, why would you put up with a job that you hate other than that you are afraid to make a change? Whatever the reason, it is born of fear. Tolerating a job you dislike for a short period is not so bad because it is being used only as a steppingstone to move you forward, but *staying* in that job too long will bring about the negative results that we have been discussing. When we do a job that we do not like, we should always be on alert and ready to change to the job that we *should* be doing. But sadly, too many of us sink deep in to the lie of complacency that eventually filters down to our children. By doing so we teach them the lie of keeping a job we hate. This complacent lie becomes an entire life's philosophy and is often practiced in many other areas of our lives.

Your job can be a blessing to your children even if you don't particularly like it. Going home to your children and telling them, with excitement, what you did at work lets them know that you can enjoy your job even if you don't particularly like it. Even if you don't particularly like your job, you can still briefly tell them what you did and why you are working there, **and** you can tell them about your future goals and dreams. Teaching children to dream realistic goals is a very good trait to teach. But, to *indefinitely* stay at a job that you choose to dislike, and to then not make attempts at changing it or not offering sound explanation as to why you are staying at a job you hate, teaches the children a very damaging lesson.

If up until now, you have stayed at a job that you dislike, you can still reach back in time and undo the damage. To do so, you need to explain to your children and ask your family to support your decision to make a change so that you have the joy in life that your family wants and deserves.

The Santa Claus Effect, *What Believing Wrongly Does to Your Child*

This important point was touched on a few times throughout the book and deserves deeper explanation. The Santa Claus tradition has become heavily embedded in culture. This is so deeply done that there is a sort of international cooperation to perpetuate the lie. When we teach our young children that Santa Claus is alive and well today, distributing toys from his North Pole headquarters, we teach them to believe a lie. This is *The Santa Claus Effect.* It becomes a method of belief for them in all other areas of their lives. We are essentially teaching them to believe lies. Many people alive today have enjoyed this tradition, but few have fully understood its roots. Some of the varying legends about Santa Claus are not as accurate as others. You may even recall the excitement of waiting for Santa Claus to come and bring *you* presents as a child!

Saying anything to possibly damage these memories is generally received with an angry response. Even the marketers would suffer if this beloved tradition ever ceased, and many children would be crushed and the world would be in utter chaos. It is felt by many that eliminating Santa Claus is an assault on humanity.

The manner in which Santa Claus is presented to our children is an outright lie—and a dangerous one at that. Let me explain why, and how we can fix this without destroying the world and making the sky fall, and still retain most of the tradition. But first, let's discuss the damage this does to your children.

You are everything to your children. When they are young, they trust you with all of their heart and all of their soul. We typically get the warm fuzzies when we think of Christmas and Santa Claus. Christmastime, for many, was generally happy because *we* as children were the focus of the attention and got all types of neat gifts and toys. We want to repeat these feelings and experiences for our own children. But because we are so accustomed to focusing on the tangible aspects of life, we have led ourselves to believe that these warm-fuzzies come from the Santa Claus tradition itself. We need not shelter them from such traditions, but we ought to teach them the truth from the start.

The warm-fuzzies have zero to do with Santa Claus and what you do with your children in that regard. The warm-fuzzies are created when *you* do *anything* special *with* your children. For instance, there are many people who are sports-crazy and have warm fuzzies about sports. The sport itself has absolutely *nothing* to do with the feelings they have. The feelings are typically because the family was together watching the sports, eating chips and pizza, and drinking sodas etc... *and* sharing excitement *together—as a family*. For many, a father's only quality time with his sons is when he takes them to a special sporting event. It is the quality time with the father that brings the warm-fuzzies to the child, sadly the sporting event ends up getting the credit as being the warm fuzzy fun thing to do and we miss the fact that it was our time *together* with them that felt warm and fuzzy. This misdirection of credit causes us to obsess about what we wrongly believe brought us the good feelings, always seeking more in attempt to achieve those feelings.

To lead the way for our minds to understand the solution to undoing the lies about Santa Claus, we first have to realize that these fond memories have little to do with the tradition of Santa Claus. Those "warm fuzzies" are there because *you* had a special moment **with** *your family* and loved ones and because someone cared enough to make the place all clean and specially decorated with beautiful decorations, pretty lights, and delicious treats. You may even have had extended family that you are fond of come to for a special Christmas visit, and maybe even had a special meal prepared. Santa Claus has nothing at all to do with those feelings. We typically and mistakenly relate our experiences of love and togetherness with our memories of our physical surroundings that we encountered during the experiences of love and togetherness. Often the *surroundings* are given the attention, such as Santa Claus or the aforementioned ball game.

Someone could argue, "Then why was my child so disappointed when they found out Santa was not real?"

The disappointment is because *we* lied to them. We have built up a tale in their minds that has become so big and deceitful to the innocent children, that even the department stores and the weatherman get involved with the tale.

Billions of dollars are spent to promote the Santa Claus tradition every year. More money is spent on Santa Claus annually than is spent in a most elections. Much of this is to get the children to believe that Santa Claus exists, so that the parents buy them presents. Our fond memories and money are what drive this damaging rouse.

Very convincing movies are made that show the doubt people have about Santa, and then, later on in the movie, comes the revelation that Santa Claus really does exist and then even the parent in the movie finally believes. This is very compelling for children, especially when Mom and Dad are in on the hoax. Are we proud that we have duped a three year old? Oddly, many people who indulge in the Santa Claus hoax tell their children that God is *not* real and then become angry when someone tries to tell them that God is real. Is this not totally contradictory behavior?

For adults, the Santa Claus movies are mere entertainment because we watch a lot of fantasy movies for an escape, but the difference is that we go into watching such movies with a full understanding they are not true or real. However, when our children begin to doubt the myth of a currently living Santa Claus who is headquartered at the North Pole, we then go out of our way to perpetuate this international lie. It seems cruel when it comes time to reveal to our children that this is not true. But why? And how does this harm them?

Recall the chapter "*The Faith of a Child.*" Children believe whatever their parents teach them during their early years. They trust their parents with all of their heart, mind, and soul. Whether what we say to our children is true or not does not matter to them because when they are young they believe us *unconditionally,* regardless.

When they have no reason to believe anything other than what we tell them, they *will* believe what we tell them with the whole of their being. With their entire mind, heart, and soul they believe their parents. If you recall, with "*The Faith of a Child,*" it is the fact they have accepted something to be true and that they do not question it that is the important point about their faith.

"Blind faith" lurks wherever the faith of a child is found, in an effort to try to step in and usurp the innocent child's faith. You teach your child to have *blind* faith when you promote Santa as is traditionally taught.

And now for the problem of the Santa Claus Effect: At some point, your child is going to find out that *you* have lied to them about Santa Claus. While they may not hold you to this lie or make an accusation against you, you have still violated a fundamental principle within their lives that, whether you choose to believe it or not, has, in some way, helped to destroy their ability to accept anything as absolute and true. Their faith has been abused and broken by *you.* You have boldly broken the natural expectation of trust that they had in you when they were born.

This might seem petty to many people, and few will say or admit that they themselves have been destroyed because of Santa

Claus. The problem is revealed in our future faith—that is to say, our ability to believe what is true.

The Santa Claus, as presented by tradition of the twentieth and twenty-first centuries, is an utter and outright lie, with a flying sleigh, flying reindeer, elves, and a magical workshop where there is no land mass beneath it at the north pole. I understand that this view appears cynical, but this is what we are telling our children with the help of the marketers, movies, and even the weatherman showing Santa Claus' location on maps during the Christmas Eve news broadcasts.

We want to continue to believe that this has no effect on our children, but it does—and it is a serious trust issue. When taking part in and promoting the lies about Santa Claus, we teach our children how to believe lies when they are very young. Then, when they begin to figure out the truth, we teach them more strategies to ignore the facts that they discovered. We convince them to use those strategies to hide the truth and ignore what they actually see.

Just like the primary languages we spoke of earlier, these strategies become a primary language in themselves and are taught at very young ages.

This is the most heinous lie we have ever perpetrated on our children. Do not teach your children to believe lies. It would be different if we were mistaken, but we are not. We know full well that we are lying to our innocent children who get *all* of their preliminary and fundamental information from their trusted parents—us!

Similarly, the tales surrounding Easter with a bunny, and the tooth fairy all do the same thing to children. It is better to *not* lie about any of these or similar traditions. We should at least notify the children that these are only imaginary play games and that it is the parents who do all of these wonderful things for them. With this approach you will not continue lying to them about what is true.

So how do we stop this lie and **not** destroy the world economy and collapse the sky at the same time? We use the *truth*.

Take Credit for Your Gifts to Your Children

You can still put money under your child's pillow when they lose a tooth and it can be *from you*. They will be no less excited and they will likely love you all the more for thinking of them and making the event special for them. The same is true for most of the holiday or special event traditions for which we dupe our children.

We all love fond memories. If you think back to when you met your spouse I'll bet that those memories rival your childhood Santa memories, and for most of you, Santa was nowhere in sight when you met your spouse. It is almost certain that you no longer believed Santa was real and alive at that time in your life when you began dating your spouse.

These warm fuzzy feelings are there for one reason and one reason only—Love! Or better stated—Truth. We have the most joy in our lives when we are with people who are treating us fairly, respectfully, and when we are sharing with them and they are sharing with us. Our memories have added feeling if someone took the extra time and effort to make the setting perfect. In the case of Santa Claus and Christmas, that would be doing something such as decorating the house and offering gifts in kind gesture. Or while dating, getting all dressed up for your date and going out somewhere special to eat. The gifts, settings, clothes, and food are not the things that are special. It is *the special attention* to the details that *you have done* as an act of kindness for the other person that makes those memories fond or special to them. Surprises and anticipation, and then fulfillment of good things are a powerful means of validation.

With our courtship memories, many people think the feelings are from the clothes worn when they met or the place they met at etc... but when we try to duplicate those circumstances by going to a place or dressing with certain clothes and listening to certain songs, the feelings are really the offering and acceptance that we had felt with our spouse which we are trying to reproduce, and often successfully do.

You could have done any one of a million things differently and those other million choices would invoke just as fond of memories as what actually occurred. We are not in love with those events; we are in love with the way the other people made us feel. The Santa Claus Effect is no different. The warm fuzzies are not Santa Claus, they are from the special treatment and the care in selecting the gifts and the fact that someone thought enough of another person to give them something special. When someone does something special for you, is the gesture not a good feeling?

The first step in reversing the Santa Claus effect is that you, as the parent, should be taking credit for those gifts your children get. After all, you are the one who has worked for and spent the money and time to pick out and purchase those gifts; additionally, let them know that it is the Creator who grants us the skills, talents, and desires to keep and do our jobs. Take credit for your gifts. Your children will love you all the more for thinking of them, and their devotion will be rightly aimed at *you*!

The benefits of understanding the source of the warm fuzzies are obvious and you deserve the credit. If you have children and have shared the Santa tradition in the customary way with them, then you have wasted a great deal of joy. The sooner you stop, then the sooner you can reclaim what rightfully belongs to you, and stop your child from suffering from The Santa Claus Effect.

So, what's the next step to take in order to make sure the sky doesn't fall? Let's try the truth!

Santa = Saint
Claus = Nicholas
Chris = Christ
Kringle = kinder (German for "child", as in kindergarten)

You can tell your children where these legends came from and about the man we call Saint Nicholas who had a reputation for secret gift-giving. You can also tell them about the German word for "The Christ-child", pronounced Chris-kind who is the traditional legendary Christmas gift-bringer in some regions of Europe. Telling them the origins of the Santa Claus tradition *enhances* their lives and helps to build their trust in you. But be warned that when digging into the various Santa legends there are parts of the tradition that they don't need to hear that are a bit darker in nature depending on the cultural path you follow while researching and would likely frighten your children.

Honesty about Santa Claus can still cause problems if you have taught your child things wrongly. There is no need for your children to go about telling other children "Nu-uh, there is no Santa, he's dead; my mommy and daddy said so, that's all fake!" This is unproductive and damaging to the other children and their families. If your child behaves in this way you have failed them and it is time to make the needed corrections in your example to them.

Barring your children by means of *militant* removal of the Santa Claus tradition could, and likely will, cause problems for you in the future depending upon how you do handle the task. You can play the Santa game and pretend that Daddy, or even Mommy, is Santa; you can even dress up like Santa if you would like and still have just as much fun, and more, rather than participating in the North Pole Santa Claus hoax. Your children will be able to be a part of the tradition and they will still have the warm fuzzy feelings and the stores will still get their business and the movies can still be made, but the only difference is simply that your children will *know* that the movies are fake and are fantasy movies and the Santa tale is all for fun; plus you will not break trust with them by lying to them.

You will never have to deal with having been a liar to your children, and the world will live happily-ever-after! There is no need to become angry about this tradition and speak hatefully against it. We need only to correct our approach, so that we are not lying to and deceiving our children. It's okay to take part in such traditions provided you're honest. There is no need for hatefulness or malice or lies.

Then there is the actual meaning of the reason that we actually celebrate *Christ*-mas that is to say: *Christ's*-mass. You may want to explain that to them also. You know the story, the Christmas story about the babe born to show us the way to truth and light, the one that's in the Bible.

There is no reason that we cannot be honest with these sorts of customs and still be able to partake in them without lying to our children.

Some people choose to tell their children about Santa Claus but then struggle with the world because the custom is all around us. What you choose in this regard is your own choice, but the custom will remain. Please keep in mind that the issue here is not Santa Claus, the problem is all of the deceit about it and the fact that we break our trust with our children because when they ask about the truth then we typically deliberately lie to them about it.

The damages caused by breaking trust with people runs deep and wide, but the damages caused by lying to your children runs the deepest. Broken trust causes a rift in their ability to accept anything as absolute—Broken trust destroys their ability to understand Truth! Some children make it through this and later grasp truth, but many do not fully grasp it. When we, the parents, set up an elaborate hoax and dupe our children, then how can we expect to create a person who is capable of believing anything as absolutely true? We cannot!

Don't be Unaware
Pay Attention to what Your Children Watch

What your children watch greatly affects them, but what you tell them about what they watch affects them even more. Similar to Santa movies and having you lie to them about the reality of the Santa tradition, the other shows that they watch affect them also. Your actions and interaction with your children matter.

When we allow our young children to experience any form of entertainment without *us* first using our own judgement to filter it for appropriateness for their ages, or if they watch without us being there to explain what they are seeing as they watch, we may be subjecting them to a great deal of material that is against what our own values are.

Some of the entertainment for children has, admittedly, subliminal information in it. This sort of thing is difficult to detect but the more open and obvious subliminal effects are your larger concern. Entertainment and commercials have messages within them, if they did not, then there would be nothing to see. Often, we are too caught up in the cuteness of the characters depicted in the entertainment, and so we are willing to overlook the disturbing, underlying principles being presented in the messages conveyed within the entertainment. There is a price to be paid with regard to what you allow your children to watch. The question is not *if* there is a price; but rather, the question is, how much will you and your children pay overall for the messages that you allow to be poured into them?

TV has become a horrible form of entertainment that has captivated the hearts and minds of the world. Yet it is not really TV that is the problem, but rather, it is our excessive use of TV and the programming that *we choose* to watch, or more importantly, what we allow our children to watch with or without our supervision. Children are empty vessels that are being filled with whatever they experience in life.

TV can bring messages into your home while **you are not there** watching it with your children. Often, children come home from school while the parents are away at work, and they can watch anything they wish. Their options are even more of a risk when you have cable or satellite TV as many people do. It is your responsibility to utilize the parental locks that most of these devices have, but few people use.

TV is a tool when you know how to use it properly, and just as a knife can be used to cut a potato or to harm a person, so it is with TV. What your children watch has a lasting negative or positive effect on them, but that *choice* is yours!

Cartoons

Cartoons seem to be a favorite with children. Many cartoons have very bad messages in them. It will do you and your family good to analyze those cartoons and their messages before you allow your children to become accustomed to them. Decide whether or not what is being shown or presented is good for your young children, and then enforce those decisions.

Everything that you allow your children to watch matters to their life's direction and thinking. If you are remiss in teaching your children, and you further allow them to watch shows that do not agree with your family's values, then you can **expect** problems in your future with regard to your children and with regard to your relationship with them.

> Your absence in this matter
> is as good as your approval.

If Mom and Dad are not saying anything, then it must be okay! This is the message that we are giving to them when we fail to care enough to monitor what entertainment they watch. Adult-level sitcoms have increasingly taken the after-school children's-viewing time slots. This varies depending on the programming schedules of the local transmissions to any one community and the channels being watched.

Movie Horror

Horror movies... why do we watch these? It is mostly a teens-to-twenties demographic that drives this malicious market. Is it really a good thing to have children, or anyone for that matter, be entertained by these movies? Teaching our children malice in this way is not good.

It only takes one child to become distorted in their thinking and act on it to cause serious problems and loss for many as we have all too often seen. Additionally, horror movies cause children to be unnecessarily afraid and have issues with feeling safe and secure. This is far worse when we ourselves are foolish enough to subject our very young children to this type of entertainment. Regretfully, this is something that many people do.

Some of these movies are so poorly done that they become a laughing stock; and in that, they become "cult classics." Under that guise, we foolishly approve them for our young children to watch.

Additionally, many of these movies associate sexually intimate moments with the malicious acts of murder. Do you really want your child imagining that when they get their first kiss in the park, that someone is going harm them? Is this good for them?

The images and messages that are shown in such entertainment will be hiding somewhere in their mind and it *will* affect them, but to what extent is uncertain. Is this a risk that you want to take with your children? Do you want them to live in fear?

Video Games

What can be said about video games that has not been addressed so far? Unlike horror movies, not all video games are bad. Companies have actually been making some games that can be physically and socially beneficial, yet a good amount of games are explicitly violent, malicious, and sexual in nature.

To deny that this affects your children is to choose ignorance. There is nothing that any human being experiences that does not become a part of them and affect their behavior to some extent. If your children's behavior, or anyone's for that matter, was not affected by entertainment, then we would never repeat the words from that entertainment, additionally, all commercials would promptly cease to exist.

The video games your children play *will* affect them. To what extent is unknown, but not facing this truth by you not monitoring your children's entertainment, puts you and your family in the spotlight for much unwanted attention if any of your children decide to terrorize their school or any other place or person(s). Many people feel that this only happens to *"other people's children"*, but we need to keep in mind, that this is the same way the parents of the children who harmed others felt before the problem occurred.

Internet

Of all of the forms of entertainment, the internet is perhaps the most useful **and** the most dangerous. The internet can be a wonderful tool, but gone unmonitored it becomes your worst nightmare. There is little that is not available on the internet. Allowing your children unrestricted, unmonitored access to it is reckless and dangerous. It is as if you dropped off your five-year-old at a drug infested brothel where murderous gangs linger outside the neighboring crack house.

It's all up to each family to decide what is best for their children and family. Having TVs and computers in each of your children's rooms more likely serves to separate them than bring them together. If they have computers or phones that are unrestricted and unmonitored in their bedrooms, then you have created a gateway for everything imaginable to enter your home without your knowledge. I would have added, "*or consent*", as in: without your knowledge and *consent*, but since **we** are the ones who place the computers, phones, and TVs in our children's rooms without restriction, and without monitoring their use, *we* have given our consent, and *we* will suffer the consequences for doing so.

An additional note that should be pointed out about the internet is if your child does something foolish and you place a video clip of their embarrassing moment online and it goes "viral", you could destroy your child and make them a laughing stock of the world for years to come. There is also the problem of, typically girls, being taken advantage of by their boy "friends" where pictures are taken of intimate moments and then these pictures are subsequently shared and passed around online or are posted online for the entire world to see. Be careful with these tools so that they do not turn into weapons against your own family.

It seems cynical, but not everyone's motives are pure. People have been and are unfairly treated due to the power of the tool of the internet. Society will pay a heavy price for the trust it places in putting too much personal information to be accessed on the internet. And your children will pay a price if you fail to teach them truth and how to use it in life. It is not an easy task to try to get your children to understand the perils of society without turning them in to cynical people. Understanding truth helps a great deal in this undertaking.

Before the internet, you had to work hard and must have been able to show responsibility to be published or broadcast. However, now with the internet and other technologies, anyone can, at no cost to themselves, say anything and have it be available for the world to access, even if it is all lies and malice.

Everything that your children experience becomes a part of their life. They trust **you** to keep them safe and guide them.

Their perspective, which they are typically unaware of, is that if *you* do not object to it, then it must be okay for them to see it, and if it is okay for them to see, then it is also okay to do. What they experience is mostly allowed and orchestrated by us—their parents.

The internet is a useful *tool* that deserves to be used with respect. When we place too much information out for public viewing, then we put ourselves in a very vulnerable spot. Learn to respect this powerful tool and teach your children to do the same, and then use it for things that are helpful to your family, and for things that won't harm others. Teach them to use it to improve society.

Allowing your children unrestricted access to any form of entertainment is going to have a general effect on them of exposure to lies, misinformation, and general bad behavior. This is not what we want our children to learn. Doing so teaches them to believe lies. There is much great information for them out there in the world, and some of it is even in entertainment, but it is *your* responsibility to make sure that *good* information is the type of information that they are accessing. Adults, and especially children, are constantly repeating lines from movies or TV shows. Repeating these lines in itself is not a problem, but many people can recite lines from entertainment and commercials, yet cannot even make a single accurate quote from a Bible. It's not wrong to repeat these lines if they are not harmful, but denying this abundant evidence illustrating that children **are** affected by entertainment does deliberately ignore reality.

Regardless of whether it is the Santa Claus Effect or simply the entertainment you allow them to take part in, in the end, it is all the same; if it is not true and good, then it is a lie. Make sure your children are not blindly following lies, and just as important make sure you are not the cause.

Chapter 17

Schooling

The schools we choose to send our children to *will* affect them, and so will their teachers' values, the values of the classmates, and the curriculum values. Over their school years, your children will learn, but will also be subjected to an assault of *less-than-*good examples coming from all around them.

Knowing what and how you teach your children will prepare them for that journey. If your parenting and life approach has been rooted in things that are not true, then your children will *not* have the needed skills to detect when they have come upon lies. These lies could be in the school's curriculum, from friends, from their teachers, or maybe even from the empty promises of drugs and alcohol in effort to dull their emotional pains. Teaching your children to stand for what is actually true will cause nearly everyone in their class to learn more, and will make them and everyone around them better and more understanding people.

Your foundation will make the difference of what *they* are able to get out of school. Do not leave this to the school, because schools are not designed to teach your children truth. Schools have become trivia learning centers, and they typically teach your children a bunch of facts that have little bearing on life. It is you and *good* teachers that will reveal to them the life lessons and the practical application of the trivia that they will be subjected to in school.

The School Bus and School Yard

Ah, the school bus! That dreaded ride to and from school. For some students it's not so bad, only a few minutes each way, but for the unlucky souls who are at the end of the country bus route, the ride can be over an hour *to*, and over an hour *from*, school. While enduring this ride, your children are un-chaperoned because the bus driver is too busy trying to safely drive the bus—a bus that contains forty plus passengers chattering with loud voices and entertaining themselves with all of the debauchery that accompanies a typical school bus ride.

With children of all ages riding together, from the most innocent to the most brazen, there is little you can do about what your child will be exposed to, short of driving them to school every day yourself. The school bus and the schoolyard are where many children pick up their "street" information.

For those of you who rode the bus to school, recall your experiences, and then prepare your children for *that* daily ride by teaching them how to choose what is good and true. This does not end when they jump off of the bus and onto the schoolyard—because the same is true of the schoolyard. We must also prepare our children to deal with things that they will be exposed to while on the schoolyard by teaching them what is true. The same goes for the classroom, and while there are many good teachers, not *all* teachers are good, and not all information being taught is accurate and true.

Home, Parochial, or Public?

So, should you avoid the bus and schools altogether by homeschooling your children? That all depends on *you*. You and your spouse both need to want to homeschool, *and* you both need to be disciplined enough to carry through to do it properly. Depriving your children of the fundamental skills with which to learn is cruel. Homeschooling is a wonderful approach, and when done well, advances your children far beyond what any public or private school offers. Typical schools must divide the teacher's time between upwards of twenty students, where *you* on the other hand, can teach them one-on-one.

Most homeschool students excel because of the one-on-one teaching that they receive from their parents. When done properly, it takes *you* little time to teach them. This could be done by you simply including your children in your daily life. Public school is meant to prepare your children for daily adult life, but frequently fails on that account. Whether or not a school is able to successfully prepare children for their adulthood has no bearing on the fact that it is ultimately the parents' responsibility to do so. Bringing them into your world and then, along the way, teaching them in everything you do, teaches them skills that they will *never* be able to learn in *any* schools. School does not prepare people for actual life experiences. There is no replacement for actually experiencing life.

This is especially true for families who run a small or a home business. Do not make your children your slaves, but include them in your work and teach them all of the aspects of your work. Have them be a partner in what you do, and incorporate their school lessons in doing so. After all, this is why they are going to school to begin with—to learn enough to be able to earn a living and function well in society and maybe even advance it. But remember, you are educating them, not preparing them to take your place in your business; that decision must be theirs alone. Anyone who runs a business properly will be dealing with mathematics, reading, logistics, spelling, letter composition, and business and mechanical maintenance etc., all of which are the most excellent teaching and learning tools.

The difference seen between standard curriculum and— homeschooling in an inclusive manner—is that they get real-world practical application lessons while they learn at home. This reduces your children's additional homeschooling needs to only those subjects that your work and life do not normally cover. Plus, *you* will learn a great deal along with them.

If homeschool is not your game, then the private or parochial schools might be an option for your family. Many people would choose parochial schools if they could take the tax money that is required to be paid to the public school system and use it to pay for the parochial tuition of *their* choice. But since this is not going to easily happen, most people have taken the route of least resistance and now use the public school system for their children.

Parochial schools offer one key element that the public schools do not, a freedom to express your family's religion, which to some people, is very important.

Parochial schools are not innocent by any means. Talk to any former parochial students who are now grown and you will find that parochial schools rival the public school system in student antics and debauchery. Send them to parochial schools for the right reasons. Thinking that they will not get exposed to bad things there is naïve.

The difference between public and parochial schools is that in parochial school they can learn something about your family's religious beliefs and your values without getting the godless lessons of the public schools. Although, you should have already taught them about your family beliefs and the sound reasoning as to why you believe what you do.

Public schools could be great learning places and for many students they are. However, since the big bang and evolution theories dominate the science world, the public school system has often become a puppet of those godless philosophies, thus forcing that agenda on to vulnerable innocent unknowing school children. When we have come to a point in society that teachers and administrators misunderstand the laws of the land to a point where they are foolishly willing to censor the freewill free-speech rights of the citizens' religious viewpoints, then are we really "teaching" the children at that point?

We need not specifically teach religion in the public schools. In fact, we must not teach a "religion." But to stifle discussion about religion and the obvious possibility of Creation, is both foolish and dangerous. Discussion of religion in public schools would be very beneficial to all students. Allowing discussion of the possibility of intentional Creation, versus teaching religion, are two completely different things. Those few teachers who are anti-religion zealots who stifle conversation in public schools and universities can only maintain their power through their control of your voice. Take back the power from them.

"Wrong" information is somewhat a matter of opinion. The "wrong" information we are discussing in this situation is about our beliefs. As discussed earlier, the level of—the skill of evaluation of facts—with which you send your children to school, is going to determine how much they can be affected by any wrong information that they learn.

Both parochial *and* public schools have evolution being taught in them, but neither seems to be able to determine what is true. How could they, when the churches and scientific community can't even agree on the, who, what, where, when, and why?

Your children will get their share of bad influence no matter where they are schooled. It is your ability to teach them about weighing *all* information on the scale of truth that will allow them to be able to easily choose a right path regardless of where they are taught.

Higher Education

The time where many parents lose their children is when they move from childhood to adulthood in the college school system. This is where The Santa Claus Effect shows up most prominently.

Many university professors are believed to be highly "educated." They have diplomas showing various degrees of how much trivia they have learned. They have been taught debating skills and how to craft clever hypothesis in order to persuade people to agree with them. This is not a bad thing—until it contradicts *your* family's beliefs and morals; but more importantly, until it contradicts *the truth*. Some political and religious information being taught in the college system, all too often, is doubtful at best.

Political and religious views are two areas where the university system has become proficient at convincing the students to go down a path *you* might not agree with politically and/or religiously. When the parents are paying the bill and signing the paperwork, then the responsibility rests on the shoulders of the parents who send their children to these colleges and pay the tuition. When you blindly send your children to these learning venues and pay the tuition, you are essentially agreeing with everything the professors say. You are confirming to your children that the professors are correct. This is shown by your supporting the professors by paying the often overpriced tuition that pays their wages. This allows the unrestricted professors to promote agendas that are not in agreement with your family's beliefs. Some of the responsibility also sits on the shoulders of the professors who you allow to teach your children.

A child who is sent to college with weak understanding usually comes out of college with beliefs that are different from their parents' beliefs with which they entered college, and, often, this is radically so. If your values are Christian or "conservative", then your children will be in for a very tough battle unless you have given them the ability and skill to balance facts and seek what is true.

There are two key things that stop them from departing from correct beliefs. First is foolish-blind-stubbornness, which makes them potentially just as deceived as some of the churches, some scientists, and some of the professors who will be teaching them. But foolish-blind-stubbornness will be a snare to them in their life somewhere else even if it holds up against their college instructors.

The best method, and the second key, is a rock-solid foundation that is able to quickly weigh the facts and opinions on the scale of truth and is thus able to stand against lies being forced upon them by "higher education".

The Erosion

This world is full of clever thinkers and books written by clever thinkers—some right and some wrong. Assaults against belief systems have been raging on for thousands of years.

Whether it is the naturalists "proving" that the creationists are wrong, or the creationists "proving" the naturalists are wrong, these sorts of debates still have been raging on for thousands of years. Everyone seems to be pointing fingers with hostility saying the other side is "wrong, wrong, wrong!" Sadly, they are pretty much all wrong.

This is being boldly stated because we cannot hide any facts and be considered "honest" in regard to the subject we are *hiding* facts about. If we see a conflict in some of the facts presented to us, and then because of that, we choose to decide that the facts are irrelevant, then we may be, and are likely, **wrong**.

Two witnesses can feel the temperature of a bowl of water and one can say it is warm and the other can say it is cool, but both can be right because hot versus cold is a perceived value. Both are speaking of the same water, but perceive it differently due to their most recent experience of a comparable source of stimulation (very hot water versus very cold water.)

The only thing that any of us need to concern ourselves with is truth. Without truth, the world, and especially the college university system, often erodes our *correct* values that are typically falsely propped up. Children that go into the school system strong, come out of the system stronger; and children who go into the system weak come out of the system weaker, damaged, distrusting, and defeated.

Typically, the universities only take the brightest students, and then brag how great of a job the university is doing. This is deceitful and disingenuous! Brag if they will, but at least be honest since colleges are institutions of "higher" education.

Universities build their prestige based upon how well *you* raised *your* children and how much money they can get from you for expansion of their facilities and to pay for their staff. A *truly great* university would only take the children with the lowest grades and poorest attitudes and teach them how to become brilliant students and successful business leaders—but they do not do that. They steal the glory of great parents and call it their own.

Schools, politics, religion; it doesn't matter, it's all the same—it is *people* that make the difference. If status were not what it is all about, then the universities would accept *any* student, but they do not. In their arrogance they use the reputations of the highest performing students who are typically the only ones they allow into their universities. The credit assumed by the universities belongs to the parents and their children, **not** to the universities.

The universities themselves are just buildings with resources and should be thought of as such. Your children should extract as much learning that enhances their lives and interests as they can from the universities, but leave the rest of the junk at the college. Going to college with this attitude will gain students much, but doing so, while leaving college arrogance behind, will advance them more!

Chapter 18

What to Teach Your Children

This chapter lists a few important issues that create a lot of difficulty for parents. There are many books with many methods of dealing with these types of issues, so we will limit the discussion here and only touch on the more prominent issues that test most parents.

Your examples and your teaching affect the direction your children choose in life. What then, should we teach our children? When your children get into their teens and early twenties, you are no longer going to be able to be there for them in the same way that you can be there while they are learning their primary languages. Winding back the clock a bit to when your children were in diapers, if you have trained them for *The Santa Claus Effect*, then you have also likely used the same "Because I told you so" methods for teaching them their religious and political beliefs.

When our children believe *anything* in a Santa Claus Effect manner they can be easily deterred even if what they believe *is* correct. When our children do not know *why* they believe what they believe, then they cannot state their case well enough when someone proficient at debate challenges them in their beliefs. This causes them to appear and feel foolish. It's like when a child is told by a friend from school that there is no Santa Claus and the whole class laughs at them for believing that there is one. This is what happened to the Church. The Church arrogantly said, "*This* is the way it is," and then a handful of people who like to think "freely" came up with a list of *alleged* conflicts in the Bible and proposed alternate theories about the origins of man that *appeared* to make more sense.

The students are then challenged and told that there is no God and are subsequently mocked by the entire class and professors. This is because they have no basis for their beliefs other than "the Bible told me so." So what should *you* teach your children? Just about everything! All interaction you have with your children teaches them something. Whether that "something" is good or bad, is up to you. Teaching your children to weigh everything on the scale of truth enables them to engage in intelligible dialogue, in for instance, the debate about evolution-versus-Creation, without being humiliated.

We've discussed the schooling aspects, but there are other basic aspects of life that are also critical, such as health, eating and hygiene; some of which start at very early ages.

Teaching Clean - Soap and Water

Giving your young children a bath at least two or three, or more times per week is a good idea and teaches them cleanliness. The obvious—cleaning themselves with soap and water for good hygiene—is always good to teach them; and like any primary language, it too, is something that should be taught young. Good personal hygiene habits start young and should be taught to them right away by you doing it for them until they learn to do it on their own. It is important to teach them to get at the hard to reach parts and the delicate parts. Failing to teach this primary language can get you unwanted visits to the doctor's office in order to deal with preventable rashes and infections. Simple things like making sure to teach them to clean their faces and genitals *before* they clean the dirtier areas, such as their feet, can stop the spread of unwanted infection and virus. Cleaning behind the ears and the back of the neck, and behind their arms and legs are all areas that can easily be missed by them. If they don't form these habits when they are young, then they are more likely to miss those areas, or wash in the wrong basic order when they are grown up. When a child is young it is not as much of an issue what order they do things in, but when they are grown and work all day long in hot, sweaty shoes, then it is especially important for them to wash their feet last in sequence after they have washed their genitals, etc. Cleaning methods of this nature are especially important for women to recognize. Many people do these things out of pure logic on their own, but not everyone thinks about it enough to realize that it matters, and failing to do so can cost us dearly, causing infections and viruses in all the wrong places.

Teach cleanliness young. Make these times enjoyable for them. We parents have this nasty habit of turning these simple tasks into an unpleasant chore, and then we spend years and years nagging the children about tending to their personal hygiene and cleaning tasks. Do the basics of life *with* your children and make it a game. Make it enjoyable! Create the warm-fuzzies for them while doing these tasks.

In general, our perception of *clean* is going to be based upon what we were taught and what our house was like as a child; though some people can escape this even if they were taught poorly. Teaching our children *clean* by keeping them, ourselves, our home, and our cars clean and ordered will be carried with them into their own adulthood. Teaching them to wash their hands and face after eating helps them have better manners when they are grown. If your children have a dirty face, mouth, or nose when they leave the house, then don't be offended when people look at them and shake their heads thinking them to be seventeenth-century orphans. Teach them how to properly wash their face and clean their ears, teeth, etc., and you will keep their risk for disease and infection low all of their lives. They will be more respected when they are clean.

Potty Training and Bed Wetting

There are as many different opinions on potty training as there are parents. But there is one thing that is certain. The longer they go not being potty trained then the more difficult it is for the parents to train them and take them out in public. And the older the child is, the more work it is to clean them up. Potty training is a tough balance for parents because if we yell at children for wetting their pants or not making it to the potty fast enough, or for wetting their bed, thus causing extra mess, the more negatively the child will feel about the entire experience.

Encouragement and *example* are two very important tools for potty training children. Incentive is also a very good tool. It seems that making it somewhat unpleasant for the child when they mess their pants is good, but the problem that we have is that while *we parents understand* why we are rebuking the child for doing so, the *child does not necessarily understand* why we are angry. If, in the child's eyes, they are not connecting messy pants with being yelled at, it comes across as irrational to them. There is no perfect solution to this issue, other than to realize that children might not understand what it is you want of them. When we understand this then we are able to adjust our approach until we get it figured out. Typically, parents have their children potty trained by age three. If it goes longer than that it is time for the parents to pause and diligently review their approach and promptly make some adjustments accordingly.

Here are a few things to pay attention to. Regarding bed wetting at night, don't feed your children right before bed. Often we allow the children to have something to drink just before bed. While some children can hold their bladder through the night, or rouse themselves to get up, others will not. Allowing them drinks just before bed fills their bladders and increases the chances of bed-wetting by a factor of ten or more. It is best to have a gap of one or more hours after eating and drinking before they go to bed, thus allowing them time to adequately empty their bladder *before* bedtime. If you find that an hour is not enough time then increase that gap. Also, the type of foods and liquids they consume can affect the timing by which their bodies absorb and release water. For instance, salty items can cause you to retain water, but at some point that water retention is released. If that occurs in the night, it can be a problem.

The same holds true when you are planning to go away. If your child drinks anything shortly before you leave home, the child will inevitably need to empty their bladder at some point during the brief trip. If you allow your child to drink before bed and before leaving home, then expect them to have to go potty at some point. And, as is common with children, they often will not ask or cannot make it to the restroom in time. In this case it is somewhat unfair to become frustrated or angry with them because it is the parents' own fault for giving them drinks at an improper time.

If parents take the time and effort to think upon any unpleasant situation with children they will almost always find out that the problem is not with the child, but rather it is with the parents. This means that the parents need to stop, think, and then adjust accordingly. Problems are warning lights telling you that you are doing something that needs to be changed in order to properly address the problem situation.

A good rule of thumb regarding eating and drinking before bed, is to *not* allow any drinks less than two hours before bedtime. This allows their system to process the foods and beverages, and gives the bladder time to fill enough to have them able to go potty and empty their bladder completely just before bedtime.

Brush Teeth

Washing up and brushing teeth can be as warm and fuzzy for your children as Christmas day if *you* are there doing it with them. It is your love that they want, along with your approval and your admiration.

Children will do almost anything to get their parents' approval. If you don't *give* them your approval then they will *take* your attention, and that is never good. Show them your approval by spending time with them and by teaching them during life's simple tasks.

Teaching your children good hygienic habits keeps your doctor bills lower and nearly eliminates all dental bills. There is no reason your children cannot get into a full set of adult teeth without a single cavity. Not having your child drinking soda and imitation fruit drinks at meals, never letting them eat food or candy after nighttime teeth brushing, and not allowing them to take food or drink to bed or at naptime saves you loads of money on dental bills and keeps your children in their own good teeth until they die of old age. Your children will be cavity-and-filling free for life! There is no downside in doing so.

Eating Well

Eating *well* and eating *when*, are important. Teaching our children to eat healthy food, *in proper quantities*, at proper times keeps them healthy and fit. This helps them to learn those good habits for later in life when they are on their own.

If we spent a lot less time at the workplace just so that we can afford health insurance, and instead, spent a lot more time learning about and teaching good thinking, eating, and health habits to our families, then health insurance would not be nearly as important because it would rarely be needed. Health insurance and life insurance are actually sickness insurance and death insurance. They are okay to have, but it is as if we believe that we will soon get sick and die if we do not have these "insurances."

Teach your children good eating habits when they are young and they will likely follow the example when they are grown. When they eat too much, their bodies process the food and most of it goes to waste right through them. The book *Dream Thin – The Weight Loss Repair Manual* explains how most families could drastically cut their food costs and reduce medical expenses if they would only get their family's eating right.

Healthy eating has obvious benefits. But even when your children have *you* as a good example for their eating habits, at times they may still not want to eat what you are serving. Children have their own set of likes and dislikes and those differing tastes can sometimes turn on and off like a light switch.

When parents teach, in a loving manner, why it's important to eat healthy, it is far easier to get them to eat well as they grow up. This is best done from an early age. There is no need to be militant or deceptive about it. When a child won't eat what you prepared, bargaining with or bribing them typically will not be successful in the long run. Often it brings only *more* attention to the situation by making an issue of things; this etches negative feelings about that food and situation deep into their minds. The next time the particular meal is served they will have those negative feelings recalled in their memory.

Distraction is the best method to get children to eat. If a child has set their focus on not wanting to eat a particular food item, they usually stand by their decision and reject it. Bringing more attention to the particular food item only serves to intensify their feelings about the item. It is best to distract their attention of not wanting to eat it, and direct attention to some other topic; this often works very well when done *before* it has become a point of resistance for the child. Even if they do not eat it at that particular meal they will likely do so the next time you serve the item provided that you have not previously made an issue of it. Forcing the issue casts a negative feeling about the item deeply into their thoughts, thus causing them to more likely remember their negative feelings the next time you serve the undesired item to them. When children have decided that they do not like certain foods there typically is a reason, even though *you* may not see it. The particular reason is less important than their *focus* on that reason. If their focus on the issue can be broken, then they tend to forget about their previous reason and begin to eat the prepared food.

All too often, we make the wrong assumption that just because we like something, that everyone else will like it too. If this were true then we would all be you. Others are not you, and you are not others. Your children are not you, and you are not them.

Some of the reasons children won't eat that parents often fail to notice are food temperature, taste, and texture. Food temperature is critical! Not everyone likes hot food; in relative terms some people like it *warm*—which is a very important point for parents to know and remember.

Since hot, warm, and cold are personal perceptions of the person experiencing them, we must be careful when giving young children hot food. They might not be able to communicate, in an adequate manner, about their dissatisfaction of the burning hot, or too cold, temperature of the meal or whatever else the dissatisfaction may be, other than to reject it or cry. Beside the pain and dissatisfaction that the hot or cold foods can cause, there is also the issue of the flavor change and the texture change when food temperature changes. The differences in the taste and texture are important and they matter to us all, including our children.

A most important part to keep in mind about a child not eating whatever you serve is that the foods taste might not agree with their taste palette. If something makes you gag, then it makes you gag. We should not dictate what our children must like. As parents, we have a tendency to want our children to like what we like, but they are separate people from us, and they develop tastes that, to some extent, will vary from our own.

Be sensitive to the fact that children may be trying to tell you, in their own young way, that they are not pleased with something. If a child misses a meal on occasion it won't damage them unless they have some serious biological issues. Forcing them to shovel food down their throat is not going to solve anything, however, not allowing them to take part in the bonus dessert will. And it *does not* need to be used as a point of leverage to coerce them into eating.

There is a difference between *incentive* and *bribing*, and many parents fail to recognize this difference. The view from the outside regarding the difference for something such as a yummy dessert can be identical in the end. But it is the disposition of the child and the desperation of the parents that make the difference of whether something is a bribe, or if it is an incentive. The timing of when it is offered is also a factor.

Consider carefully the following: If you are bribing your child, then *they* are in control of the situation and they are in control of **you**. However, when a parent is in control, then the yummy dessert becomes an incentive for the child. Many parents miss seeing this difference because they have never experienced being in control of a situation with regard to their children. Often, we parents try to control them rather than being *in control* of a situation. This difference is critical for you to understand.

Of course, the eating example here is only the tip of the iceberg. This *bribing* versus *incentive* issue, typically permeates all areas of family life. In other words, if you get it wrong at mealtime, then you are likely getting it wrong the rest of the time as well.

Anytime you say to a child, "I will give you something if you do something" you are bribing them. However, if they understand that they get something when they do well, and don't get it if they do not do well; it is incentive. The difference here is seemingly small and hard for many people to tell the difference. But I assure you, the difference is very important.

In bribing situations, the parents feel the loss because the child refuses and rejects the parents' will. In incentive situations the parents stand firm and will not allow the child to have the good thing if the child fails to comply with normal and reasonable expectations. No pity is shown by the parents because the child *chose* to not cooperate; and thus the child has cheated themself out of obtaining the incentive of *their own* free will.

The difference between incentive and bribery is essentially the same as the difference between entitlement versus satisfaction of accomplishment.

These eating situations and other similar situations turn into a bribe quickly when the parent fails to stand firm. A child sees the yummy dessert and will complain about not getting it. At this point the parents have a choice to say, "If you eat, you can have dessert," thus turning it into a bribe. Where instead the parents can ignore the whining and enjoy the dessert themselves. No remarks need to be made; the child will eventually figure out the fact that the parent is unyielding in this regard, which in turn, helps the child to learn to comply with common human decency. If the parents turn it into a bribe, then the child remains in control of the parents, causing the parents to suffer at the demands of the child. Saving it for later and allowing them to eat it later if they *eventually* ate their main meal also puts them in control of the situation. They should eat with the family when supper is served. Allowing them to eat at *their* will puts them in control of you.

Trying to lie to a child that something is good or tastes like something else is either a lie or may look like a lie to them because their taste buds taste in their own unique way. They may have different taste distinctions than you. If it is not true then it is a lie and it is intended to deceive them, thus making *you* a liar. Within reason, allow them their own unique likes and dislikes. Lying to them will mess up their logic, especially when it is the parents who are doing the lying.

You are the parent—there is no need to bargain with a child to get them to eat or to do anything. If they indicate dissatisfaction with the food, then make sure that the condition of the food is satisfactory for *them*. *Your* version of warm, may be *their* version of scalding hot! People drink hot beverages or eat hot pizza that would scald the mouths of most people. How they do this no one knows, but if they are ignoring the burns then most of us want no part of it—this is no different for children.

Bargaining with children in any circumstance puts *them* in control of the situation at hand. If you are being controlled by your children, then you will have far bigger problems when they are older. Don't bargain with a child. If you do you will be bargaining with a bully while, and after, they grow up.

Not allowing a child dessert if they do not eat is not a *punishment*, it is a *consequence* of their own actions and choices. A deal or bargain should not be made using dessert or anything else. Using dessert as a bargaining tool hands all of your control over to your child and *puts the child in total **control** of you*. Place the food before your child, and then enjoy your own meal. If they pick at their food they might not be hungry.

If they are willing to eat the dessert but not the meal then one of a few situations has occurred: They do not like the food's taste, the food's condition is unsuitable (hot, cold, bad texture etc.), they have learned that they can manipulate you, or they have dessert in their eyes—and to a child, few meals have the delightful sweetness of a yummy dessert! However, for most parents that face this problem, it is the fact that the children learned that they can manipulate their parents.

Eat your meal first and then *after* the meal discuss the benefits of a bonus dessert. Dessert out of sight and out of mind is a good rule. Instead, prepare it after the meal and allow the children to help, but do not use their hope of this as a bribe.

The problem that many parents have is that they are not decisive, and when they finally choose to be decisive then those same parents are often unfairly or unreasonably decisive. Decisiveness comes from being well-grounded and knowing and understanding *why* you do what you do. When you have chosen the wrong belief system, then you will live life based upon a lie. This causes you to lack a stable index of how to guide and direct your children. When a parent has no sound foundation for their reasoning while raising their children, they will either experience confusion when the child resists or they will overreact by unfairly and unreasonably making demands of the children that cannot possibly ever be logically reconciled in the minds of the children. This is such a great area where parents can easily see the results of their actions where parenting techniques unfold in a matter of days, and often, in only a few seconds.

Eating together as a family is a very important part of being a family. If you break that honor by teaching them to have the TV on every night while eating, or you plunk them down alone, in front of the TV in the living room watching their favorite shows, then you *will* pay a price for not sitting down *as a family* while sharing a meal *together* as a family. If you do this, then when your children get older you can expect them to *not* want to be with *you* at mealtime, and you will likely become a bother to them. Sure, on special occasions it's okay to do it once in a while, but to make it a habit to not eat together and not share stories of the day or of the past, cheats your children out of a wonderful opportunity full of warm and loving family memories, and, instead, it fills them with messages that are typically not all that good. Even if the TV that they watch is generally good programming when you do this, they are still being cheated. Yes, that's right, I said "cheated." They are cheated out of your love and the richness of your life because it also tells them that they do not matter to you as much as the TV does.

Over Eating

Teaching your children to overeat is another problem area. As parents, all too often, we are trying to get our children to eat the same amount of food as we adults do.

When an adult is eating a proper diet, on a chemical and physical basis, if a child is one-fifth your size, provided neither of you are overweight, the child needs roughly just over one fifth the amount of food that you consume; and possibly less, because we adults typically consume way too much food, as is commonly indicated by our ever increasing waist size. Our bodies are chemical machines and they are consistent in the way they process energy. Count your calories for a while and you will learn very quickly how often children are forced *by their parents* to overeat.

Children are often chubby when they are young but then when they are older they thin out because their body is finally catching up with their caloric consumption. A child that is thirty pounds needs far less calories per day than a typical full grown adult. Eating more than that will pass through their body, be stored as fat, burn off as excess heat, or become a part of their body as they grow. It is good for very young children to have some extra fat on their bodies in order to protect them when they fall, but this should be a reasonable amount and can typically be determined by seeing a consensus of other children of the same age, including historical data on children's weights and ages.

Any notion that a small child should eat the same quantities as adults do is an obscene notion. A good indicator is when they are around two years old and older if, in general, they poop at least once daily then they are not being shorted. Feeding a child less (read properly) will have them needing the potty less often. If the child is overweight then you can slowly reduce their calories until they begin to slowly lose weight, they need not "diet." They just need to be taught to eat a little bit less when they eat, **and** to eat well; that is to say, to eat good foods. When a child eats properly and eats the right amount of food their weight will balance to a healthy level automatically over time.

We parents are often very inconsistent with regard to eating. Many mothers have a knack for pushing food on their children, and then when the children become overweight, the child is told that they need to lose weight. This is both unfair and cruel to do to a child. Often when this situation arises, the parents confront the child about their weight problem, and then proceed to insist that the child eat yet more food. The messages sent to our children by doing this are inconsistent, contradictory, and are all too common. This causes the child not to be able to understand why they cannot seem to ever lose the weight they put on in their youth.

We also teach children to overeat when we give them treats. Many of us miss this simple little secret: When you give a young child a cookie, or any other treat for that matter, they are just as happy with two cookies the size of a quarter as they are with two cookies of normal size. Starting at the earliest age that we give children those sorts of treats, we should be vigilant to give them a few small portions rather than an entire package of large portions.

How to Speak Correctly

Many children have gone through life with speech impediments. Children who do not speak well often go to school and are told that they need speech therapy. They are also often mocked for their poor speaking habits that their parents allowed. Typically, when a child needs speech therapy, his or her parents have failed to take the needed time to teach the children to properly annunciate their words and letters. Sometimes it may be that the child has hearing problems, and so their speech reflects that. Hearing-related speech issues are different than failing to teach your children to annunciate their letters properly. But even with hearing-impaired children many speak with near perfect clarity.

Is it fair to pin children's speech issues on the parents? You bet it is! When two people decide to have a child, it is those parents' responsibility to teach the child all of life's lessons. You are not being a good parent to your children if you neglect teaching your children how to live and speak properly, and then, later, make them see a speech therapist to correct *your own* negligence. The earlier the parents work with children to pronounce their sounds accurately, then the easier it is to correct problems. When a child learns to speak wrong, it is much like them learning a foreign language from birth as if they were from that foreign country. Every child can learn to speak any language. It is your responsibility to properly teach your children the language of your people. Do it when they are young, and then you won't have to struggle with it when they are older. It is difficult enough to communicate our thoughts to each other; children don't need speech impediments to add to the problem. Never allow your children to speak baby talk just because it is "cute". Immediately begin the correction process simply by repeating the word properly once *each time* they say it wrong, and enjoy their baby talk for the brief time they do it, but *do not* encourage it.

Being a parent includes every aspect of a child's learning. If your child is not doing well in math and reading basics, then it is *your* responsibility, not the school's, to make sure your child can read, write, add, subtract, multiply, divide, *and speak* properly.

There is no replacement for a good parent, and there is no replacement for a good parent's teaching. Always be a good parent to your children, and teach them all of the details that they need to know in life to function well and thrive!

Teach Your Children to Learn

Some people think that the more books you have on your bookshelf, then the more you know or the smarter you are. But the quantity of books that you have read or that sit upon your shelves has little if anything to do with your true intelligence. We can read as much as we want and remember as much trivia as we can, but in the end it gains a person very few useful life lessons.

If you want successful children then *teach them **how** to learn.* This might seem silly, but we are not taught *how* to learn. We are actually taught how *not* to learn. The general feeling is that there is a given set of information that should be included in the curriculum, and once these pieces of information are retained by the child, then the child is considered "educated."

Filling our children's heads with petty facts is pointless *unless* they understand how to properly apply those facts to their day-to-day lives. It is the understanding of how to weigh facts in the balance of truth that has created *all* major accomplishments, and that is what we want them to learn.

Focus Their Attention

Before and during the mid-nineteen hundreds there was a simplicity in life that quickly began vanishing around the nineteen-seventies. From that point forward, manufacturing methods became over-efficient, causing the prices on goods to drop substantially. This was especially true with children's toys, because books and electronic toys, during those times became so inexpensive that children often got more gift items for a single occasion, like a birthday, than they did in several years' worth of occasions prior to the mid-to-late nineteen-hundreds.

This has brought about something that the children of this planet have likely never before experienced—*over-stimulation.* There are so many colors, shapes, noises, and complexity that the children are almost confused at times.

Many of these toys and devices are very educational and enjoyable for the children, but don't be afraid to give some of these things away when you have collected too many of them. Consider putting most of these items in storage. Doing this allows you to frequently rotate your child's toys in and out of storage, which will cause the toys to always seem fresh to them and allows them to rediscover their old favorites. This will teach them to focus their attention, and that focus will help them later in life. Training a child to be over-stimulated by having too many toys for them to deal with causes them to behave in a similar manner when they are older. Be aware of this and deal with it accordingly. The amount of toys they are allowed is up to you and you are in control of the situation. There is no need for your children to have access *to all* of their toys *all* of the time.

What You Teach Them When You Drink

Drinking alcoholic beverages to excess in front of your children is not a particularly great example for them. When we teach our children that we can only let go and have a good time when we have been drinking alcohol, then we are adding this to their many other reasons to be afraid to excel. This does not mean that you can't ever drink.

Drinking is used improperly when it is a mask for us to hide behind or as a refuge to wallow in. If you teach your children that they need to drink alcohol in order to have fun or have a good time, then they will likely follow your example.

Using drinking as a mask inhibits our ability to feel free to be ourself without drinking. Many people suffer from this problem and when it becomes excessive or addictive, it becomes even more difficult to overcome. Vices, such as drinking alcohol, can easily be overcome when adhering to the principle discussed in the cornerstone book *Hot Water*.

Your Money Works in the Same Way

The mask of too much alcohol is similar to any mask that hides or releases us from our prison of arrogance or false humility. Money works the same. If you teach your children that they must have access to lots of money and that they must buy things in order to be happy, then you are dooming them to a disappointing life.

We should be able to feel joy whether or not we have much money at our disposal. The habit of wanting things and flashing around money leads to debt. Not having money is one thing, but not having money and then also being in debt is entirely different and it is a far more painful existence to live.

Debt can happen in ways that are not specifically provoked. But when we use money as a mask and are willing to be in debt for the sake of that mask, then we trap ourselves and our children. We must teach our children a healthy respect and understanding of money. We must teach them to be the masters of their money, rather than their money and their financial situation being the masters of them.

Our money is a representation of our time. When we work, we have traded our time for money-numbers that we can use anywhere. Inversely, going into debt is trading money-numbers for your time. Once we do this we have agreed to serve the money-numbers with our time until the debt is paid.

Debt is the culture of our world and society and has been as such for a very long time, probably always. The time that we breathe and are alive is a part of all that we have of true value in this life. If we did not have this time alive, then we would not be here because we would be dead or we would never have been born.

An unhealthy understanding of money reduces respect for those money-numbers and for your time left in life. Our true value is not in the money that we have dedicated all our time to collecting, it is in our remaining time left. If you die now, your money has no value to you because you are dead. Even if you believe in the life after death, you still cannot take the money with you.

Our money buys things, and we teach our children to be dependent upon *things* with it. Parents' teaching by example is very subtly done to a point that we do not realize we do it. For instance, electronics is one of the most abused areas of being dependent on things. We learn to use electronic items as a dependency, rather than as the tools that they are meant to be, and by example we teach this dependency to our children.

Deciding to not utilize these technological tools puts you at a disadvantage in a modern world. But technology becomes a problem when we offer too much of our personal information into the technology, and it becomes a problem when we insist that we cannot be without the technology. If a person cannot have a conversation with someone who is present with them while walking through the forest, without being interrupted by a technological device, then you know that the technology is being abused. If there is a critical situation that you are awaiting news about then it may be acceptable, but when you interrupt time with someone that you are physically with because you are answering random calls or texts from others, then you are abusing the tools and are being very rude to the person that you are with.

Whether it is money or technology, and whether or not you mean to set a particular example, your children will interpret your example only the way that each child knows how. If one child sees you spending money, they may interpret the spending of money as the key to success, while another child might not see the money as the key. Properly explaining to them the *low* importance of status items will help them to eliminate potential misdirected focus in their future. Money can be a danger to us and our children because we view it as the *reason* rather than the *result*, and we then go on to believe that we are somehow better because if it, but we are not better people because of money.

Teach Them to Stay Out of Debt

Teaching children to be in debt is *not* a good thing, and while you may not teach them directly, you likely teach them through your examples. If you struggle with debt yourself, then coming to the full realization of what truly is *necessary* to live, greatly enhances your life. For most people, debt has become a way of life, but many of the things in our lives that caused the debt are *not* needed. While sometimes painful, struggling financially for a time is often a good thing for people because it teaches what is truly *needed* and important. The slower you are to learn your true needs, then the longer you will suffer the pains of debt. In many cases, the second car is not needed, nor is the second job. What is needed is for all of us to learn what *true needs* are.

Debt is not a good thing and nothing will make it a good thing. Sadly, the world of finance has been built upon debt, and not much happens without it. This has gotten to the point where we are rated and valued based upon an arbitrary system of credit rating, which no one seems to know the methods of, except the designers who built the rating systems.

Sadly and unfairly, interest rates, discounts, and even jobs are dictated by credit scores. Teaching your children to stay out of debt is the only way to free them from being caught in this trap. If they involve themselves in the credit trap then it should only be to the extent of getting a good credit rating so that they are not unfairly discriminated against.

The commerce community created a multitude of methods to keep us deeply in debt as conveniently as possible. Many of us have fallen prey to this trap. Let us teach our children to keep out of debt's depleting grasp.

The Lessons We Teach With Our Things

Most of us enjoy buying new things and then cherishing those things. We use things everywhere in our daily lives. Few of these things are bad or wrong in themselves, but they often cloud the real message. Which is: it is not what we have that makes us great or special; it is *how we* use those things, or *what we* do with them, that separates us and makes us special.

All of the tools in the world will not make you a good carpenter. If you do not understand what needs to be done in carpentry, then no tool will be of any aid to you.

A person who is truly skilled or gifted at a task will need very few tools in order to display their genius at the task. For them, having more tools will only make them more efficient and more accurate, but they can usually succeed without any specialized tools.

Placing our children in an environment with many tools that are not appropriate for their nature, is like putting a bird where there is no air to support its wings. A sparrow can have all of the water and dirt in the world, but if you take away the air beneath its wings, then it will not be able to show its true gift of flight.

When we focus on *things*, our children see this and get the impression that they need *things* to thrive and survive. Things can help, but teaching them to be propped up in their life based upon those *things* is their one-way ticket to failure; and more importantly, it is a ticket to an unsatisfying life of unhappiness. You need not look far to see this occur in people's lives.

Our things are *things*, and if we cannot survive without them, then we have become dependent upon those things. Being dependent on *things* erodes our self-worth and makes us only as valuable as the things on which we have become dependent. These things become our status and our communication of that status to others. We flash our money and things around to others in order to display our perceived success.

Just because you get a new car does not mean that you are being showy or bragging. Of course you will want to share your excitement about some of your things with your friends. The problem with your things is your own personal self-worth's dependence on those things. If your self-worth is unaltered because of your things, then the things are indifferent in your life.

Watch for this dependency in yourself and make sure that you do not accidentally teach it to your children. Your things might be indifferent to you, but your children might possibly see you utilizing your things and get a wrong impression that you are dependent on those things, and they will likely emulate your behavior as *they* perceive it.

Teach Them to Seek Truth

Truth is your key for your family's foundation. Having a strong foundation of truth requires understanding of what is true. Truth is a learned behavior, and the sooner they start to learn it the better off they will be.

The best way to teach truth is by your example of honesty. If you are truly honest, then you have it mostly done, but make sure your children are honest too.

You can always detect honesty by observation when being challenged. If you reject having your own thoughts or opinions being challenged, then you are not honest!

A challenge to our thoughts should be embraced. When we have sufficiently demonstrated that our perspective is accurate then we need not concern ourselves with that point until someone presents another challenge that we have not yet considered. At that time we must consider the additional information and adjust our thinking to comply with what is true *if* our previous thinking is now shown to be incorrect.

Without the process of allowing challenge to your thoughts, you and your children are doomed to believing things that are not true. What is worse is that you will think that you are right when you are not—Always choose Truth!

Give Them the Gift of Choice

There has been much talk about *freedom* over the last several centuries. Freedom requires the right to make your own choices. When someone tells you a lie and you believe it, then they have robbed you of your freedom. We might think that we can easily choose to not believe lies, but a well-crafted lie is specifically designed to deceive us. Yet, in the end, it is still our own decision to believe it.

Because you believe something that is not true, you have barred yourself from the possibility of being correct. When you teach your children how to seek the truth, as previously discussed, then you have given them the most precious gift—*choice*!

Teaching Your Children How to Reason

Reason and truth are two terms that have been heavily abused over the last several centuries. The ability to reason is not necessarily truth, but it is part of the process.

Reason is the process of comparison, where *truth* is the accurate conclusion of those comparisons. If there is not enough information revealed, then a proper conclusion cannot be drawn and we will need to wait for more information in order to come to an accurate conclusion. Our society has the terrible habit of sensationalizing everything, making us feel that we are wrong when we disagree with the sentiment of the latest cultural trends and headlines even if they are wrong.

Regardless of how much pressure society places on us to force us into submission, when something is wrong, then it is wrong. The sooner we learn this, the better off we will be. We must teach our children to ignore societal pressure and evaluate a situation based upon what is true and best, rather than succumbing to the pressures that others and society places on them.

Tradition
The Blessings and Dangers

We discussed the dangers of tradition, such as Santa Claus and *The Santa Claus Effect* with regard to our views of Creation on both sides of the Creation-versus-evolution belief sets.

Teaching your cultural traditions can be a blessing and a good thing when the tradition is based in true things. For those who believe in the Creator and the Christ, Christmas is a very pleasing tradition. Family traditions can also be good because the traditions can bring our family culture through to subsequent generations and pass along our heritage.

Traditions become dangerous when they are not understood, which causes them to become filled with lies that are full of impossible demands and rituals. This serves to only further the problem of not understanding the tradition's original intent.

Traditions can be both good and bad. Determining whether it is good or bad depends on you and the way you teach and practice those traditions. It also depends upon the tradition itself. Some traditions would be best abandoned and forgotten. If a tradition does not commemorate important and good things then it might be best if it is forgotten altogether.

Living up to **Your** Expectations

Forcing your children to live up to *your* expectations has two key aspects. Often, we demand that our children do or believe something because *we* said so. The line between doing this right and doing this wrong is foggy for most of us. Often we don't realize that we are being unreasonable when we demand that our child meet *our* expectations.

Many of our expectations of our children are based on our own shortcomings that we do not want them to repeat. Forcing our children to do something only because we feel that we have failed, and because we do not want them to repeat our own failures, says nothing of what is best for *them*. Their skills and talents are likely somewhat different than ours and they should be allowed to build their life based upon their own natural gifts.

Our expectations of our children should be nothing more than that they demand truth in their own lives. This causes them to reach for goals that most people believe to be impossible. The only forcing that we need to do with them is to attempt to get them to drop fearful inhibition so that they can flourish and not fear doing great things with their natural gifts. The fear that children perceive is typically due to the fear of someone's negative and discouraging words to them.

Most of the needed *forcing* that we feel we must do with our children comes from our own lax efforts in parenting. When we start parenting with a strong foundation while our children are infants, then we will have far less problems when they are older.

Teaching our child to *not fear* by means of understanding truth is far different, for instance, from forcing them to eat a food *we* like but that *they* don't like. Understanding truth is universal and will help them in *every* area of their life.

Show Your Children that You Can Admit Your Mistakes

The key to finding truth is that you must be able to admit when you are wrong. Showing your children that you can do this will help them a great deal in life. Showing your children that you can admit your mistakes, when you have made mistakes, teaches them the primary lesson in living a life based upon what is true. Admission of error should never be confused with false humility or a declaration that you are wrong when you are not actually wrong. False humility is as bad as arrogance, and admitting that you are wrong when you are not is a lie.

Both arrogance and false humility depend upon lies. When someone gets into the habit of false humility, they then develop a dependence or false need to be built up by others. When we do so, we walk around telling how woeful a job we did so that others will feel compelled to compliment us. Arrogance on the other hand, which is false humility's counterpart, flaunts achievement for more than its actual value.

Arrogance and false humility feed each other. Often when one child is arrogant, another in the family will have false humility. Both of these behaviors are commonly exhibited within the same person in various aspects of their life.

Since the root cause of arrogance and false humility is due to embracing what is not true, these behaviors share that root and are often seen in close proximity to one another.

A good and simple thought to convey to your children is, if you don't want to regret your mistakes, then don't make mistakes that are regrettable. Having fear is the king of all mistakes and it is the cause of all arrogance and false humility!

It is important to not confuse *not making regrettable mistakes* with *not trying at all.* Many people fall into the fearful trap of not trying to do anything because they are afraid that they are going to fail. In other words, they feel it *might* be a mistake so they never even try. When we don't try something because we fear, then the only real mistake we make is allowing our fear to dictate our path.

When you allow yourself to wallow in these attitudes you trap you and your children in the lies you are embracing. The only way to teach them how to overcome this is by doing it yourself. Admit to your own mistakes and correct them as promptly as possible and then your children will witness and most likely copy your corrective nature.

Handling Rejection

Handling rejection is something that people do not do very well. Rejection is a refusal of someone and what they stand for. When we reject a person's thoughts, efforts, talents, or any other good aspect of them, then we are sending a message that they are not worthy of our attention or consideration. It is our right to do so, and we should always reject bad information and bad behavior. Often, rejection comes with an explanation, but when it does not, we are left to wonder why we were rejected. When we are rejected we should try to understand *why* we were rejected. Yet, understanding why we were rejected is not as important as our effort to be true. But this causes us to want to know why in order to figure what went wrong so that we can be certain that we have not accepted wrong information.

Getting rejected hurts no matter what. Whether right or wrong, it is still painful to us. Some rejection is not as painful as other rejection, and in these cases, it is usually because we have a full understanding as to why we have been rejected, and so it is logical to us; for instance, when we have asked someone on a date, but they declined because they already had plans.

Entire books have been written on the subject of rejection because it is a far-reaching topic. This section is only touching on the basic elements to draw awareness to our need to understand it. You grasping that there is a need to understand rejection while your children are still young, helps you to teach them to make—properly handling rejection—a natural behavior for them when they are older.

When arrogance or false humility is present in the heart and mind of a child, then rejection is severely bitter and painful to them. When life is built upon *things* or the false promises of those things, then any attack on those *things* or anything related to those things will be felt as a direct assault on the owner of the things. This includes *things* that are not tangible, such as our beliefs.

When arrogance and false humility are present, the response to rejection is often severe, vicious, and violent. If the response is not one of these, then the response will usually be even deeper false humility and withdrawal into themselves.

Our self-worth is placed on ourselves by ourselves. And even though many of us get our perception of ourself from others, it is still ourself who makes the final assessment. When our children embrace what is true, they will handle rejection better. If they are being unfairly treated and are rejected in an unfair manner, teaching them to properly handle rejection will help them to stay in accordance with what is true.

Handling rejection is best done by being able to discern what is true. Seeking what is true helps us to handle rejection, and being better able handling rejection brings you closer to seeking what is true. This circular system feeds itself and increases or decreases in the direction you choose to allow and feed.

Learn to Just Walk Away

Children need to know that they can walk away from bad people and bad situations. Rejection is a fickle subject and a fickle aspect of life. Teaching our children to "just walk away" can be a very bad thing. Walking away because we do not like what we are hearing will do us no good *if* what we are hearing is true. However, if what we are hearing is false and we have had our fill of falsehood, then a firm, kind, and reasonable exit is the best action after we have delivered the true information in a kind and courteous manner.

When we are being treated "unfairly", we are being abused to some extent. In these cases, removing ourselves from the situation by walking away is usually the best action. The definition of what is "fair" or "unfair" is going to be decided in the mind of the beholder. Those who have chosen the path of arrogance and false humility will perceive any truth that exposes their lying actions as an unfair assault against them. When we have delivered truth, and the other party proceeds to unjustly attack us, then walking away is usually our best course of action. Learning to walk away is a matter of practice. Once you start doing it, it becomes easier to walk away from futile situations filled with inaccuracy.

We should not need to, and our children should not be taught to, tolerate other people's lies. Doing so allows the person who is not truthful to continue in that behavior, and it serves to make them more definite in their errors during future encounters.

Not accepting their wrongness, and possibly offering a correction, is appropriate, but when their response is returned in an unjust manner, then walking away is typically a proper way to live and a proper way to teach our children if we want them to be self-assured and strong in what is true. There is no need to have arguments or fights, because merely delivering the truth, and then moving on, is all that is required of us. Learning to walk away is achieved by actually walking away **when** *it is appropriate*.

We Think the Wrong People are "Cool"

Arrogance is an attractive behavior to many people because pride and arrogance are often wrongly interchanged. It is our misunderstanding of these two concepts that causes the world a great deal of trouble.

Pride is a certainty and confidence that you are correct. Pride always checks itself to make sure it is heading down the right path.

Arrogance, on the other hand, will appear certain because arrogance appears as confidence, but it is not. Arrogance only *acts* as if it is certain. Often when we use the term "cool" in reference to a person's draw or appeal, we are usually being attracted to their arrogance. Although, some of these people are actually truly confident and they can actually do what they say they can do.

Respecting someone is different than our stereotypical definition of thinking that they are "cool." Cool is often associated with people who are being different for the sake of being different. When we parents place our admiration in this type of personality, then our children will likely follow our examples. The sports and entertainment industries are very good examples of this.

Attempting to keep our perception of "cool" balanced, does not mean that we should not show respect for skilled people. But consider that when we build these people up, we are teaching our children to be people-followers. In doing so, we blind our children from the humanity of those people, and then it is often treated as if those people can do no wrong. Later, when a false hero falls, as most of them eventually do, then a part of our world comes tumbling down with them. Sadly, children emulate the behavior of these "heroes."

It is important to note that in media presentations, no matter which media source the hero or idol is from, what children see is mostly *costumed* for attention. For instance: singers, actors, dancers, and all the rest are often wearing costumes on stage that they would generally never be caught wearing outside of those performances or other publicity appearances. This often dupes children into following suit and partaking in bad behavior and dressing foolishly.

When we allow our children to blindly follow these made up characters, we end up making fools of our children. Permanent body alterations or markings are a typical example of how these personalities can negatively influence the hearts and minds of children and adults in a long-term manner. Clothing is one thing to copy or emulate, but when we copy idols and heroes by permanently marking up our bodies, then we will have to live with those alterations **for the rest of our lives**, but *we* will not get paid to do so like famous people do. In fact, permanent body alteration can inhibit your ability to be hired for many jobs because it is unsightly and not respectable. You cannot easily change your mind later when you decide you no longer like the changes that you have made to your body from following this shortsighted fad. This will have a lasting impact on a person's future self-worth. These things are trends just like a pair of designer jeans or fancy sneakers are. The difference is that when you get tired of the jeans or sneakers you simply buy new ones and toss the old ones out. This is not something you can do with your flesh. It is safe to say that when five or ten years pass that many people will regret their choices in this regard. What is worse is that sometimes actors have it only appear as if they have permanent marks for movie roles, but then get to go home and wash it off. But some people who see the movie will regrettably copy the movie by getting a real one that can *never* be washed off.

False humility can also play a dangerous part in the "cool" problem. For instance, when we believe that teachers or professors are superior to us, then we set our children up to be their followers. This causes our children to follow someone who has values completely opposed to our own. As it is with grade school and high school, the same is true for glorifying the value of college.

Respecting people is fine, but it is the misdirection of our focus that is dangerous. Our focus, our children's focus, and the focus of the family should always be—to be *true*. Believing that someone is greater than you is false humility. They may have more understanding about something in particular, but they are still only equal to you. When we believe someone is greater than us, then we have devalued ourself. Doing so is a self-fulfilling prophesy.

Are You Glorifying Your Past?

Use care when relating stories of your past to your children, or they may accidentally get the wrong idea. The antics of your youth may seem to be fond memories to you, but do you really want your children to follow *those* foolish examples? Be especially cautious with your *younger* children with regard to your past.

As our children age, we tend to give our younger children more information than they are ready for. When we relate things to our older children who are ready, or old enough, to hear the information, then the younger ones typically hear it also but they may not be at a ready age for the particular information that you have just shared with the oldest child. Also, your children will often talk together in a group, and the older ones may discuss your past in front of the younger ones when you are not there to filter the thoughts for them and put those thoughts in proper context and explain to them that you made foolish mistakes. There is a time and place for everything. Make sure you choose the right ones.

Your Teaching Never Ends

All through your life, as long as you and your children are alive, you will be teaching them. Even after your time here is done, your actions and memories will still be teaching them. Our impressions on one another are eternal. These impressions can be good or bad examples, and we can learn good or bad things from both good and bad examples.

While we are alive is our best opportunity to teach our children. The age of our children is indifferent to our ability to teach them. Children will always react to their parent's examples and teaching based upon how you have taught them in the past and how you treat them now. It is your choice if you are going to be their guide of good, or their index of what *not* to become.

Our ability to guide our children is going to be directly proportional to their respect towards us. If your child is older and has children, and maybe even has grandchildren of their own, and you see them making a terrible error, then they will more readily listen to your wise counsel **if** you have gained their respect over the years. If you have not gained their respect, then they will likely not listen to your advice even if it is correct. Respect is best gained by being true and kind to your children all the way back from when they are born onward to the current moment. If you have failed to do so earlier in their lives, gaining the respect of your children is done in the same ways as if they were young. The respect is gained by being able to admit and confess your own shortcomings to them, and then to apologize for your offenses against them. You also must embrace what is true and *always* consider and process, their thoughts.

What You Teach Them They Will Be

All of the examples we set for our children, including what we allow in our home through entertainment etc., affects our children. Even if we do not agree with something in the entertainment for instance, we are still allowing it in our home; and in allowing it, we validate the message. It is vital that you are able to discuss things with them, so that they understand your feelings and the truth about what they have seen or heard.

All that we think, all that we say, and all that we do is shown in some form to our children. They will learn from us twenty-four hours a day, every day they are with us. What our children see during their waking hours is embedded in their hearts and minds during their sleeping hours. This is besides our talking and conversations that also go in their ears while they are awake or asleep.

All that surrounds them, they will typically become. We teach our children in every thought and action that we do. There is nothing that you have done, and there is nothing that you now do, and there is nothing that you will do, that has not taught or will not teach your children in some large or small way. **Everything** is an example to them either for good or for bad. Whether it will be good or bad is largely up to you.

Chapter 19

Correction, Discipline, and Punishment

Correction, discipline, and punishment are all a bit different. Understanding the differences between them clears our minds of confusion and allows us to select the appropriate course of action when guiding our children.

"*Correction*" is to call out the bad, incorrect, or false, and then direct the children to the good and true.

"*Discipline*" is often thought of as punishment for doing wrong, but it really means to teach or learn. *Discipline*, as in *disciple*, is a student/teacher type of relationship system of guidance. Discipline can also be thought of in terms of "a discipline"; in other words, following a particular teaching.

"*Punishment*" is penalty or pain. We can inflict punishment on someone even if they are innocent, where with discipline it may involve minor punishment in order to correct or teach.

Punishment is done for one of two reasons: It is either to communicate to a stubborn person, or to intentionally and unjustly harm a person to try to make them bend to our own will. If our children respond to correction then they have been disciplined— they have been taught! When they refuse to respond properly to discipline, then we often use some form of punishment as a means of communicating the importance and serious nature of their error. This is usually done with the intensity of the punishment fitting their level of stubbornness.

Punishment is a form of trying to get them to see what is true when they refuse to look. If our children make an error and we punish them and then never explain to them (teach, correct, or discipline) *why* we punished them, then we are both cruel and foolish. If this is the way we treat them, then it is as if we are randomly hitting them without cause, which is unacceptable. Not understanding *why* they are being punished confuses children. This is especially so with very young children who simply do not yet understand.

In general, when we do the right things in their early years, punishment will *not* be needed much, if at all, in their older years, but few of us do. There is nothing more critical in getting it right, than to *get it right*. In other words, understand how to teach them to—understand and balance their facts on the scale of truth. This is a primary language that will build their rock foundation for the rest of their lives.

Children misbehave and have tantrums for several basic reasons. We will focus on three. One reason is that the parent is neglecting and totally disregarding the needs and desires of the child, so out of sheer desperation the child does the only thing that seems to get the parents' attention: they scream and cry—they have a tantrum. In this case, the parents deserve the trouble because the parent is failing to give the child fair and appropriate attention. Such neglect is unfair to a child because when the child acts up in this way, the parent usually becomes angry at the child for doing so. You will quickly spot these situations when looking for them, whether in yourself or in others who are dealing with this problem.

Do not neglect your child and then become angry with them when they act out in order to get their required attention that they deserve—doing so is unfair to them. Instead, give them the needed love, care, and attention beforehand.

The second main reason children have tantrums is because the parents have not learned when or how to say "no" and stick with it.

In truth, both reasons for our children's tantrums have to do with knowing when "No" is appropriate. Some of us unfairly say "No" for no particular reason, or we ignore the children altogether, while others fail to even say "No" at all. The secret to parenting is finding the proper balance that will teach your children to respect others and still feel like they are allowed to be included in, and be a part of, something. And the third common reason children have temper tantrums is that they are overtired or overstimulated. Make sure your children get plenty of rest.

Do Not Fear Your Children!

It seems odd that a parent would fear a child, but we do. We're not speaking here of older tyrannical children, no, we're talking about those little pint sized ones who are less than a fifth our size. In general, when people get upset, it brings a peculiar command to their disposal and a fear to others who are around them, even when it is our own young children demanding their own way.

The fear we experience can be for a several reasons. One reason is that we are afraid they will scream and make a scene and embarrass us, *or* we are confused and don't know what to do about their behavior. All too often the reason is that we are just plain afraid of them. You accepting any one of these methods of fear will cost you dearly.

When a parent is afraid of their child, then the child is in control of the situation **and** *in control of the parent.* That means— ***they*** control ***you!*** This is not at all helpful to bringing up good, balanced children who will have a strong foundation. When you fear your children, it erodes anything that you have already established in your family's foundation. This leads to all, and more, of the negative issues addressed so far in this book.

When a child has crossed the line of proper conduct, they need to know, in no uncertain terms, that what they did was unacceptable. Usually, stern decisive reprimand for violating what they have already been warned against will suffice. Saying politely to your child and asking them not to do something that they have already violated once before, and have been warned about, will only cause them to test us further in the same and other similar situations. At some point, a parent must take a firm non-negotiable stand.

Approaching repeated violations with a half-hearted effort ends in unneeded argument that becomes a futile bargaining session for the parents. <u>Parents: *no* means *no*!</u> Children test the limits in order to learn what the limits are. They *want **and need*** to know what those limits are. If we don't tell them, then who will?

It is a parent's job *and duty* to lay down the limits for reasonable behavior for their children. When this is not done then the children will grow into adults who do not know or understand the concept of being *reasonable*. Those new adults will also have children who will do the same. This problem typically worsens in the subsequent generations if no one stops it and says, "Not in my family!"

Crying Babies - Knowing When

Our fear of our own children begins at their birth and is born out of our own uncertainty. Bringing a beautiful brand new baby home is a great bit of responsibility for new parents. When the realization hits that *we* are responsible for this new life, it can be frightening, leaving us in a state of uncertainty.

Because this responsibility is new to us, and we want only the best for our new baby, we run to them at any peep while they are newborns. In addition to this, we *want* to pick them up and hold them and know them, which is very good!

While babies are in our care in their early days, they receive a great deal of comfort and love, but within days they are able to turn this in their favor and in their control without them or us realizing that it ever happened. There is much that we do while alive that we are not aware of. These unknown acts are deeply important, and, at times, deeply troublesome for us and our families.

Infants are not intentionally trying to manipulate their parents, but they do manipulate us when we parents allow it. Picking up a child *whenever* the child begins to cry traps a parent in an unhappy life situation if the parent does not promptly take decisive action to begin to move the situation in the right direction over time.

When we pick up our infants and young babies at every peep they make, then we are teaching them to cry for every bit of attention that they desire. The cries seem to be all the same, and we tend to have no distinction as to why they are crying.

When a child has learned to cry whenever they want attention, those cries are often equally as intense as the cries that they use when they are hungry, wet, tired, or sick. The similarity in intensity of the crying makes our job tougher, and we then must try to differentiate their needs on our own.

Some children cry in a slightly different manner for different needs and some parents detect this and can use it to their own advantage in discerning their babies' needs. However, for the rest of us, we need to run down our own checklist, such as:

- Have they been fed?
- Are they wet?
- Did they nap?
- Did they get their love?
- Are they teething ?
- Are they having tummy problems?
- Do they have a fever?
- Is some noise in the night rousing them?
- Plus other critical items that is on your own family's childcare checklist.

Once the checklist has been covered and the child is still crying, then we might check with the doctor and the doctor tells us that there is nothing more we can do. This is the point where we need to realize that we may have picked them up a little too often in their first few weeks when they cried. The sooner we tough it out, then the sooner we can contain the problem and reclaim our nighttime rest. This problem generally does not get better on its own. It takes decisive, loving action from the parents to remedy this, and the sooner the parents do it, the better. There are various ways to do so, and that choice is yours; but, doing nothing is certain to create very undesirable results for you.

It's good to comfort our children, especially when they are infants, but for their own good, we must set reasonable limits on complying with their *crying* desires. It is not wrong for them to ask. Our problem comes in when *we* **always** say yes. Infants are not making plans to manipulate their parents, but we teach them to do so when we run to them *every* time they cry. You can see how this becomes a problem, as infants have a natural born ability to cry as a means of communication to their parents. After several months, a child should generally be sleeping through most of the night.

Sometimes you have to wean a crying child from their poor sleep habits. Doing something like laying them down instead of holding them when they cry, but maybe rub their back or some other comforting action and then do it less and less with each passing day. It's not that there is some specific technique, but rather it is that you make efforts and move towards your end goal. The point is that we must do *something* to make progress. But what that "*something*" is can only be the parents' decision.

Crying serves many purposes, but with regard to you, the most important purpose is communication. The rest of communication is learned. Infants do the only thing they can do to become satisfied— they cry.

Their intent in crying is this: "Satisfy my desire," or maybe just "satisfy" whatever the particular desire is: food, love, comfort, etc. In many cases it's the "whatever" part that gets us into trouble as parents. When the *whatever* is them becoming demanding, and when we choose to serve their demand, then we have done them a great disservice.

If we fail to taper off our attentiveness to their *every* cry, a problem will develop in the long run and eventually we get very little sleep. It's not bad to pick our infants up when they are crying, but it is up to the parents to each determine their own child's survival and love needs. Most parents have the required instinct to know that there is something wrong that requires a doctor, versus the child's crying because they want to be picked up in the middle of the night.

Once your own family's infant checklist has been gone over and the child is still insistent on crying, then it might be time for Mommy and Daddy to take assertive action by coming to an agreement of standards about tending to their crying child. Taking assertive action can be done at any age, but doing so earlier makes things easier for your entire family in the long run. If you are unsure about this, ask your pediatrician.

The longer we parents put off dealing with any problem, then the more we reinforce the child's problematic behavior. The more we reinforce their behavior, then the more they behave in that way. The more they behave in that way, then the more we tend to patch the problem and put it off rather than dealing with the problem. In doing so, we reinforce their behavior, and the more we reinforce the more they will do it, and on it goes round and round. You can see where this will go. It is a dangerous cycle that feeds itself.

In general, infants, babies, and children *do* deserve to be picked up, even when nothing is wrong and they're *not* crying at all. It is important to pick them up for no particular reason because they desire to be loved for the sake of being loved, as we all do. It's also okay to pick them up on occasion when they're crying and they simply want to be held. It's good to give them love—we all need love. But again, the problem comes with the frequency of, and the reason for, picking them up. It is obvious that we need to take care of them when they're wet and hungry etc., but things are not so obvious when they only want to be held. It's a good idea to pick them up when they're *not* crying, in order to help them learn that crying is not the only way for them to get attention and love.

Finding a proper balance, and catching these trends sooner rather than later, makes parenting a pleasure rather than a nightmare. Finding a proper balance is a big part of what parenting is all about. Accepting this truth makes dealing with this issue simple. Accepting and dealing with this problem might hurt at first, and may tug at your heartstrings, but, shortly after, it brings peace and joy to your home no matter what your child's age is. In the end these thoughts are here only for you to consider; it is only the child's parents who truly know and can decide what they need to do to accommodate the child's needs.

To clarify, it's not so much how often you pick them up, but rather, it is *why* you pick them up. If, on occasion, you do it for the wrong reasons, it will not become a problem. However, if you *always* pick them up for the wrong reasons, such as succumbing to needless demanding crying in the middle of the night when they are getting older, then it can become a very long-term problem for you.

Each family must determine these limits on their own. If you see that it is developing into a problem, then start making proper adjustments right away in caring for your child. Inaction on your part will become a problem. The interesting thing about this is that, to remedy the situation, you actually have to do nothing. In other words, when this is the problem you might simply allow them to cry themselves to sleep when you know they are okay.

Be deliberate when you are parenting. This means that you take note of your day-to day circumstances and the take specific actions towards solving any problems. Doing so will greatly guide and affect the outcome of your children. Good children are *not* an accident. They are deliberately created by parents who realize that they need to, and take the time to, do what it takes to teach and build a great family and great children.

With regard to the baby crying issue, you adjust to suit *your* family schedule, but not necessarily the common accepted sleep patterns of society. What is important is that you consciously, and in full awareness, work to move the child in a direction that suits your needs, rather than doing nothing. It is important that parents realize that all child-rearing efforts are done to meet the needs of the child *and* the family, with the important thing being consistent action with constant influence towards your goals and needs to solve the problem. The problem that many families have is that we fail to do anything at all and we fail take any action, or we simply do not see that it's something that we're doing or not doing that is causing our child's improper behavioral problems. These opinions are only meant as springboards to make you aware for you to better understanding your course of action, an action which must be designed by you, the parents, and implemented as *you* see fit.

Why Do Children Go Through the "Terrible Twos"

When we fail to properly address the primary language of crying for attention when they are infants, then we are ushering in a time of trouble for each major age level that follows. The crying topic we just discussed becomes a true nightmare for parents when children are around the age of two if it was not handled properly earlier.

Two is the age in their life where children begin to really grasp the concept of independence. They begin to have thoughts of their own that are completely independent of ours, and they begin to realize themselves as *apart* from us. This is all good, and they will test us during this time in their life just as they did when they were infants. If we have failed to properly deal with them as babies, then when they are two, they might become seemingly unmanageable when we continue our same bad parenting behavior in how we tend to them.

Just their newfound two-year-old independence in itself can be challenging for us parents. By this time, they are walking and often potty-trained and can climb things faster than we would like, allowing them to get into lots of mischief very quickly!

Each of our lives is a lifelong experiment, and our children will be pushing the limits of experimentation, thus testing our patience and composure. When we have done our job in their early days, then they will give less resistance to proper discipline during their two's and beyond.

If we have allowed them their way every time they made a fuss in their early days, then we can *expect* that same sort of behavior to continue during their two's, and we can add to that the chaos that even a *happy* two-year old can create. Even if a child has been handled adequately in their early days, they can still offer a great deal of resistance during and around their two's, which is an age where parents often lose their parental control of their children.

Using the same technique that you should for a crying infant, you can also bring the situation back under control with a two-year-old. **You** are the parent; be fair, firm, and steadfast in your decisions.

Your Mommy Powers!

Mommy powers are something that most Mommies do not realize that they possess. Daddies also possess Daddy Powers and also seldom realize it. What are Mommy and Daddy Powers? These powers are your ability to have your children quickly obey your reasonable requests. When a child offers resistance and you comply with their resistance, then you have compromised your Mommy and Daddy powers. This works similarly as when a three- or four-month-old cries. If you pick them up every time they cry, then you are teaching them that crying will get them anything they want. Similarly, if you ask them to do something when they are older and they decline and you comply with their dismissal of your request, then you have taught them that they do not need to listen to you.

Do not compromise your Mommy powers. When a reasonable request is made by you, it should be followed by your children, such as when a child does something wrong and you tell them not to do it anymore. If you allow them to continue doing something after saying "no", then to them, you have taught them that it is okay to defy you. You taught them that your "no" *does not* mean *no* and you have lost some of your Mommy powers.

Later, when you have had enough and say "no" again and they take it to the next level, then, if at the new even higher level of their resistance, you again comply with their dismissal of your instruction, once again you have taught them that they need not comply. You have taught them that they only need push a bit harder and then you will give in and they will once again get their way. **Do not** lose your Mommy powers **or** Daddy powers! Besides direct cruelty to our children, this is perhaps the single biggest error parents make.

Is it Bad to Always Say Yes?

Sometimes parents want to have their children experience many things in life and in doing so they will say "yes" to most everything the child asks for. This can present a problem for the child in life and it is a difficult thing for those parents to balance. If a child asks, and a parent always says yes, then the child will have far more difficulty understanding at times when the parent must say "no." Typically this eventually catches up with those parents. You will see this in situations where the parent says "no" for little, seemingly insignificant things, and the child resists and sometimes has a tantrum.

This is a problem because if there is no particular reason to say "no" to the child, then why not say "yes"? Right? Because when a child never hears "no", the child expects to *always* be allowed to do or get whatever they asked for. Then when the parent says "no" for some small thing then the child has a fit. This is a hidden danger because the parent might never give in to the child, but because the child nearly always gets what they want they make a fuss for the little things. This catches those parents by surprise because they believe that they do not give in to their child. The reason they feel they never give in to their child is because they don't. Instead, they unwittingly say "yes" to *everything* that their child wants and thus, never have an opportunity to experience the child's resistance and so the child never learns to grasp *restraint.* Then when something seemingly insignificant comes up and the parent must say "no," the child proceeds to have some level of a tantrum. Surprise!

There is a cost for *always* saying "yes." When you allow a child most everything they ask and then you say "no" for something insignificant, it comes across as unreasonable to the child, because if you *always* let them have the candy bar at the store and let them ride the little car or merry-go-round in the entry of the store, but then say "no" to them having a healthy snack just before bed because it is too late at night, then that simply does not compute in their little minds.

Be careful with this and do not go to extremes. Just realize that it can be problematic and say "no" on occasion if for nothing more than to teach them restraint and moderation. You will be pleased that you attended to this problem

Dealing With Terrible Twos' Tantrums

When we fail to take care to stand firm and we allow our children to have their way too often, then they *will* have tantrums on a regular basis anytime they are not getting what they want, and sometimes, they have a tantrum even when they do get what they want. This is where things can really go bad for families. When parents are being otherwise reasonable about allowing a child enjoyment and fulfilling their children's needs, then a child who *gets his or her way* by having a temper tantrum *is in control of* the parents and the parents have forfeited all of their Mommy and

Daddy powers. When this has happened, even if the parent shouts at the child and spanks them, the child can still dominate, torment, and manipulate the parents. It is the interaction between them and the disciplinary methods used that makes the difference between whether or not a parent is **being controlled** or is **in control**.

For instance, if a child wants candy at the supermarket checkout and we say "no," and then they proceed to have a tantrum, then we might shout at them or even give them a slap on the butt as a form of discipline. But if the child continues with the tantrum, and at any point we give in to their tantrum, then the discipline just done was for nothing and the child remains in control of you. And, again, we lost our Mommy and Daddy powers!

No means *no* and it must remain so! Saying no, and then later giving in to the child's tantrum, is showing them that *no* means: cry and scream some more to get what you want and then *no* means *yes*! This is the same exact function that happens when a child is an infant and is picked up because the parent succumbs to the child's demanding unreasonable cry. This can start at any age. When a parent finally has had enough of the crying from their toddler and decides to let the child cry themself to sleep, then the child will cry louder, and when the parent gives in and picks them up again it is like the supermarket crying example given in the previous paragraph.

PARENTS:

Your "No" should always be reasonable.

No means **no**, and **it must remain so!**

Anything less has compromised *your* authority as a proper parent and you have lost your Mommy and Daddy powers!

It is very easy to end the "terrible two's" or temper tantrums. Know what you mean, and mean what you know. Say what you mean, and mean what you say. Say what you will do, and do what you will say. **No** means **no**, and **it must remain so!**

Follow through with reasonable loving action. Failure to do so brings heartache for you and everyone involved, and even to those watching.

Children need and desire constancy! Constancy is that truth which we have been discussing so far throughout this book. When we say "no," and then give in to our children's tantrums, then we have lied to them.

Child: "I want candy!"

Parent: "No!"

Child: "Whaaaaaa!"

Parent: "Okay, Okay!"

No **was not** no! In the dialogue example just given "No!" was really "Yes, alright already!" and so the parent initially lied, and at the same time, threw away their wonderful Mommy or Daddy powers.

Parents must give clear messages to their children and stick to those messages. If you change your mind because they had a tantrum, then you are *not* giving clear messages. Daddy and Mommy, you are their rock and their foundation!

> There is *nothing* more important than your being *constant*, *loving*, and *fair* as a parent.

Your constancy and consistency should be for what is true, and proper. Following this simple guideline can eliminate most of the troubles encountered during the twos, and most of these troubles can be eliminated inside of a week's time when the parents understand the importance of the *constancy*. Then your Mommy and Daddy power can be regained and restored! The same holds true for children of any age. Also note that the constancy regarding the children must match between the parents. If it is different then you will experience the aforementioned problems

Be constant, but be reasonable. Here is an example: It may be a good idea that after several trips to the market and after the child has learned to behave and *not* ask for the candy or have a tantrum, that on occasion, you ask them *before* they ask you. Once they have proven themselves to be able to behave, then **before** you get to the checkout, you could ask them if they would like to pick out *one* item (list your limits, gum, candy bar, small toy, or trinket, etc...)

Allowing them a treat on occasion, at **your** *discretion*, will be incentive to them and will give them something to look forward to. **Do not** offer it as a conditional term where you say "**I will** get you something *if you* behave." But rather, simply ask them if they would like to pick out an item. They may be disappointed if you don't offer this on another occasion, but then those times when you do make the offer, they will be that much more grateful and appreciative for it. It is their ability to *appreciate*, that we want to teach them. Appreciation shows them value in life, and with it, you will take back your Mommy or Daddy powers!

In discussing "no means no", we are focusing on the idea that when you have parental reasons for saying no then you must stick with it. "Parental reasons" are for things like disciplinary reasons, safety reasons, health reasons, behavioral reasons etc.

Just what is a Spoiled Child or Spoiled Behavior?

This topic is somewhat in the eye of the beholder, but the consensus is that when a child screams and cries to get their way, and then gets it, then they are spoiled. But wait... there's more! A child need not scream and cry to be spoiled. "What?" you say, "How can this be?"

All of what we discussed, the tantrums, the crying, and the screaming are all the same. These are all a form of coercion or manipulation, and are an effort to get you to stop resisting them, or are an effort to embarrass you into giving them what they want. It is typically not specifically knowingly done, because it is more of a habitual response that you taught them.

Some children do things like hold their breath, or when they are older, threaten to do harmful things to themselves or others. These foolish games can even become deadly when they are allowed to get out of hand, as is sadly sometimes seen in the teen years.

Manipulative behavior escalates. When we choose to resist them, they *will* escalate their efforts. When we give in, they have defeated us, and again, we have lost our powers. In this, they have learned that they only need to increase the stakes because then *we* will forfeit our resistance to their behavior. Once manipulation by escalation has been learned by them, then the problem has become very serious indeed! It is only their own personal limits and respect for themselves and others that will limit what they will potentially do to get their way. **_Do not_** let them get to this point! Take back your Mommy and Daddy powers immediately! And always use fair, just, and loving decisive action.

Spoiled behavior can also turn into a form of punishment. Merely having a fit in the store is not so bad, until they have learned that they can "**get you**" by doing so. In other words, if you have said "no" and meant no, but they have come to an understanding that *they* will "teach *you* a lesson," then they are going to embarrass you to punish you for saying "no" to them and refusing them their demands.

This form of punishing you is very closely associated with manipulation, but this form of unreasonable punishment will happen to us even when we are consistent in saying "no" but are not consistent in the rest of our lives. This part is usually learned from us by our example to them, where manipulation is being taught to them by giving into their demands. When punishment to the parents and manipulation are learned and utilized by the same child, then a parent's life will be very unpleasant.

Beneath the tough surface, children want to be guided, and they want loving, reasonable, and fair guidance to follow. When children have gone over the edge, they often get into serious legal trouble and may need counseling. As parents, we devalue our authority and our worth when we allow our children to get to this point. Additionally, in doing so, we have lost our parental powers and as a result we have devalued our children.

Brought on by ourselves, once our children have lost respect for us, then we have no power to guide them. When our children are sent to some correction hall or counseling, the counselors can typically deal with them more easily because the counselors have not forfeited their authoritative powers or *respect* to the problem child.

No means *no*, and *it must remain so*! This should start when they are only months or even weeks old. No does not always need to be spoken, as it is also shown by your action of not doing. Such as, not acknowledging a tantrum and/or uncalled for crying. Sometimes firm action needs to be taken when they have a tantrum. That action is always each parents' choice.

If you ever lose the respect of your children, or if you have lost their respect already, you need to understand that it is because you have not been consistent and/or fair with or to them.

The only way to regain your children's respect is to be fair and consistent by not wavering on your "No." This will regain your parental powers, but in doing so, you must understand that your *no* must be *fair* and *true*. And of course, you must always be in full consideration of their health, safety, and well-being.

Tantrums
Stop It in Its Tracks, and the Sooner the Better!

The notion that a parent should not pick up a *needlessly crying* child is a difficult one to tackle with words in a book. This is because there are many reasons that a child will cry, and if the parent is not noticing a true problem, then the parent might mistake the child's crying as *needless* crying when it is actually an urgent cry. That is why no book can tell you what you must do, but rather you must figure this all out on your own with regard to your own child. What a book can do is to let you know that this sort of thing occurs with some children in some families and with that knowledge you can then consider the information and better evaluate your own situation.

Babies crying for necessity can quickly turn into frequent crying *only for the purpose of being picked up* as long as the parents submit to that crying and pick the child up to comfort them *whenever* the child cries.

This creates a dependency, and it is up to the parents to determine what is "picking them up too much". Continuing to pick babies up every time they demand so with their crying, if gone unchecked, will have the child in temper tantrums well *before* they are two years old. Tantrums are a form of coercion and manipulation. This is not something we want to teach our children. And if they get to that point, it is your own fault. It is a primary language. Remember, it is more important as to *why* you pick them up, than it is how often you pick them up.

Dealing with spoiled behavior is best done sooner rather than later. The younger we teach our children *properly*, then the more pleasant everyone's life will be and the better they will function, and as a result, the more successful they will be in life. It is damaging to our children to not deal with their spoiled behavior. The unpleasant result of our failure is our own fault!

If we really love our children, then we must do the important things that seem so hard for us to do. Once we have learned this easy parenting skill, it becomes effortless and we will no longer find it difficult. Additionally, our children will be better behaved, making our lives even more effortless and joyful. All of your actions should be firm, fair, loving, kind, good, and safe.

Parents can address this behavior at any time in their child's life, but the longer we wait the more risk there is that serious troubles will arise. Stop this sort of behavior while you have your children's respect. In doing so, you will *keep* your children's respect. There is not an age limit on correcting or disciplining your children. As long as they respect you, they will consider your words, even if they are fully grown adults.

Parents who apply such disciplinary measures must be certain that they do not abuse these measures and wind up neglecting their child. Children should never be harmed when spanking is used—watch your own strength and *do not* use objects to spank if you do it.

Dealing With Their Tantrums and Their Will

Children cannot be allowed to have their way when they are demanding it. When a child is allowed to build their *will* in this manner, they become unbearable, demanding humans; it is this type of will that must be broken. But parents must be able to discern between a child's demands and child's needs.

When children are wanting to do something wrong or improper and we allow them to do so, then **we** are supporting their *will* for what is **not** good and what is **not** true, and we are supporting what they are doing.

Often we confuse saying "No" to their false will, with our ruling with an iron fist. We begin to say "No, you can't do this" and "No, you can't do that." Saying "No" for no particular reason does a disservice to the child. If you break their *will* entirely, then they have no purpose in life. A child must have a *proper* will. The problem we face is to understand what a "proper" will is, and this is where we fail. We don't understand the difference between a *proper* will and a *false* will. Knowing that there is a *proper* will and a *false* will is the beginning of understanding this problem.

The will of a person is very important! If we lose our will, then we typically live a lackluster life and will contribute very little, if any, to the world and to those around us, and typically we will heavily burden others. When we lose our will, we become nothing more than a machine that consumes, and we offer nothing back to the world or to those around us. Our *will* is important!

Distinguishing a *proper* will from a *false* will is done in the same manner as understanding what is true. If a will wants anything other than what is good and true, then it is a false will built on what is not good or true.

A false will is propped-up arrogance, and it is supported by those who allow it. When we parents allow this sort of will by giving in, when we actually know better, then their arrogance is created *because of us*. If in their youth a child thinks that they are above their parents, then they have a false will. If this is the case, then they often step outside of their parents' guidelines. *False* will is broken by being constant, certain, and true, and then you can properly regain your parental powers.

There are cases where the parents are so misdirected that the children can actually become wiser than the parent while the child is yet under the parents' care. Make sure that you are a wise parent *by actually being wise.*

Creating Bullies

This entire chapter has been dealing with the underlying subject of manipulation and coercion. Manipulation and coercion, in their worst form, become bullyish or terroristic. What's worse is that this can be in your own home with your young or older children, or even your spouse.

The cornerstone book *Red Hot Marriage* discusses, in deep detail, offensive bullying behavior and how to stop it in your marriage. The difference between a *terrorist* and a *bully* is the weapon that they use with which they cause physical and or mental harm to others. The difference may also depend upon your own definition, and possibly your political agenda as well.

No matter what we define a terrorist as, the underlying concept and motive is the same. Bullies and terrorists want it their way for *their* own good, regardless of any harm they do to others. They will hurt anyone who gets in their way or who they do not like. Bullies and terrorists will falsely accuse a person who is correcting or disciplining them regarding being a bully or terrorist and that accompanying behavior.

We parents create bullies and terrorists when we allow them to have their way with their false will when they are younger. The behavior starts young and is supported by *us* through the years. When a child, who has been allowed to always have their way, is fully grown, they will then bully and terrorize others. When those others, for fear of their safety, submit to the demands of the terrorist-bully, then that behavior is reinforced even more. This gives the bully the false illusion that they are right or correct in their actions. It is only when everyone stands up together against this sort of behavior and says "No", that the bully can no longer function. It is in this way that people regain their powers over evil. This problem becomes worse when you are not living in truth because the child will be even more irrational. On the other hand, if you still fail in regard to your child becoming a bully but you otherwise were living in truth, then the child will likely not be nearly as offensive.

When we submit to someone's demands, then we have handed them our power and our freedom. When we place our freedom in the bully's hands, then *they* have *our* power. This makes them stronger and able to bully or terrorize even more innocent people.

The above paragraph holds true whether it is a two-year-old having a tantrum, a school yard bully, an abusive spouse, a state leader passing an unjust law, or an international terrorist threatening us. The underlying behavioral function is all the same.

Do not submit to a false will—***ever!*** Doing so only makes the false will grow and feeds the bully beast.

Choose Your Battles with Your Children

Choose your battles with your child and never choose a battle that you are unwilling to win. Does this mean to let them do what they want? No, this is not a pass on the tougher situations. The point is this: If you are not going to stick to your position and be firm, then do not start the fight to begin with. Choosing a battle that you are unwilling to win will quickly cause you to lose your Mommy and Daddy powers.

> ***Say what you mean <u>and</u> mean what you say!***
>
> ***And be reasonable.***

If you ask your child to clean up their toys, and then they refuse, and a shouting match begins, then you should follow through and *work with* them until they have completed the task. Do not do it for them! Backing down teaches them to **not** listen to your requests. In this case, you said that *no means okay* and, in that situation, you would have been better off *not* asking them to clean up their toys to begin with. *Follow-through* is a parent's most important task and it is our most important tool.

Unfairly starting battles out of reflex is another thing that we often do to our children by saying "no" just because we are too accustomed to telling them "no." Getting into this bad habit makes you very unfair, and you *will* appear unfair to your children. Then your unfairness might later be used as a weapon against you when they are trying to demand to have their way.

If your child has been well-behaved, and all is well, and they want some harmless thing to do or to play with, or whatever the case may be, then regularly telling them "no" for no particular reason will likely have two effects: First, they will eventually figure out that this is not quite right and may begin to fight it. Second, it will take away their purpose in life. If a child cannot ever have any joy when all is well and they are behaving properly and doing good, then they will lose their desire because they know that they will always have their hopes crushed by you. When they learn this as a life habit, it becomes a primary language to them and it is difficult for them to escape. Thus, they will gravitate toward unfair relationships and have little ambition, causing them to not accomplish much in life. Learn to properly balance your saying "No" for no reason.

We should always be attentive to our children's situation and be in constant consideration of their well-being. Choosing *when* to fight the battle and which battle to fight can be easily known by understanding what is good and true; then you will maintain your Mommy and Daddy powers.

Stop Rebellion

Stopping rebellion is slightly different than stopping our children from having tantrums, from becoming bullies, or from becoming hate filled terrorists. Rebellion can certainly involve tantrums, bullying, and terroristic behaviors, but rebellion is usually due to lack of consideration on our part.

When we talk to our children, if we "Tell it like it is" then, even if we are correct, they may rebel. You must be able to offer sound reason behind your actions when explanation is due. Making statements that have no reasonable foundation causes your children to have much doubt *of you*. Even if your statement actually has a good foundation, it can still cause them to have doubt *of you* if you fail to deliver the statement with a reasonable explanation—and deservedly so.

Even if we "tell it like it is" and we are correct and deliver the information well, we can still create a rebel.

> The most important thing, with regard to rebellion, *is to hear other people and listen to and process their words.*

Listening and processing is often how leaders calm crowds, by hearing them and having it at least *appear* as if they considered those thoughts. When we are being honest in our considerations, then considering other people's thoughts works well. When we disregard their thoughts after hearing and possibly even considering them, then it is only a matter of time before the rebellion will begin again. Be honest in *telling it like it is* and allow them their thoughts in return. You are not required to agree, but you should hear and mentally process their words and then respond accordingly. It is a great time for teaching and sharing life lessons.

The importance of the proper and full consideration of our children's thoughts gives a near perfect guarantee of *not* creating rebels against reasonable rules of conduct. When we utilize proper and full consideration and teach them what is true, then they will only rebel when it is just and proper to do so, which is when their true freedom is being stolen from them by a terrorist or bully. This is our ultimate goal as parents and humans—it is called truth—it is freedom!

The Iron Fist, Correction Without Reason

"Correction" without reason is ruling with an iron fist and always includes an unfair punishment. Correction without reason can be seen two different ways, and both are unfair and unkind.

In the first way, a child may actually have done something that needed correction, but they were not told what they did wrong and were punished anyway. In this case, it's not as bad since the child *did* actually do something wrong. Not clearly informing them of exactly what their error was, and why it was not good, is unfair to them and leaves them behind in the dark about truth. Without knowing what they did wrong, they will not know what changes to make in order to make the needed corrections in their own behavior, thus causing them to repeat the blindly-erred behavior again and again. This situation is more common than we choose to imagine. We might think that we have told our child their error, but if *they* did not grasp or understand our explanation, then the punishment did no good and the child will be left confused. This exponentially increases the probability of creating an unjust rebel, or a withdrawn underachiever who very much lacks self-confidence.

The other type of correction without reason is when they did something that was *not* wrong, but *we* didn't like what they did, or worse, they did not do anything wrong at all, but they were punished anyway. In these cases, punishment is usually severe and absolutely undeserved. This is commonly found in physical abuse situations. But any situation that uses this method of child rearing is unfair and unjust, even if it is only verbal. Using such tactics destroys your children and creates hostile angry children who will likely repeat this behavior against those around them, and against their own children and spouse when that time comes.

Iron-fisted parenting is often seen as an attempt to break the will of a stubborn child, but if the child did nothing wrong or was not taught or *properly* corrected in their errors while young, then any punishment that is not properly explained will be unfair and unjust and is perceived as such by the child. In the long run, this leads to a rejection and the disregarding of the parents. Additionally, it creates unjust rebellion in other parts of the child's life as they grow up. **We** must teach them *properly* and be fair and just with them.

Breaking Their Will and Building Their Will

Breaking a *stubborn* will, while not using an iron fist, is our goal. It is the *stubborn* part that we must tame and not the will itself. When we use an iron fist and break a child's will altogether, then we have done them a great disservice and have stolen from them a very precious thing—*their desire.*

Allowing children to call the shots causes you to have to bargain with them. Once bargaining starts, you have doomed yourself unless you put a stop to it. If you allow your children to call the shots when they demand so, then they will develop a dangerously strong and arrogant will. Our means to understand the difference between their stubbornness or false will, and a true and good will, is *truth* and *necessity*. If our children demand their way and there is no purpose for their demands and we allow this, then we are failing our children. We know what is needed, so then we should do it! Failing to do so creates a monster.

Building our children's *will* through truth, understanding, and reward can pay your family great dividends of joy for the rest of your lives. A reward is not something that is done as an incentive or bribe. A reward is a bonus for doing right and it is the option of the giver, not a right of the rewarded. The rewarded person should desire to give their best most creative effort and then they can hope for a reward, but they should not expect it from you. When they receive their reward, they will have the joy of that reward. The best reward a child can receive is the love, consideration, and praise of their parents. Anything more is a bonus for them.

Separating the Iron Fist from a Guiding Hand

Separating an iron fist from the hand of loving guidance is hard for many of us because of how *we* were taught as children. If we were brought up with an iron fist, then we will likely do the same with our children. When parents use an iron fist to love and guide their children, then things get confusing for the children, resulting in making it more difficult for them when raising their own children; and even more difficult for them when their own children are adults.

Iron-fisted parenting allows little consideration of those being ruled. It is a "Do as I say" method. It might appear successful, but the resentments that are borne in to the children because of it eventually comes back to haunt us at some point.

A loving hand explains things and hears and considers their words. Then, through just and true analysis, balances those words against what is good and true, and explains the details to them. A loving hand is a gentle push in the right direction rather than the iron fist's unfair smack-upside-the-head. The choice is ours and it is dependent upon every choice we make. Our choice is either true and good, or it is damaging, bad, not true, and unjustified.

The effects of teaching a child to have a proper *will* and *desire* touches every area of their life. Allowing a child their own will allows you to teach them how to discern things. If we fail to teach this skill, then we can expect that they will make many poor choices in life, possibly even making an unwise choice of a mate when they are grown. This all comes about because they have not learned how to be discerning.

How to make good decisions is ultimately what we are trying to teach our children. Good decisions cannot be made without balancing *everything* on the scale of truth. Teach them to balance everything on the scale of truth through your example, correction, and discipline, and then you will not need to do much punishing, if any is needed at all!

Allowing Bad Behavior

For every person, the realization usually comes at some point in life, that allowing any behavior will typically cause that behavior to continue and/or increase. This can be either good behavior or bad behavior. No matter who it is: you, your children, or other people, if we are doing something and we don't sense any resistance, then we have no reason to stop what we are doing. The world is able to function precisely because people resist bad behaviors. If we did not, then our world would be a very, very dark place to live.

When we go around insulting or violating other people, we are typically met with some amount of hostility from them. It is this hostility that keeps us in check and causes us to realize that we have been offensive to others. If we want to be accepted by other people, then we need to quickly realize that we must cease behaving so carelessly and maliciously towards others. When resistance is absent, then there is no signal for us to stop and change our behavior.

In general, this basic system of being kind and true, and being resisted when we are *not* kind and true, has allowed humanity to increase and survive for millennia. When any society fails in this regard, then the society's collapse is imminent. The same is true of your family. Generally, most of us realize that when someone is offending us, at some point we must resist. But the situation changes a great deal when the offender is our own self.

When we insult ourselves and/or think lowly of ourselves, then who is there to resist? Many of us are down on ourselves and talk badly about ourselves. Eventually, this self-malice drags us down and makes us feel even worse.

As individuals, we should not allow others to attack us if we hope to ever stop their behavior; and this is no different for families. Also, when we allow ourselves to demean ourselves by believing that we are not worthy or by insulting ourselves, then we have become the bully to ourself. We must stop ourselves from doing this.

Bad behavior is bad behavior, and no matter who is doing it, it is wrong and destructive to the person who is being unfairly attacked. Speaking love, kindness, and firm discipline to ourselves and to others is the only way to make our families and the world a better place.

Our children follow our examples, and typically emulate our *bad* traits more easily than our good traits. Making sure that we treat ourselves with respect teaches our children to have self-respect. And when they have self-respect, they are far less likely to allow others to treat them poorly without resistance. This is the key to a better world.

Chapter 20

What Matters Through Their Ages

When our children are grown and leave the house, we realize how short this life truly is. Stop and take the time to enjoy all the days of your family life, and all the days of your own life. Use them wisely, there are too few days in a life. They are all that each of us has while alive. Whether you believe in an afterlife or not, is not an issue in this regard because even only these earthly days of life in themselves are important to each one of us.

If we believe that there is not an afterlife, then the value of this life is all that we believe we will ever have and it is best to use these days to the best of our ability because then this life is that much more precious. If you believe in the afterlife, then you also probably understand that the way in which we treat others here and now affects your future afterlife position. No matter what we choose to believe, the truth is, where you are mentally and morally at this moment will affect the rest of your life whether here on earth or in the hereafter. And your behavior during your lifetime can and likely will affect your descendants to some extent after you are gone.

We learn through our experiences and through the experiences that our choices have brought about. As parents we have the luxury to guide, teach, and explain life to our children. We have the opportunity to show our children good things. We have the opportunity to teach them truth and how to weigh facts on the scale of truth. We get to teach them *how* to *understand.*

If our lessons of "understanding" are built on things that are not true, then we can fully expect that our children will believe lies and accept inaccurate information, and that is not our goal. The following sections detail why things tend to get off track in some families and what to do to correct the problems.

Pre-Conception

The theme of us all facing what is true, is deeply embedded in all four of the cornerstone books mentioned throughout this book and listed in back. There is nothing more important in anyone's life than to face what is true. The negative effects of not being able to see this simple truth costs us and our families dearly.

These effects can be felt in our health, in our successes, in our accomplishments, in our thinking, and in our interaction with others, but to get an understanding of the magnitude of this, we need to grasp the origins of our choices.

Often we have a simplistic view of the complex, and a complex view of the simplistic. This causes us to miss out on a great deal of the wonderful aspects of our lives. The complexity of our bodies does not stop at a single cell. The complexity goes far beyond even the chemical aspects. The complexity goes all the way down and into atomic and subatomic particles as discussed in the book series *The Science of God*, but to keep this focused regarding parenting, we will only discuss what surrounds the important chemical aspects required to discuss the topic.

Typically, parents quickly find out that their children are each born with a particular temperament. Our children can share similar temperaments, but they each have their own. The question is, *when* are these temperaments developed? While this section is not necessarily scientifically provable, it is most certainly worthy of consideration by everyone who has decided to have children.

In an earlier chapter, we discussed how our body's chemistry is irrefutably affected by what it senses, due to the fact that everything happening in our body is a chemical reaction. If you are at rest outside with the wind blowing by your ears and you hear the whoosh of the wind, then your body has sent a chemical chain reaction of events that has gone from your ear to your brain, and subsequently, your brain has responded with another chemical chain reaction that will cascade throughout your entire body. This is not in question at all and is obvious upon the slightest consideration.

If the wind was cold, which is also a chemical signal sent to your brain by your sensory system, then another chemical reaction *will* cascade through your body, likely causing goose bumps. Even if the wind is warm, you may still get goose bumps when you have a unique thought that "gives you chills." This can even happen when your environment is neutral. Merely thinking certain thoughts can give you goose bumps. *Everything* that we sense **and think** affects our physical chemistry.

When we are with other people, conversing or in any way communicating, then we are becoming part of one another. Hearing a song or reading a book makes the singer, songwriter, author, musician, and artist's work a part of your physical body. Everyone and everything we interact with has affected us to some extent and becomes a physical part of what and who we are through these amazing chemical reactions in our bodies. Someone could debate the level of the effect of any one interaction, sensation, or thought, but this is chemically, scientifically, and logically so; and it is quite obvious when we apply even the slightest amount of thought and reasoning to it.

All that you have seen, heard, felt, smelled, tasted, and thought since you were born has affected you chemically and is somewhat a part of, or has affected, your body today.

The next level of biochemistry to consider is that all of these chemical elements are *very* heavily reacted upon when we meet our mate and begin our relationship. What we sense continues all the same, but the chemical reactions are far more intense when we have these sorts of intense intimate feelings towards the person who we have chosen to pursue. The causes of the increased feelings could be debated, but it seems logical to conclude that the part that is **us** causes the body to produce the exciting chemistry we sense.

There are two sides of this topic. There is the receiving of the sensation, hearing, and seeing, etc., and then there is the response. The question this brings up is: do someone's intentions affect *our* sensation at all *if* we are *unaware* of their intention?

If we are unaware of the feelings a person has towards us, and that person touches us with the intent to catch their balance, is that touch going to be received or sensed differently by us than if someone specifically has an intimate interest towards us and does the *exact* same action in order to catch their balance?

This question would be difficult to scientifically prove, but it is entirely possible that we could sense the difference without realizing it. From a purely physical perspective, the person who has an intimate interest in you would have their biochemistry being affected simply because they are near you and are seeing you, which will cause their body reactions to be different, such as body temperature, sweaty hands, etc. We may pick up on these differences in a subtle and, likely, unaware manner, but it is the area beyond these signals that is important here in this discussion.

Our brains do have electromagnetic emission, and these emissions are likely detectable by others. The question is: do we emit a vibe, aura, spirit, or some other *nonphysical* essence of us? This may be a difficult or even impossible thing to test for, but the possibility is very real. As discussed in the cornerstone book *Understanding Prayer*, our bodies are chemical, but our brains seem to emit electromagnetic signals. Our brains have repeatedly been proven to be effected in various ways by electromagnetic signals, so it is very likely that we *can* sense other people's intent towards us in some form and to some extent via that mechanism.

Setting aside the purely spiritual possibilities, just the scientifically measurable electromagnetic and chemical effects of this are immensely important. Since we realize that bad things are bad for us, and good things are good for us, we need to determine what *bad* is and what *good* is. In our purpose and understanding here: bad destroys, and good creates or sustains.

Since our feelings are usually very intense when we are thinking about and sensing the sights, sounds, and such with regard to our person of intimate interest, then the reactions attributed to those sensations are also more intensely utilizing our biochemistry. We become a part of our intimate interest in very deep, intense, and powerful ways, and all of this affects us.

A women is said to be born with all of her eggs, but the environment in which those eggs are kept until they are released is affected by the chemical reactions within her body.

With regard to a man, his reproductive cells are said to be produced almost on-demand. In his case, they can be greatly affected by his *current* chemical state during the moment of production.

When these two cells, the female egg and the male sperm cell, finally meet, then the egg, in a sense, chooses which sperm cell to allow into itself to become a part of it. This is a micro example of exactly what we do in our own lives. *She* must allow *him* into *her*—this happens on many levels in a male-female intimate relationship. If you have a desire to read more on this the cornerstone book *Red Hot Marriage* goes into more detail with regard to the nature and physical design of men and women and how and why it affects their marriage relationships.

Clearly, all that we are, all that we are doing, all that we have done, all that we have thought, and all that we were thinking at conception, potentially has affected the newly fertilized egg—the new life that we have created.

Do not be fooled by the picture of the simple looking transparent single celled newly fertilized egg that we often see in pictures. The complexity in this single cell of life has a depth, scope, and beauty far beyond the imagination that most of us are willing to expend upon it. A cell is not a single thing, it is a complicated micro machine that is richly full of intensely complex chemistry and brilliantly designed mechanisms.

Stepping beyond the chemistry for a moment, we reach the atomic and the subatomic stages of each chemical component of the cell. Beyond that we get into the theoretical physical realm which only brings about a multitude of additional questions—questions that people dedicate their entire lives to trying to answer and understand. And yet, conception occurs all around the world at nearly every moment of every day without effort or thought.

Understand that there is, at minimum, a very real and provable chemical effect, from our thoughts and sensations, on a single newly-fertilized cell (the pregnancy with a new baby). What we sense and think matters! Our resulting actions are also sensed by us, along with the reactions from those actions, and it all affects our thoughts and our thoughts affect our actions. All of this affects and becomes a part of our body chemistry and therefore becomes a part of us. It also affects and becomes a part of the body chemistry of those around us and therefore a part of them.

Conception

Once an egg is fertilized, the egg is held protectively in the womb of the mother. As discussed in previous sections, her chemistry is affected and those chemicals are instrumental in building and creating this beautiful tiny new baby machine—a soul that is alive and dwells within a living human machine body. Everything the mother encounters, including her own thoughts, is impacting the construction of this tiny and wonderful little chemical machine all while it is being created and growing within her womb.

Referring to a baby, or even any person, as a machine seems cold. However, realizing the rough details of our chemical existence should serve to increase your appreciation for the beauty of humanity, of children, of life, of the human body, and of the soul.

All that the mother senses, thinks, and does, becomes a part of the life within her womb. The interaction between her and her husband affects each other's moods and body chemistry. What the husband says to his wife becomes a part of her chemistry and therefore has eternally altered the chemistry of the child that is being created within her.

The *moment of conception* brings together these two thinking beings, the mother and the father. Scientifically and logically, we know beyond a doubt that the sensory chemistry is a chain reaction through each person or entity, including the baby. The question then is, does our spirit, soul, mind, the way we think, and the actual thoughts, or any other less tangible aspect, also transfer in a non-chemical way? I say that it does, but since we cannot physically hold tangible evidence of such, we each need to form our own hypothesis and choose our own belief in that regard. Your observations of those around you who are planning to start their families, will offer additional insight for you about this topic. Pay attention in life, because life is very interesting!

Gestation

The period of time that new life is being created or built within the mother is an intensely chemical event. Not in a toxic chemical sense, but in a very real and beautiful manner.

Every moment that life is in existence within the mother, the life is exponentially increasing in complexity. Each cell created is affected from the chemistry that is creating it. Think of this in terms of a mother building a house and she is leaving her chemical fingerprints on every single brick that she touches that goes into the house. If the bricks are made from poor or low quality materials then the house won't be as strong as it could and should be. What the mother senses, thinks, and does matters to that new life. The interaction between her and her husband is very important. A mother's chemistry is likely going to be more impacted by the words and actions of her husband than it is from any other source beside herself, likely even more than from her own children.

Once the cell has become fertilized, it begins to multiply by dividing. The fertilized egg cell is fueled by the chemistry of the mother—chemistry that is affected by all of the things she encounters in her life. As these new-life cells continue to grow within her, they are not only experiencing the mother's chemistry, but these cells also are experiencing *their own* life experiences, or senses.

Just as we can hear the heartbeat of a fetus, so too, the fetus can hear and sense the heartbeat of the mother, and the fetus also experiences the other senses of sight, taste, touch, and smell. This includes the sounds outside of the mother's womb. While taste and smell are possibly not well utilized or needed in the womb, sight, touch, and sound are. The baby will hear sounds and possibly see some faint light and feel the movements of the mother. The obviousness of this is so blatant that we need not waste time demanding proof. The only thing that we need wonder is the *amount* of effect that it has on the baby. These chemical effects on the developing child continue the entire time that the child is within the mother.

It is when we step in to wondering about the spirit, soul, or mind of the child that we are left without "proof." Until someone can produce irrefutable proof, we will be left to wonder and have to withhold our final conclusions. But it is fair for us to speculate on these things. Without speculation nothing would ever come to be because we would have no desire to actually research anything to draw our conclusions with. We research and then study what we speculate on because we are curious.

Many mothers will testify to a temperament of any particular child while the child was in the womb and that the temperaments often differ from child to child. Could some of this have been developed before conception, at conception, and during gestation? The answer is likely, all of the above.

Then there is that additional and fundamental element of *who* we are, which is our temperament that is a part of our *who*. But is it all entirely chemical? Not likely; *thought* is an elusive subject that humans have been discussing, debating, and fighting about since as far back as is recorded in history and likely beyond that.

"What makes you—you?" is a very important question. Obviously all that we encounter affects us, but at the three earliest stages of a created life (before conception, at the moment of conception, and moments after conception) is there more going on than just chemistry? Can the spirits, souls, minds, or thoughts of the parents blend and be joined as one within that life in addition to the chemical part of the process?

For many parents the answer is a distinct and definite "yes!" As parents, we often see things in our children that do not make sense, but seem to be passed to them somehow. How could they do something that is so odd or unique as to be like something we ourselves did as a child, something that our own child would not have been privy to or ever have seen us do and is something that is not typical of all children? We can all have our own speculations on this sort of similarity to the parent, but it is wise to at least not throw it out or disregard its possibility.

Everything that has been or is, or has been in our life or is in our life, has affected our children to some extent whether or not we choose to believe it. The possibility that we also pass spirit to these new minds is highly probable.

Birth

Once a child is born, there is little question of their mental and physical formation and how it occurs from that point forward. They now are subject to the environment that surrounds them. This new environment includes anything or anyone that can be sensed by their senses, including the potential electromagnetic and electrochemical aspects of life previously mentioned, and possibly even a realm beyond that, such as mind or spirit.

These tiny new people, that we have made, are affected chemically just as we discussed at the beginning of this chapter about how *we* are chemically affected. All that they experience from this point forward is obvious in that it will alter their life, body, and thinking.

First Week

Earlier we discussed, at length, the importance of understanding that children learn to get their way by crying. The seeds of crying, in order to manipulate, can be planted in the child during their first week of life while *outside* of their mother's womb.

However, the problem is not the seeds planted in the child in this first week, it is in the parents' *choice* to feed, water, and nurture those demanding crying seeds in the following months and years.

Do not mistake feeding and nurturing the seeds of manipulation for feeding and nurturing your child. It is good to pick your newborn up often, and show them care and love, especially those first several weeks and months. Enjoy them and take joy in being with them and in loving them and sharing with them. I sometimes hear people commenting that "They (meaning the baby) do not know" referring to the baby's ability to grasp things. This thinking is a terrible plague on mankind and is utterly wrong.

Babies can smile the first week. They can see, and their hearing is incredibly sharp. Just because they have not yet fully grasped how to utilize these senses, does not mean that they do not sense things with them. They have brains, bodies, and minds and everything else that we have, and it is entirely possible that an infant's rate of learning is far greater than any adult's learning rate is or needs to be.

Talk to your baby, look into their eyes, smile at them, and tell them you love them. Touch and hold them, love them, sing to them. And do all of this frequently with joy and love in your heart, mind, and soul.

First Month

If our thoughts affect our brain signals, then these electromagnetic signals are received to some extent by our infant. From a scientific standpoint, it is not *if* they are exposed to these signals, the question is **when** they are, *how much does it affect your infant?* Beyond that you have the spiritual/mind aspects of life. Do we humans connect on a level that goes beyond this physical and scientific realm? Our electromagnetic brain signals are physical and are a somewhat tangible element because we can measure and detect them in a laboratory.

But the concept of mind or thought is a bit more elusive. We ought to consider the potential that there is a very real possibility that our infant can sense something more that is beyond the physical electromagnetic signals. If our thoughts or mind is in a bad or negative state, then we are potentially teaching the child *negativity* or *bad* without realizing it. This is obviously true in the electromagnetic realm, so it's wise to be real and true with our children. Putting on a happy face may not be enough. If we are hurting or frustrated inside, then our frustration and pain are likely detected in some form by our child.

If our child can sense our mind and we are in a negative state of mind, but we are putting on a happy face for them, then we, in a way, are deceiving them. This is not speaking of mind-reading or reading someone's thoughts, but rather sensing a state of being that is good or bad, positive or negative, constructive or destructive, true or not true.

Whether or not we communicate on a spiritual level, our physical connections are obvious. There is nothing more important than loving and tending to, or caring for, your infant. But we must be aware that during their first month we can develop something in them that can take root and become stronger every time we feed the seed of over-attentiveness. By doing so we are essentially letting them have their way.

Often new parents want to know specifically how often to pick up their child when they face this situation, but there is no specific answer, rather there is only your awareness of the issue. Being aware of this is what gives you the ability to have insight as to what to do and when to do or not do it.

To briefly recap what we discussed in earlier chapters, when we consistently pick a child up at their every peep, then we build a pattern for them to follow as they grow. Our seeds and the watering of those seeds of picking them up and comforting them for *every single peep* they make creates a dependency on that sort of comfort. This means anytime your child is awake they will have learned that crying is the only way to be picked up and held, which is getting what they want—to be comforted.

The balance, here, is up to each one of us. If we are too cold, then our children will potentially be distant. If we are picking them up too often when they cry then they potentially become too demanding.

It is important to note that it is not actually the fact that you are picking them up that is a problem. The problem is in your picking them up *because* of their crying for no good reason. What this does is to tell them, by your actions, that when they cry they will always be comforted. It is not so much how often you pick them up, it is *why* and *when* you do it that determines your outcome.

Planting these seeds is difficult to *not* do because picking them up is a good and natural thing with regard to their general care and love, but it is our persistent *planting, watering,* and *feeding* of these seeds that gets us into the trouble that some families experience.

It's good to give a child a hug and hold them when they need it, both chemically and spiritually. But once they have learned to get their way by crying, it is supported by us when we are not decisive and firm in our actions. When we submit to their crying to be held too often, the dependence is forged and is reinforced with each occurrence of our action.

We must be able to separate their demanding crying from their crying for true needs and their need for reasonable love. The crying may not be able to be differentiated, so once our family's checklist of obvious problems has been exhausted, then it might be time to tough it out and allow them to cry themselves to sleep. But only the parents can decide that.

> Remember:
> It is not only how often you pick them up,
> it is when, how often, **and why** you pick
> them up that creates a problem.

Since our babies are a very serious matter, because they are living human beings, we will detach a bit and think of a very young and new puppy. For anyone who has ever had a new puppy in the house, you are likely familiar with the advice to let the puppy whimper and whine during the night and *not* pick them up in the middle of the night when you first get them. If you do pick them up, then you doom yourself to having a pet that will be very whiney whenever they want attention at night. They will build a dependence upon your attention and will always cry and whine in order to get attention at night when *you* want to sleep.

With a puppy, we realize that they will be fine if we leave them whine and cry. They won't die, and if they make a mess then they will typically sit across the cage or box from it. When we tough it out and don't tend to them in the middle of the night for only a few days, then they stop the nighttime whining and we live happily-ever-after with our new pet.

It works similarly with people, but with babies they need certain care, such as diaper changes and feeding, and tending to those needs in the night. We *must* tend to those needs. We also just need to know that babies also will cry for nothing more than attention and comfort at times. Picking them up to get them to "shut up" confirms to their innocent little minds that the response to screaming at the top of their lungs is you comforting them. Supporting their belief by doing so builds their dependency on it and doing so makes *demanding via crying* a primary language for the child. They learn this quickly and they learn it well.

Enjoy your baby and give them great amounts of love and care, but realize that meeting demands of their crying for no particular reason can cause unneeded longer-term toil for you. Knowing that this is often a problem for parents is the beginning of correcting the problem. But only you, the parents, can make the determination of when, how often, and why you need to pick up your infant. No one else can judge that for you, it is your own responsibility as to how you handle your child.

First Year

The seeds that we plant in the first month of our children's lives, as we figure out the nature of our new infant, are easily controlled during their first year, provided that we are aware that this occurs. It is a stunning statistic how few of us know that we ourselves even plant these seeds, and worse, how few of us figure it out until it is too late to peacefully make the needed changes.

The longer it takes us to understand that *we* planted and nurtured these demanding seeds, then the longer it takes and the more turmoil it causes us while correcting the situation and reversing the habitual behavior of them *and* us.

Impressing this topic into our own heads is important because this problem is the seed and root cause of most troubles in our lives. Teaching a child to get what they want by having us pick them up because they are screaming when there is nothing wrong, seems insignificant, but I assure you that it is not insignificant. It is the single most dangerous seed that we mistakenly plant in our children.

But the bigger and more troubling problem is that if you do it here then you likely do it just about everywhere else in their lives.

We teach them to *demand* by eventually succumbing to their demands. This is a primary language that follows them all through their lives if it is allowed to continue; and they will learn to speak it more fluently with each passing day.

We could think of their crying in terms of an actual word, and that word is "*ask.*" In general, our perception of *ask* is to go to someone and make a request by saying "would you please [*whatever*]?" But, when we break down under the pressure and give into a child's demanding crying, then we have taught them that the word "ask" means to *demand* and *force* others to comply through the child's loudness and brash actions. We parents get to choose what the underlying definition of the word "*ask*" will be for each of our children.

First Two Years

In the first year, the effects of caving into their demands are very noticeable, but the penalty is mostly paid *after* the first year *if* we continue to teach and allow them to perceive the wrong definition of "*ask.*"

We, as adults, confuse the concepts of *command* and *demand.* In the word "*com-mand,*" *com* means *with* and *mand* means *mandate.* With the word "*de-mand,*" *de* means *away from* or *apart from,* and again, *mand* means *mandate.* One of these words states we are working together and the other states that we are doing it "my way!"

Because a *demand* is often done in a decisive manner with intent and intensity, we mistake it as an authoritative action and behavior. Most of humanity hates demanding behavior. Even if we ourselves don't do it, we still hate it when someone else does to us.

Command is different in that it has people coming together and doing what is best for the good of all. A command is often delivered by a decisive person who has a good ability to convey the message with power and certainty. You can see why this gets confused in our minds, especially when you consider that we either demanded in our youth or likely lived with someone who was demanding.

We have learned to **not** notice that there is a difference between *command* and *demand* because we have become too used to it and too familiar with the confusion; this causes us to completely ignore the differences between the two words. This is similar to when we get comfortable in the water when swimming, and eventually it does not feel as cold as it did at first. The water didn't change, but our perception of it did change. The particular difference between these two words is important for parents to have a hyper-awareness of.

The first two years, and especially the second, is our greatest opportunity to correct the problem of *demanding*, before it gets out of hand. It is after the first two years, in those "terrible twos" where we truly feel the pain of our shortcomings of the first year or two of our child's life.

By the time the first two years have been completed, we sometimes have it figured out and have already made the needed adjustments. If we have not, then we are in for a ride that is going to be fairly unpleasant, but which can generally be dealt with in only a few weeks' time if we understand when and why to pick up or attend to our children when they cry.

When a child has been spoiled *and* does not get proper love, it then becomes more difficult to solve these problems. However, if the child gets good positive love and is still having spontaneous tantrums, then it is usually easier to solve the problem.

By simply rejecting the behavior and disciplining the child, the problem will quickly go away. Giving timeouts and catering to the child will only reinforce the child's bad behavior and spontaneous outbursts. If ignoring behavior has not worked, then sternly but fairly rejecting the behavior and reprimanding the child is a fair course of action. Parents often have trouble in this area because they do not understand the simple dynamics of children's behavior. Children who have not been receiving proper love see this reprimand as attention, and they will likely take what they can get if they have not been getting their needed love at other times. But when the child gets a fair amount of proper, positive attention and love at other times, then a stern reprimand will be comparatively unpleasant for them and discourages the child from having spontaneous tantrums. Parents often fail at this because they are trying to reason with a child who is being unreasonable.

> You cannot reason with
> people who choose to be
> *unreasonable.*

If a parent responds to tantrums that have become habitual for the child, and the parent proceeds with any attempts to get the child to calm down by being *too* gentle and *too* kind, then it feeds the child's bad behavior because the child got what they wanted—their parents' kind attention. Parents need to establish clear limits in their own minds and understand that the children will unknowingly push the limits of the parents because that is how children learn. A parent that allows a child to push them further with each subsequent tantrum will find themselves in serious distress while the child ages as this poor behavior is reinforced and grows. A parent will slowly lose the respect of their child, and as the child ages, it becomes increasingly more difficult to solve the problem.

Make sure your child is getting the proper love at other times, and then stand firm against spontaneous tantrums. Tantrums are fed when parents do not resist; but tantrums are defeated when parents reject the tantrum behavior while it is occurring. It is okay to get reasonably angry with children who are misbehaving; spankings are one thing, but never use violence or abuse.

Up to Age Six or Seven

With each of these stages, the child's falsely propped up *will* becomes stronger and more deeply rooted, requiring you to have far greater strength to pull out the roots of the troublesome weeds.

Take bargaining for instance: You could follow all of what has been discussed and be a firm, loving, and kind parent, but if you bargain with your child, you have lost all of your credibility with them. For decades, I have been watching generally good parents make the "*bargaining*" error. Typically, this is done when the tears start pouring (An injured child is different, and that is not what I am referring to here). If we bargain with a child when they cry because they are "spoiled", then the child has just gotten their way. We typically *do not* need to tell them to "shut up and stop crying", but we can certainly let them know that that sort of behavior is not allowed and is not acceptable. Here's the part that is tough for most parents that have fallen into the bargaining trap: Many parents have grown up with bargaining in their own lives and therefore we do not realize that we are doing so with our own children. And because the children have become so accustomed to it, even when the parents finally decide to challenge them, and *not* bargain with them any longer, the child cries as if their world is coming to an end. It is at this point you need to summon your parental fortitude and be strong for the good of the crying child and for the good of your entire family. Use your own good judgement when doing so.

Let's not confuse parental unfairness with the children's crying. Sure, "the parents are the parents", but parental guidance must make sense to the world, to yourself, and to your children—it must be fair. The important part in this is that it is you, the parent, who conditions the child in regard to what is "fair" and reasonable as they are growing up. *Unnecessarily* giving into a crying child from birth onward will not produce true joy in the child or in the parents, and doing so skews the child's perception of "fairness." Anything that you perceive in them as joy when you foolishly give in to their unwarranted tears builds a precedent that becomes so unpleasant that it will suck the life out of an otherwise good family. The more you allow this sort of behavior, then the more often it will occur. It is a very ugly cycle.

Bargaining is often overlooked because the parents do not need to do it in words, because bargaining can be done by the look in or on your face. Children are the most brilliant people that you will ever meet! Sometimes it seems that we get stupider as we age. Children can read a parent's subtle facial expressions in an instant, better than we adults can imagine. When you show any weakness in your face they pick it up and use it to their advantage; I have witnessed this a multitude of times over the years. Any weakness that is seen in your face is a form of bargaining. **No means No, and it must remain so!** This includes the facial expressions and any other body language or words that you exhibit. If you have mistakenly uttered "No" for no solid reason, then apologizing and correcting your action is important. But when the "no" is fitting then you must stick with it.

Now here is an important key to understand and remember: Those seeds and roots were planted by us—the parents. This means that since they were planted by us, they started in or from us. The problem is not the child, *it is us*—the parents.

It is us who have planted the demanding seed in them and allowed it to grow. As long as we feed that demanding seed and supply it with water and food it *will* flourish. This root is not a child problem, it is a parent problem. When the parent stops feeding the problem, the problem *will* wither and go away. (In reference to "feeding" we are not discussing actual food, but rather actions, attitudes, and information.)

The ages up to six or seven, are the years where most torment is felt by us if we fail in this area. This is mostly because our children are home all of the time and we get in the habit of supporting and nurturing this primary language. Mothers tend to be more susceptible to this problem because: one, they are more often the ones caring for the child at this age; and two, because mothers are, by nature, typically less decisive and less stern than fathers. However, this is only a rule-of-thumb and it may be completely opposite in your own family.

All ages of children are a true joy when we have the demanding-seeds aspect of life and the primary languages under control. If you're experiencing a demanding child, then you can be certain that you have missed this very troublesome and common primary language.

Adolescence

Once our child has reached the age of adolescence and we have not managed to control our servitude to their demands, then the primary language of demanding morphs into blatant defiance. Getting their way when they become angry or upset allows the child to believe that they can do whatever *they* want to do. When they begin to realize the independence that comes with age, then they will have thoughts and ideas of their own.

Their independence is not a problem if what they want happens to be in full alignment with our values and common social limits and decency. However, when it steps outside of our limits, then we will have a battle on our hands. Children who have learned in their earliest years, that they can yell and scream to get their way, will also do so in non-family situations. When we have never stood our ground in the past, they have no reason to think that other people will not do likewise in this case.

When we finally do decide to stand our ground and say "no" then it is only their respect for us, or their fear of us that will stop their defiance. However, if they only fear us, then they will likely defy us in secret after they have had their tantrum. This is why the previous parts of this book are all so important to understand. Creating and keeping the **respect** of your children is an important key for parents to understand.

When a parent finally starts to stand up to a demanding child, it is usually done during this adolescent age if it was not already done in their earlier days. Deciding to suddenly take a stand against their behavior at this age is often done because the damage that they can inflict on themselves and/or the family becomes very real and serious.

Gaining the respect of your children is very important to do when they are at a young age. Their respect for you is directly proportional to this primary language that you have taught them, *and* it is proportional to how well you fully consider their thoughts, ideas, and opinions.

When a child does not respect a parent and they have not been taught that tantrums are unacceptable, then we have lost all of our parental power and forfeited it to our children. This is often turned around and thrown back at the parents around the age of adolescence, usually in the form of threats of some sort of doom meant to inflict pain on the parent in order for the child to get their way. In truth, these are their calls for us to step in and take that needed and serious action to become a real and true part of their life by guiding them and teaching them true love. This is done through our words, actions, intentions, and positive attention.

Their defiance will come when their will does not agree with our will. For many parents, this is very difficult to weed through because, all too often, our will is arbitrary and has no distinct line of reasoning or pattern. In other words, *we like what we like* and what we like is based upon our own demands and has no basis in truth. Even though what we like might not be bad, it can still be terribly inconsistent. When our inconsistent *will* meets with our child's inconsistent *will*, then they have no reason to follow what *we* want, and so they defy us. When we are inconsistent in this way, then to our children, life does not make any real sense and comes across as very arbitrary. This is often why some children become unstable in their rationale during their teen years.

Teen Years

Attacking this issue heavily during the adolescent years, if it has gotten that far, is far more easily done then than in the teen years. The teenage period is a great time to teach your children many wonderful lessons about life that will shape the rest of their lives. With each successive age group reached, our children gain more and more freedom, and with each level of freedom the dangers of the trouble that they can cause increases immensely. This is why it is so critical to get this done early when they are one or two years old. In their teen years, they are driving and dating and exposed to all sorts of substances and devices that can cause them or others a lifetime of hurt.

In this regard, the teen years are much like the adolescent years with the exception that the freedom, attitude, danger, and difficulty are all increased considerably. These should be some of the most wonderful years of their lives, and your lives, where you can teach them many wonderful things. We get to show them how to live and we can share parts of our life with them that they were not ready for in their younger years. Our skills, talents, and knowledge can all be shared with them doing hobbies, work, leisure, and at play.

Getting to the point where we have this under control will take our time and dedication. Then we can spend that time and dedication with them in true joy. Money cannot solve the problem, only our time, love, consideration, and action will solve it.

When the situation of a child being demanding has gotten to the point of rebellion, we may need to deal with our failures of the past, but the solution and the action is the same whether you already did it right in the past or you are only now starting to do it right.

Spending time with your children, considering all of their thoughts, and discussing those thoughts in an open and free manner with no prejudgment is the way. Showing them and yourself what is true and how that balances against their thoughts and your thoughts—is the only *true* way to live to begin with.

Once our children have reached their teenage years they become greatly influenced by their peers and society. The more *we* fell short in the past, then the more the negative influence of some of their friends' negative behavior will have on our children. Well-guided children are our choice, and when we teach them truth, then they will typically stand by that truth and will be largely unaffected by the negative behavior that will, at some point, surround them. It is better that your children learn to guide wisely than to be unwisely guided by unwise influence.

The bottom line in all of this is that we *will* be spending time with our children. We just need to decide if we want to spend that time *shouting* at each other, or *teaching* each other. A truly open parent will probably learn more from their children and from raising them than their children will learn from the parents during this or any other time of their life at home with you. Learn as much as you can from your children and teach them only what is true!

Adult Years

By their adult years, our children will often have shed some of our failures, because, in general, society is not going to accept an adult lying on the floor kicking and screaming, though that does unfortunately exist.

If tantrum behavior *is* exhibited by them in any way when they are older, then it is likely to get them fired—thank God for necessity! However, this can be dependent upon their position in a company or job. If they are lower in the ranks, then they will likely get fired for bad behavior. But if they have obtained a power position and have poor attitude, then they will make other people's lives miserable. We need not look far for situations of a ruthless boss or manager. If we are not the one doing it, then it is probably being done to us or to someone we know.

As you can see by the progression of this primary language, it is common and unpleasant to overlook tantrum behavior. Since our entire culture seems to be immersed in this to some extent, we hardly notice it in any detailed manner. We complain about the effects of this type of behavior that we see in society, but seldom do we realize the depth and extent of the origin of these manipulative and demanding problems. Children go from brats to bullies to terrorists all in about twenty years and it is us parents who make the choice of whether or not they will follow that path.

It is so easy to deal with the problem. However, just because it is easy to deal with the problem does not mean that our life will be painless, but it does mean that life can be far better and far more joyful than what it often is.

During this adult age group, your children will likely find a mate, and that mate is typically chosen based upon how you have taught and treated your children through the years. Their choice will also be based upon how you have brought them up *and* upon *your children's perception* of how you brought them up and treated them. The cornerstone books *Hot Water* and *Red Hot Marriage* reveal a great deal about this and about how what you do *now* will affect your future and your child's future. Your child's spouse is going to become a part of your family. If that spouse is a troublemaker, a gossip, or has a negative attitude, then the spouse's behavior and attitude will weigh heavily on your family and possibly even tear it apart.

Children typically marry people who have many of the same attributes as their parents, whether good or bad. Just as we become accustom to the water while swimming, we also become accustomed to behavior while interacting. When we are accustomed to certain behavior, (including both bad and good) two bads are often put together and it becomes hell for the family and for the extended family. Eventually, your children will have children and then everything that we have discussed in this book all starts over again with *their* own children and family. And you will suffer the consequences all over again as you watch your own children make your same mistakes.

It is our job and duty as parents to give them sound direction that is built upon understanding and what is true. It is also our job and duty to live this way ourselves. In doing so, you have mostly guaranteed that your children will pick mates who will be of a similar nature to you, thus bringing similar joy to your own life for years to come.

Older Age

There is no age where this chapter is not true or does not apply. Bad behavior and the solutions for it ranges from our children's conception and birth, until their deaths. Notice, I did not say *our* death, but rather, *their* death; this is because our words live on forever in their behavior. When we teach our child a behavior, whether good or bad, it affects their children and their grandchildren and their great-grandchildren and on and on, until someone finally takes a stand to stop the bad behavior and only teaches the good behavior, or until someone neglects everything and, in so doing, teaches bad behavior. Even when you're gone, your words are echoing in the hearts and minds of your children and ultimately their offspring, whether they are nine-months-old or ninety-years-old.

This transferring of behavior is without end until humanity ceases, and it is each our own choice what we will allow into the next generation's thinking. *You* must say "Enough! Not in my family." Teaching them what is true offers freedom, but when we have decided to teach what is not true, then we have bound our children and taught them to believe what is not true. If we follow a lie of wrong information, then we cannot make truly good decisions, and this will be reflected in our own behavior *and* in their behavior.

It is important to understand that our successes in life have far less to do with the things we chose to do, and far more to do with not making wrong choices. Wrong choices and wrong direction bog us down in unneeded toil and strife. Indecision is not a particularly good trait, but making no choice is often better and less damaging than making a bad choice with painful, long-lasting ramifications. Failing to address the fundamental issues discussed in this book is a wrong choice.

In this chapter, we stepped through the various major stages of a child's life to give you an idea of why the described behaviors occur, and how to effectively deal with them. If we failed our children in their younger years, we can still address the problems and make things better in subsequent years. This is true during any point in their lives when you have obtained their respect. And it is important to note that, regardless of whether or not they respect you, your words will affect them for good or for bad. While you are alive, even after your own children have become grandparents, your words will still affect your children's thoughts, and your wise counsel can still guide them. Through that guidance you can even guide their children and their grandchildren; this is true even after you have passed on. Our words and actions matter for a very, very long time! Love and guide your children well!

Chapter 21

The Fortress

As children, most of us have witnessed our parents building walls around themselves. We, in turn, learned from that and built walls of our own. When we are young, not only are we often allowed by our parents to be demanding, but often we were hurt by them as well, thus building our walls more sturdy with each unpleasant encounter.

As a parent, allowing our child to misbehave will cause them to unjustly demand our attention while we become frustrated with the behavior that we have chosen to allow. And as we discussed in an earlier chapter, when this happens, then there are often name-calling labels unfairly placed on the child. The particular damaging labels that we are referring to here in this section are specifically about their behavior.

We feel powerful when we use labels, such as dumb, idiot, fool, stupid, etc. When we have a low self-worth we step outside of good logic and often name-call in this way in our attempt to make ourselves feel better about ourselves. Even though those labels might be somewhat descriptive and possibly true, they are still nothing more than mere name-calling. It is not the specific words that are a problem, but rather, it is the *when* we use those words as labels that it becomes problematic.

When a parent labels a child as lazy, spoiled, a big baby, etc., then it is the parent who has caused and allowed that in the child to begin with—it is our own fault. And being the parent, and likely the cause of the problem, it is *our* job to correct that within them.

When we continue to pin a label, or even an accusation of behavior, on our children, they begin to build a wall of protection around themselves. There is nothing that cuts a child deeper than negative words from their parents. This is especially true when it is done in an undeserved manner such as with jealousy towards the child or misdirected frustration of the parent onto the child.

Often, this is accompanied by an attitude of "I don't care." When these attitudes go on long enough, then the wall that the child has been building eventually becomes an impenetrable fortress. This fortress is their form of protection against hurt. If they have begun to build this fortress, then when you do finally decide to embrace truth and attempt to teach truth to them, they may still misunderstand things because of the previous errors that you taught them. This means more effort will be needed to remedy the situation. Our children will see things through their old incorrect filter until they finally come to understand rightly. The period in-between can be somewhat painful for them, for you, and your family until corrections are accepted and fully implemented and understood.

Quickly Learn Who You Should Ignore

Understanding who to ignore is a skill that we have been taught to *not* know. All of the negative behaviors previously discussed require that we should pay attention to those who are unjustly demanding of us and cause us pain. Many people will come into your life and your children's lives over the years and you must learn to ignore and depart from those who are damaging to you and your family. We must overcome and teach our children to do the same. The negative behaviors being discussed are prominent also in all forms of media and entertainment.

When we believe that we must tolerate other people's bad behavior, we have then bought into their lies. Just as a parent must learn to sometimes ignore a well-tended to and well-loved baby's cries or the screaming and crying of a toddler in a tantrum, we also need to ignore the demands of other tyrannical and demanding people. But at times, we must take punitive actions against them to teach them truth.

"Ignore" should not be thought to be to *"just walk away"*, and then still put up with the behavior that inflicted pain on you in order for them to get their way. No, not at all. Ignoring their behavior and allowing them to continue their behavior is what caused their condition to begin with. When they have no power over you, then walking away strips them of the power they are trying to wield over you. Only our submission to them gives power to this sort of behavior. The action of—ignoring but allowing—is why bullies and terrorists gain strength to begin with.

There is no good reason for anyone to tolerate other people's violations against them. If there are any people in your life who repeatedly cause you irritation because of their errors or violating ways, then depart from them. This of course, is aside from your spouse and children. Bullies gain their power through the *fear* harbored by those whom they terrorize. The situation is different when the demanding person is someone near to us, such as a spouse, sibling, child, or even a parent. When people who we have family-type interest in proceed to unjustly demand their way, then our best course of action is to kindly state our case. Then we, in a firm and decisive move, must ignore their vindictive retaliatory demands and we must stand for what is actually just and true.

In general, walking away stops their behavior. However, to our children and spouse, we owe a kind and brief description of how their behavior is wrong. If we do not inform them of their errors, they might never be able to realize their own errors, and then we will have to endure those errors and poor behavior all of our lives. Intolerance with regard to their horrible behavior is the only chance to remedy these situations.

All people deserve to be told at least couple of times, what it is that they are doing wrong. Beyond that, we are wasting our time and are then best served to decisively ignore their behavior and **not** submit to it and then depart from them. In some cases, we even need to take assertive action to protect the innocent and ourselves from their destructive attitude and behavior.

It is only our *in*correct response to a bad behavior that feeds that behavior. This same thing holds true for people outside of our own family.

When someone has a tyrannical or bully-style personality, people often flock to that person and become an ally for two main reasons: First, they are blinded by the person's arrogance and second, they are afraid of being attacked by the bully, so instead they take what they believe to be the "safe" position of becoming the bully's "ally". Without one of these two reasons, a weak, fearful person would normally have no association with the bully at all. Their acceptance of the bully's behavior serves the exact same function as when a parent allows a young child to be demanding and caters to those demands.

With each new minion that the bully acquires, the bully gains a perceived strength that makes them believe that they are correct. This false support only serves to increase their demanding behavior and arrogance and power over the foolish people who serve them (that's us). The more quickly we realize that we must walk away, then the more quickly we strip their false power from them.

Teaching the skill of—dealing with a bully—to our children allows them to live in a fortress that needs no walls because their internal army will always be prepared to stand for what is right, just, and true!

Offenses

Who cares if we offend people? The other people and the Creator do! It is the demanding and rebellious who have chosen to not understand the Creator. It is the demanding and rebellious who have the audacity to say that they do not care about being offended.

This "I don't care" fortress wall that people have built in their lives is not true, because if they truly did not care, then they would not condemn others who stand for personal freedom and dignity.

Anytime anyone stands against a bully, they will usually experience the bully's irrational outburst of vicious behavior and words.

It's true that we should overlook most minor offenses because it's easy for any of us to offend in minutely petty ways. It wastes our time and energy, and fighting these petty offenses is typically not worth our time or trouble. However, if these offenses become too intrusive, and too frequent, then not standing our ground against them will create a monster that will be difficult to dismantle.

Attacks

In our context here, we are thinking of the word *offense* as *violations* against us. *Attacks*, on the other hand, are the bully's *unprovoked* action against you. Any person who has been allowed to be demanding has been building a wall around themselves ever since they have been allowed to be demanding.

Depending upon all of the many circumstances encountered while growing up, the fortress walls being built can be either used only as a form of defensive self-protection, or can be used offensively as a shield of defensive protection during their attacks against others. When we have built these walls and learn to attack in this way, we have done it for a reason—these walls do not build themselves! The mortar and bricks are passed to each of us by those who surround us as we live. In other words, *we* hand the bricks and mortar to our own children to build these dangerous walls brick by brick.

Be aware that these walls exist and that we parents are typically the ones who teach our children how to build them. The understanding that this occurs is the beginning to ridding ourselves of these dangerous walls.

Self-Preservation

We often teach our children to have "thick skin," in other words, "Don't let things bother you." The sad fact is that almost all of us have been building our "thick-skinned" fortress of protection against the offensive attacks from others. We do this for self-preservation. The offenses we receive and the attacks we make upon others are all because of our own labor to build our own fortresses.

It's logical that we would do this because it is a natural response for us to try to protect ourselves, but building such a fortress does not protect us from others because no matter what we think is happening, we are still hearing what is being said about us and we understand what is meant. What we are really building is not a fortress at all, but rather, it is our own prison.

The importance of teaching our children what is true cannot be understated. Accepting what is true is the only thing that will tear down the fortress-prison that we built upon a foundation of what is *not* true. Reject all lies and accept only that which is true and then no walls are needed. When you have and understand truth, you have no need for "thick skin".

Safety in Not Caring

The lowest layers of our own self-made prison are the building blocks of not caring. Some of our lack of caring is due to our own nature, but most is due to the way we were treated by others as we were growing up. When a child is repeatedly attacked, it lowers their self-worth, and often that response is shown in their presentation and words. This type of self-destructive false-humility can be shown in several ways.

Keeping a distance by choosing to be "ugly" or "lazy" is safe. No one can hurt you because you have already set your course, but this is not the way to keep from getting hurt. It is not "safe" and you only hold yourself back—this is a very common thing for young women to do. When we choose to dress down for this reason, then we have already taken our stand. We are creating a way where—when others intend harm to us—we can feel as if we are immune to their attacks. There is no risk of rejection when you have already chosen to be rejected through self-rejection. We believe we have beaten them to the punch and hope the offender will then go away. It is perceived by us to be a "safe" route when we have chosen to do so. This is a part of the offense fortress-prison, and it is a dismal failure to do so.

This not only applies to beauty, but it also applies to achievement. When we fear failure, we typically choose to *not* try at all; in doing so, we have chosen failure deliberately and we are being lazy or afraid. Choosing this is to choose the lie that we *will* fail. The only way to truly fail is to choose to fail by not trying or by quitting. When we choose what is true, then we have chosen success; and even if there are perceived failures in the process of accomplishing our vision, we will not stop our quest for truth. Thus, we have not really failed in the long run. Truth cannot ever fail; people can only perceive it that way because of their deliberate blindness.

False Safety in Rejection

Rejecting others feels safe to us because, in our own eyes, when we do so, *they* cannot reject *us* when we have rejected them first. This is where the "I don't care" attitude thrives with our children. We see this demonstrated heavily in the "I want to be different for the sake of being different" behaviors. You can think of this in terms of "I will harm the other guy before he harms me." It is a part of our attack fortress-prison. If a child adopts the position of saying "I don't care," and acts that way, then their hope and protective perception is that people will leave them be because no insult appears to harm them because they have already rejected the others first, in a bulk manner, via their rejecting attitude towards the others.

The underlying problem with rejecting everyone, is that the rejecter will feel badly about themselves regardless. And the more they reject, then the more they trap themselves in their self-made inescapable prison.

Sheltering versus Protection

As parents, we do not need to teach our children to have "thick skin", use malicious attack tactics, or to withdraw into a self-insulting state in order for them to protect themselves. It is good to stand up for your children, but if they are wrong and you defend their wrong position, then you are seriously damaging your child, and you are essentially a liar. Thus, *you* are teaching them to be a liar.

If someone offends your child by properly disciplining them and you engage in sarcastic remarks about the person who was doing the required discipline, then you are holding your child back and are doing them a very serious disservice. You are teaching them how to build an attack fortress-prison that will bind them in chains until they find the internal power to escape—*if* they ever do. You are teaching them to lie about themselves.

Similarly, if our child fails at a project and we encourage them to quit so that we can protect them from further future disappointment, then we also have taught them to build an offense fortress-prison, and again, we have taught them to lie about themselves.

Our children will have enough trouble in this world coming at them in all directions from people around them, all while dealing with all of what has been discussed here. They do not need it from the most important people in their lives—their parents.

Sheltering a child is an attempt to keep them from feeling any hurt, and it is an attempt to keep them from reality; where on the other hand, *protection* is an effort to stop others from destroying them before they are prepared for the battles that life will throw their way.

When we teach our children truth, then they will have fewer battles and will not be imprisoned behind the sheltering walls of a fortress that truly offers no protection and only serves to hold them back from being truly great.

The walls of any fortress that our children build around themselves serve to hold them in place when someone wants to attack, making them an easier target for their attacker. The walls offer little else.

Teaching our children to build a life set upon a foundation of understanding and truth crushes their wall of lies and frees them forever! This will allow them to embrace the world and to lend their skills and talents to make the world a better place.

Be There When You Are There

Life is too short and seems to go faster and faster the older we get. We only get about twenty years with our children at our side to love and guide them while at home, so use it wisely and be there when you are there with them.

All too often, when our children are little, we are too busy to pay attention to them *even when* we are actually holding them in our arms. How many times have we ourselves, or have we seen others holding a child as the child is talking to them, but we, or the parent we are observing, are too preoccupied with something else and only utter, "Uh-huh, Honey," when the child says, "Look Mommy," or, "Look Daddy." Our children's feeling about their thought is as important to them as our thought of what we are thinking about is to us. If someone disregards **us** in this same way, we typically either get angry, or we go away hurt. Rest assured, if this goes on long enough, our children will do the same.

It is understood that we cannot always be there for our children to constantly be giving them our attention, but what we are talking about here is the very short and relatively few moments in life that we are physically holding or are with our children. Sure, we respond to our children, but we are not really there because our mind is in a different place. Most of us are guilty of doing this and at times it is unavoidable.

When these moments occur, stop yourself and give your child those few brief moments of yourself. **Be present**! This will connect you to them in a profoundly deep way. Generally, children just want their portion of love, and they want to share something with us that they view as interesting.

Be There When You Are There.
Be Present!

If we are with them, then we may as well be *with* them. Look into their little eyes when they speak, and then hear and consider what they are saying. Doing so is something that will always be appreciated by them, and never forgotten or regretted by either the child or by the parent.

Chapter 22

Our Children's Self-Worth and True Love

Our children's self-worth is directly proportional to the amount of effort that we spend in teaching them how to understand what is good and true. This is a primary language, and it is the language of their self-worth. All of the walls that we build in life are an effort to hide ourselves from hurt, but those walls do not *hide us*, they *hold us hostage*. Our only escape is to embrace what is true.

Embracing truth exposes our lies and causes those lies to flee far from us. It is when we have accomplished this task in ourselves and are able to teach it to our children and others, that we have seen true love within ourselves. It is only then that others will see true love within us. Self-worth is built on accepting truth. Anyone who believes otherwise is most certainly living an arrogant life or a life of false humility.

True Love

To start, *true love* needs to be defined. We need to define love because, in religion, there is much rambling about various types of love. In truth, there is only *one* Love.

It is the perversion of the definition of "love" that allows us to think that there is more than one kind of love. All "love" is based upon one irrefutable truth. There are no exceptions and there are no rules, there *is* only what *is*. What *is*, is the only thing that is true and the only thing that can be relied upon. To understand this, is true love.

True love reveals itself and it will not hide. It will be shared and it will share. True love is simple and it is unconditionally true. True love loves all truth and exposes lies whenever anything untrue is compared to it.

We often hear people saying, "How could such a loving God do such horrible things?" or "How could a loving God allow this to happen?" Yet, we never see a person who has been truly repentant saying such things. When these sorts of statements are being made they are almost always accompanied with much bitterness and hatred and with little acceptance of personal responsibility.

According to the Bible, the people were always warned and told that it would be better for them if they changed their ways, but the people declined and typically threatened the messengers with death. You don't even have to believe in a God to see the stupidity in this type of behavior and attitude. True love takes decisive action and warns others of impending trouble.

Let us imagine that some amateur scientist saw that a comet was headed towards earth and anticipated that the comet would directly hit and destroy a small village of about five hundred people. If the novice astronomer discovered this comet and went into the village and started telling the citizens to pack up and leave because there was doom headed their way, then do we imagine that they would all listen and evacuate the city immediately? His warning serves himself no good whatsoever. He does this out of care and love for his fellow man.

They would likely mock the person if no other renowned scientist would confirm the findings. Then, if the comet hit and destroyed the city, will the other people from the surrounding area and the few possible survivors of the city in some way blame the messenger who told them all about the asteroid and the impending doom? Some likely will find a way to blame him for the now destroyed city's people's own unwillingness to heed a concise warning; such as saying, "*He* should have *demanded* they flee." But would it not be better if they, in understanding, lamented that the people would not heed the words of the wise but amateur scientist? This was an example, with the "God" element removed, of how people often act. If we take the time to analyze human nature, we realize that this scenario is not just possible with regard to the citizens' reaction, but it is highly probable. We see examples of this on any particular day when we simply look at what certain preachers are saying about our collective behavior as a society. At some point, it is likely that society's ill behavior will catch up with society.

True love will discipline when needed, even when it hurts the feelings of the offending party. In the Biblical accounts of such destruction, the people were murderous and were violating humanity in many unspeakable ways. Since this is in the Bible, and as we discuss this story for the purposes of this book, we will all assume that there *is* a God, or Creator, that has reached the limits of tolerating horrible human-behavior done of their own free will. The Creator took the time to warn the people, but all of the warnings were *rejected* and the destroying armies were sent in, or fire and brimstone rained down upon the people who would not heed the warnings that were presented to them.

So, whose fault is it? Is it the fault of a just and fair Creator who offered the ample warning that was rejected, or was it the foolish and ignorant choice of the citizens who made their freewill choice to ignore the warnings? I suppose a person could argue that a "loving God" would not destroy a city. But then we have to ask ourselves if we think that it is okay for people to rob, rape, plunder, and murder people in cold blood without any justification?

Parenting is not much different. True love is not about vengeance. It is about correcting wrong behavior and about teaching truth. When we allow our children to harm others, or if we allow others to unjustly harm our children, then we are failing to teach them true love. But there comes a point when true love can be undermined by parents. When a parent claims to "believe in God", but then reads the historical accounts in the Bible and proceeds to tell their children that "it's all a bunch of made up stories", they undermine their own credibility and the Bible's credibility in the mind of their children.

As you are reading this, a decision needs to be made. Either we believe it is all untrue, *or* we accept that there is a Creator as stated in the documents. Complaining about the cruelty of the Creator, and then saying these are all made up stories, is contradictory thinking and is usually done in a malicious manner. Most of which is because we refuse to accept or grasp the errors of the people spoken of in the Biblical events and because we refuse to admit our own errors.

We need to make up our minds and stop living in contradiction. Our contradiction is taught to our children by our words, actions, and beliefs. Either we believe it all and are going to seek the ultimate truth about it, or we are going to continue to be indecisive about it, causing us and our families to suffer from our own indecision and from our bad decisions. When we do this we teach lies and then true love departs from us and from our families.

True love is you being strong enough to stand up for what is good so that the other person is exposed and is forced to come out of their fortress prison and show themselves for who they *truly* are. Does this mean that we draw them out and mock or condemn them? No. Rather, it means that we invite them out to be their best and do their best, and to be what they were Created to be— *beautifully Created in truth*. Only this will bring out the true Creativity in them.

To **love** is to show your existence to others and to the world— that is true love—that is true life! Without this, we are dead in hell; we are painted over with lies and falsehoods; and we are concealed in the darkness of these lies that hold us captive. There is but one true love and it is **Truth**! When you reveal your truth *then* you love.

Their Self-Worth

As stated earlier, our children's self-worth is directly proportional to the level of understanding and truth that they have within them. This has largely been taught by us parents. The brilliant sparkle of truth, makes gold look as if it is a worthless metal. Our children's internal value is a reflection of accumulated truth; and the more of it that they have saved up, then the more of it they are capable of saving.

A single lie believed can cause our children to voluntarily forfeit all of the truth that they have saved up. In the Bible it is said, "My people perish for lack of knowledge," or for lack of *knowing*. The people do not perish because they do not know the meaningless trivia we teach in our schools today. Rather, they perish because they do not know the unknown truth we are speaking of here in this book—a truth that is spoken of throughout the entire Bible.

A child's self-worth is greatly affected by their parents' words, actions, and attitudes. For instance, if you have a child who is overweight, telling them that they are getting "fat" and that they need to lose weight is going to diminish them. They already know that there is a problem. Instead, teach them through love and understanding. Eat healthy, properly portioned meals *with* them, take walks *with* them, discuss it lovingly *with* them, and create a solution *with* them. We are talking about *your* children here. Let them know that they are loved, beautiful, smart, and most of all, worthy. When our children are overweight, especially when they are young, it is our own fault, not theirs! *We* are the ones who give them access to an abundance of high calorie, low nutrition foods. It is our fault and it is our responsibility to correct the problem with kindness, love, dedication, and truth. When a child knows, through our actions, that they are loved and cared for by their parents, then they will have a healthy self-worth.

The gift of truth is the gift of life. When we teach our children to understand truth and to weigh everything on the scale of truth, then we have made them rich; and then the riches of Heaven are also theirs—this is true self-worth! Anything else that makes us feel valuable is a lie and a fraud; and when it is revealed, it will be worthless and you will feel worthless. Truth can never be stripped from you without your permission, and it cannot be stripped from your children without their permission. It is our task to teach our children this truth.

Give Them Their Love

Regarding *being there when you are there*, give them your love and look into those little eyes because they are a reflection of you. You will see yourself in their eyes. And as you see your actual reflection lighted in their eyes, so too, will you see your image reflected in their form, in their heart, in their thoughts, in their words, and in their actions.

Reveal your true self to your children and teach *them* to do the same for *their* family and the world. We all have wonderful gifts to share. Invite your children outside of their walls and allow them to reveal themselves to you, and then consider *them*—consider their heart. Take in their life and their beauty, and then they will invite *you* into their heart. You will then become a value of joy for them and them for you.

When you are there then be there for them. Hear them and share in them, and share yourself with them. *Not doing* this will guarantee you much strife in your home with only random moments of bought happiness. Where on the other hand, *actually doing it* will guarantee you much joy in yours and your children's future, and it will bring about a multitude of other abundant benefits that are natural to truth.

How to Proceed

We're often afraid to attempt the first step, much the way a child who is getting ready to walk is afraid to take his or her first step. Our fear to step forward is our own biggest hurdle to overcome. It is as if we feel that we are going to come to an end by opening up to reveal ourselves while standing for truth; when in reality, it is when we do the opposite by hiding away our true feelings and true self that we will destroy ourselves.

Most of us have been living untruthfully most of our lives We have dug in so deep and defended our unjust fortress for so long, that we fear the exposure will cause us embarrassment. This is *humiliation* not *embarrassment*. Humiliation is to be humbled, which is to be humus, earth, or dirt, and that is to be human. Our food comes from the earth, and, as we grow, we eat the food—we are from the dirt. And one day these bodies will die and turn back to dust and will return to this earth. We all know this; yet, just like Adam and Eve, we hide instead of saying "Here am I Lord, take me and shape me. Show me what is good."

Our children cannot be taught to come out of their fortresses if we ourselves do not come out of our own. This is why the cornerstone book *Hot Water* was written—to help us escape from our own troubles. It is an amazing thing to watch and to see how others grow and change in their lives and in joy when they come upon this realization. Their confidence rises, their understanding rises, their creativity rises, their truth rises, and their joy rises! And then most of their troubles vanish.

Opening Our Eyes

When we feel inadequate, we must *decide* to search, ask, seek, and learn. When we feel down and are hurting, it is only because we have lost sight of what is true and good. It is true that it's very difficult to *see the light* or what is true when others are trying to keep us in darkness. No matter what they say, it is still up to each one of us to open our own eyes and to teach our children to open their eyes. When we do this, we break the chains that hold us in our self-made prisons.

Show your children that it is easy. Once you start and open your eyes, then your eyes will become accustomed to the light and it is no longer difficult to hold your eyes open. Opening our eyes allows us to see everything. We live in a beautiful world and it is our choice if we want to teach our children to be mean, sarcastic people who feel lowly about themselves and tear others down in order to feel higher; or we can choose to teach them to be joyful, smart, eager, kind, and loving people who will do great things in this world. It is all *our own* choice.

We must remember for ourselves and also teach our children, that when we feel down or low and when we attack other people and are unjustly angry, it means that we have lost sight of what is true—we have allowed ourselves to be defeated by the lies of others. Our bad actions and mistakes are a sign to us that we have turned away from truth.

Properly Understanding Control Versus Guidance

"Control" was discussed earlier to an extent. However, here it is not *control*, but rather it is *guidance* that is being referred to. We parents often don't know this skill because we didn't experience it as children. We demand that our children listen to us and obey, rather than teaching and guiding them.

Guidance is a simple term meaning to *guide* or to look after or to know them. Even the word *lamb* in ancient form means to be guided; as in, being guided by the good shepherd. The term *obey* means to hear and come to.

Controlling others is forcing or coercing them to do our bidding and forcing them to follow all of our demands. Demanding others around is to be controlling of others. But to be **in** control, is different. It is what *guidance* is. Guidance is calm, gentle but firm decisive action to show them to follow what is true. You cannot guide when you are controlling others. Only when you understand how to have proper control can you guide.

Obtaining Absolute Power

Some of us think that power, or absolute power, is to be able to silence others. But in reality, that is actually *fear*. The only true power is the freedom that truth offers us. Obtaining absolute power is typically our goal when we have been allowed to have our way most of the time. We should not allow excuses for anyone's errant behavior, because then we are allowing someone to be able to continue in their error. However, we can make a slight exception; the excuse here is that we don't know any better. We have all been exposed to oblivious error since we were young, and we then lived it and passed it on, or will pass it on to our own children without realizing it. And, in turn, they will pass it on to their children, and on it will go until the end of days, **or** until someone takes the stand and says "**Not** in my family! In my family, **it ends today!**"

The illusion that we can obtain absolute power over anyone, other than ourselves, is very arrogant indeed! Think about it: someone wants to control us, or we want to control someone else. We know too many people that can't even handle their own lives; isn't it ridiculous for anyone to want to try control another life? The absurdity to think that anyone can control anyone is only an illusion in the minds of the person who is trying to control others and in the mind of the person who believes they are being controlled.

True absolute power is when we are in control of our own selves. To obtain this, only one option exists: To embrace truth with all of our heart, and with all of our soul, and with all of our mind.

Hear and Consider Their Thoughts

Children need their *parents'* approval; not our approval of the questionable things they might choose to do, but rather our approval of their truth. This is truly what children seek from their parents.

All of the trouble they might get into is from them searching for the simple and free gift of truth. It is when they get their parents' approval in this regard, that they can be certain that they have achieved this very important and critical goal. When we ourselves are uncertain, then how can we tell them that they have found this wondrous treasure of truth? We cannot!

To start, we must hear and consider their thoughts; this is the big secret of it all. But in truth, it's not a *secret* at all, it sits before our very eyes since the beginning of time, but we have been blinded from seeing it due to generations of darkness—it is "The blind leading the blind."

> All *we* have to do is to hear and *consider* the thoughts and ideas of our children.

All of the rest will reveal itself once we have chosen this path with open hearts and open minds while seeking only truth.

When parents hear and process their children's thoughts, it teaches the children to relate and compare, and then relate again, allowing them to be sympathetic to other people's pains and experiences. Without doing so, our children will be cold and uncaring, and they will learn to ignore the truth that sits right before their very eyes.

Building Their Self-Image

As touched on earlier, we must make sure to teach our children to resist when people violate them. If they allow other people to treat them badly, then we can make a fairly safe assumption that the violations will continue. Similarly, when we insult ourselves or think poorly about ourselves, we teach our children to do the same to themselves. There are few, if any, people who will come to children's defense if they feel lowly about themselves.

If children get into the habit of insulting themselves, it can become a sort of addiction. This is especially so for girls because there is no shortage of messages that will cause girls to question their self-worth. If a girl (or any person) reads an article about some particular part of their body, it raises their consciousness of that part and what the article unfairly negatively pointed out about it. This instills doubt into her mind about herself, and then to compensate, she might seek compliments by insulting herself, hoping to receive supportive comments in return. This happens with boys too, but is usually about their physical abilities.

Sometimes people insult themselves in order to receive compliments, but they don't actually believe their own self-deprecating comments. While another person makes similar comments, and this person actually believes the way they speak about themselves. Typically, we can tell the difference in the way that they physically present themselves.

As parents, it is important for us to make sure that the messages that our children get from us and the world are kind, loving, and creative. Being aware of this and actively addressing the problem will make a tremendous difference to your children. If you yourself, have now, or have had in the past, experienced this type of self-image problem, then you very well may be able to reflect upon your environment as a child and pin-point the source of your own self-doubt.

This type of self-deprecating-image problem is most commonly seen with females in conjunction with their body image. As discussed in the book *Dream Thin – The Weight Loss Repair Manual*, self-deprecation and fishing for compliments is a common problem. Some people are very good at fishing for compliments, and they receive them; but others fail to achieve the desired compliments, and because they fail at receiving the compliments, they begin to believe that what they say in their self-deprecation is true about themselves. Then when they feel badly about themselves, food is often their comforting solution, which in-turn, eventually proves their suspicion as they gain the weight that they so feared. But food and weight may not be in the equation at all, it could be some physical trait about their body that is either abnormal, or as is more common, it may be normal, but for some reason they have become hyper-sensitive about it. In this case, they cannot make the *perceived* problem physically worse, but they can make it worse in their own mind.

Building a great foundation for your children when they are young will assist you a great deal in them not falling into the poor self-image trap. Always tell your children that you love them and that they have life-value. Daughters whose fathers let them know that they are beautiful and loved will be more secure, self-assured, and have a much better self-image as they age, and thus, they will not need to be validated by poor sexual relationships.

This same type of effect applies to boys as well. Some children come upon these inaccurate assessments of themselves on their own with little or no help from others. In this case, it can be very difficult to detect because they will say little and may not even fish for compliments. One thing that these children often lack is the meaningful positive messages from the most important people in their lives—us parents. Children who know they are loved and who are told that they are good, kind, and attractive, will have better self-images than children who do not hear positive messages about themselves. To have a lasting positive impact on your children's self-image and self-worth, speak good and true things to your children. Your efforts will not go unrewarded!

Chapter 23

Teaching Your Children about Sex

What would a family book about bringing up great children be without a section on sex? Sex education should be done by the parents, not the school or by the church. Sadly, most of us either know too little about the subject ourselves or we fear saying anything because we are just plain afraid or embarrassed. Our children often learn more about sex while they ride the bus to school than they do from their parents. Ask yourself, "Is this really good?" Is it really good that the gym teacher is instructing *your* child as to what is or is not good concerning sex? Even going to the movies can be more accurately educational at times, than some gym or sex education teachers might be.

We parents would be the best sex educators for our children if we could get beyond our embarrassment and learn something ourselves. If we did this, then we parents would be like walking sex encyclopedias, passing down our skilled information learned from what we were taught and from what we figured out on our own. But we are not walking sex encyclopedias because sex is hidden away in shame because we do not understand it properly. Instead, sex is abused by those who irresponsibly partake of it, producing countless unwanted pregnancies and much disease, littering the landscape of humanity with many broken hearts, broken dreams, and broken lives.

Sadly, we perceive *"private"* as *"shameful"* and have in this way entirely missed the point of intimacy. A little known fact is that many of the so-called "dirty" sex terms that we consider "slang" are ancient words of intimacy and description; but these ancient words have become seen as bad because the words were being publicly used in a disrespectful manner causing people to be embarrassed. This would be much like if someone was to start disrespectfully and *publicly* sharing what occurs in the privacy of *your* sex life in your own home. Using these ancient words in a disrespectful and public way is felt as similar to having sex in public, "Shhhh, don't say that word out loud."—it should not be done. These words are private and intimate, and using them improperly and publicly is disrespectful to their original intended purpose and meaning.

These slang sex terms have gotten an unfair rap and are thought of as "dirty words" due to people's disregard for the intimate nature of these words. It is not the intimacy or the words that are dirty, it is how the words are understood and are used in such a low regard and disrespectful manner that is dirty.

A couple should do whatever *they* please in the privacy of their own home and bedroom, and they should enjoy doing so as they whisper these things into each other's ears. Somehow, our culture has husbands and wives afraid to get wild in their own bedrooms while uttering these same ancient words to one another, but some of our children will do anything, anywhere, with anyone, anytime that they wish while saying anything they want. And oddly, there seems to be no inhibition from using these words publicly in a disrespectful and derogatory manner—Is this not both overboard *and* backwards?

We have come to a sad day when our children can tell us more about sexual creativity than many of us parents know ourselves, especially when we consider that they are not even married yet and might still be in high school or even grade school.

Sex is not shameful, it is *private*. And when a person has selected a mate who they have decided to be truly committed to for life and marry, then they should have sex, and lots of it, to their own satisfaction! They should enjoy each other as the gift and companions that they were intended to be to each other when they promised in marriage. If we parents would all take such an approach and view of sexuality, then we could teach the important sexual lessons to our offspring, so that they could both partake of, and enjoy their sexuality with their spouse without regret of past errors, and have desire without inhibition of intimacy in their own homes with their own spouse. And please understand that we are not speaking of sharing your specific details here, but rather the general *good* knowledge and lessons on the subject you have acquired.

Beating the School to the Punch

Parents, teach your children about sex *before* the school and the school yard do. Truly I ask, is it good to leave this open to chance? Don't lie to your children about sex, explain intimacy as their age permits. Tell them what is true, and explain the moral issues that accompany it all as you teach them.

Lying to them will cause *The Santa Claus Effect.* Often, when our children are young, we foolishly say things to them about sex, such as, "Oh, that's yucky, you don't want to *ever* do **that!**" This is done assuming that, at some point, they will *properly* figure things out on their own. At some point, some sort of experimentation *will* likely take place. Once they discover that something is not as "yucky" as they were lead to believe, then our credibility with them in that regard will be completely gone. Then they will likely indulge in the activity because they were not given the tools of understanding, but were instead given lies about the subject. In believing the "yucky" lie that we told them, they have been robbed of making the freewill choice with diligent deliberation and discernment of good solid information of cause, effect, and the consequences thereof. And so goes society.

We need to be honest in all things with our children. Not all things are of their concern, so we need not share the details of the specifics of our own bedrooms with them. However, we can speak in an open and honest manner with them on this subject and answer their questions, *not* specifically about what *we* do, but rather, about what is appropriate and the creative things that can be done when it's time to discuss that as their age permits. They need *not* know your own specifics.

Parents, it is our time to stand and be heard and bring our children to the door of understanding and truth. Sexuality and intimacy should be known by us and taught to our children by us through *proper* explanation at the proper times and ages.

The Difference Between Boys and Girls

There are fundamental attributes that differentiate boys from girls. These differences are attractively obvious to us all as we begin thinking about dating. These differences should be celebrated because without the differences between male and female, we would all cease within the lifespan of a single generation. If we do not see that this is a testament to us, of—the stringent natural design by which we are formed—then we have chosen to be very blind indeed. Be not deceived by perversions of this simple truth.

In teaching our children about sex, we have to battle some very strong teachings about sexuality-alternatives that are opposed to our own beliefs and understanding. So as to not dictate to others what they can and cannot do, we each must live our own lives as we see fit; but this includes us, and our children as well, and it includes the ramifications of our actions. We need not have our children subjected to teachings that oppose our own understanding, and more importantly, that oppose truth.

Let's view this from two perceived opposing perspectives, the Biblical and the natural, that is to say, the Created and evolved. From a Biblical perspective, we must choose if we are going to believe the Bible or not. It's all-in or shut-up! If we are going to believe it, then any "alternative sexual lifestyle" is a fundamental violation of Creation. It is an abuse of the design with which we are Created, and we are very specifically instructed *not* to partake in such behavior.

It is still each person's choice, but the Bible's message is clear: husband and wife are to become one flesh and multiply and populate the earth. In the Biblical perspective, the Man is in the image of the Creator, and the Woman is like the people and is also "in the image of." The man is waiting for her to invite him in. That is their joy. The obvious nature of this pattern is shown in their design all the way down to her eggs and the resulting child that will be born in their image. Defying this design defiles our purpose and is found to be "detestable" as stated in the descriptions in the Bible.

If you do not want to consider the Bible, then we can look at the naturalist or evolutionary perspective. In this case, there is no god, and it all started with a random single cell that morphed through eons and eventually become man and all other life forms. Yet, with regard to mankind, there is only man and woman who reproduce as set forth by nature itself.

In this case, nature has built this model so incredibly rigid that the male-female model is found in almost every aspect of living nature. Additionally, since nature is believed by many to have brought us forth, we should respect nature and her design. From a naturalist perspective, a male goes into a female and places his seed inside of her *if* she feels that he is strong and attractive enough to offer her good and strong offspring.

Does this fundamental design stop there? No. It goes down to the very moment of conception when the man's sperm cell must be strong enough, and then the egg somehow allows the most desirable sperm cell into it. Is this not what the actual man and woman do? This model is shared amongst the entire animal kingdom. Is it not then a violation of nature itself to breach this natural progression? Any other lifestyle choice will eventually annihilate itself without adherence to nature, making it by technical definition, unnatural. The only way to perpetuate such alternate lifestyles, is to lie about this natural truth and cheat the design by having someone be either the host for the egg for you, or to be the donor of the sperm cell for you. Neither of those two options are in accordance with the natural progression of natural selection and are unnatural.

Only each one of us can answer the obvious nature of our design in our own hearts. We must decide for ourselves which lifestyle version we will choose. Additionally, what we must ask ourself is, if we choose a sexuality-alternative, are we then being true? But that question, we must answer ourself through our own chosen actions. We will be paid according to our actions—we judge ourselves by our chosen actions. But we do not get to decide what is true and real; we only get to decide if we will open our eyes to, and acknowledge, what is true and real. We cannot change what is right or wrong. Rather, we, each ourselves, can choose to agree with what is right or wrong. If we so choose to be wrong, then it does not matter how we rationalize our choice because, in the end, we are still wrong.

Eventually our actions will reveal what is truly in our own heart, and we will be accountable to ourselves and to nature or to the Creator; and possibly, accountable to both nature *and* the Creator. These choices are up to each one of us and are not able to be made by others. Only we ourselves can choose for ourselves whether we will embrace lies or choose what is true and good.

Understanding Desire

Before we can understand desire, we need to understand that there are other factors to consider as well. When a child has not been feeling loved at home, then feelings of low self-worth are often the result. When a child has low self-worth and poor self-esteem, it often leads to premature promiscuity, which can lead to poor marriage relationships. A child that is not feeling loved will try to experience feeling loved in any way that they can. Parents need to build their children's self-esteem. When parents fail to give their children reasons to love themselves, then the children seek to extract any love they can from life in any way they can. Doing so often comes in the form of promiscuous sexual interaction.

Sexual promiscuity is difficult enough for teenagers to resist, but when sexual promiscuity is built on a foundation of low self-worth, they are seldom able to resist. It likely affects boys and girls equally, but we tend to notice this more with girls because boys are generally thought of as the pursuers. And more notably, we also notice it more with girls because it is the girls who become pregnant and carry the newly Created life.

There's a born-in natural affinity that we have for the opposite gender. Whether Created or evolved, this affinity is critical to the continuation of humanity. If the desire for the opposite gender vanished, then the population would likely vanish within the lifespan of the longest living person of the final generation. As previously discussed, any affinity for the same gender is self-defeating and such choices will not survive "the survival of the fittest" from an evolutionary naturalist perspective. Our improper lusts are desires void of truth.

Desire in the realm of nature, or evolution, makes less sense than it does within the realm of Creation. In evolution it is the survival of the fittest. This means that our desire is purely selfish in the naturalist perspective. It cares nothing of anything or anyone but itself and perpetuating its kind.

However, in the Created realm, desire has a reason and a purpose, and it is a thing of immense beauty. Desire is a primary concept and our bodies are designed in the image of this desire. We are designed to know that this truth, which we have been discussing, is our desire. When we clear away all of the lies and things that are not true, then we are left empty until we fill ourselves with truth. If we do not fill ourselves with truth, then eventually we will be refilled with more lies.

We desire to know truth. This is why the colleges are filled with students who seem to be lost and uncertain in where they want to go in life. We desire! It is Created into us to want to *know*, or better stated, to *understand*. The vain quest for trivia in our education systems is mistaken for the understanding of truth. This erred quest typically teaches the students trivial information rather than teaching understanding and truth.

The gender-based model for desire is used in the spiritual or mind area of existence as well. In the Bible, it often says, "and he *knew* her" when referring to people engaging in intercourse. "He went into her" is another term used.

For a couple to truly experience joy, a woman must invite her husband into her; this applies to both the physical and of the heart—She must invite him into her heart. If this is not her desire, then the marriage will be troubled and painful for at least one, if not both, spouses. If a husband or wife cannot reveal their true self to their mate, then they *will* have problems. As discussed in the cornerstone book *Red Hot Marriage*, it is each our own task to draw one another out in truth and to reveal our inner and outer selves to each other in our marriage.

Crushing desire is a simple task that we have become very proficient at doing to our children, and it is something that we have repeatedly discussed throughout this book. Desire is in our design—whether Created or evolved we have natural desires, and these desires are common throughout our world and are shared by the vast majority of the humans in this world.

This inherent desire is a very good testament to the consistency of the design of desire. Without desire we will not achieve or seek anything.

Unless we teach our children to seek what is true, teaching our children to desire is an incredibly difficult task. The task becomes difficult without seeking what is true because seeking what is true is what **true** desire actually is.

Primary Functions of the Body

Desire is what the human body is designed for—to learn and understand! If we were not designed to desire, then we would not need a brain or an ability to recall memory. Our ability to collect experiences and share that truth with others is how we are designed. We can sense information in various ways, such as sight, sound, smell, taste, and touch. We then process this information and relate or share our experiences with others. We are supposed to be sharing things that are real and true.

Desire strikes us at our very ability to recreate. When we are stimulated by a human of the opposite gender, it creates a cascade of chemical reactions that result in our physical desire for that person. No physical touch need have happened for this physical side of our desire to occur.

The natural reactions of the body tell all about the desire and the purpose of that desire. It makes our bodies' design and the purpose of that design undeniably evident for those who care to consider and understand this fundamental aspect of our existence.

When is it Okay for Your Children to Have Sex?

Culturally, this question has remained uncertain in our minds for a very long time. The naturalist perspective is, when a girl begins to menstruate then her body is prepared; but there is also the emotional side of the question. Sex is a very personal and intimate act. A woman must invite the man inside of her body, and the only thing that is more personal than that is when a woman is ready to invite a man into her heart.

Our real self is not this body. Our real self is what is in our heart. This is the most personal aspect of any human being. The body and its functions are only a representation of that being. A representation of our *self* is the purpose of the body and what the body is modeled after. And our "*self*" is modeled after the Creator.

Physical intimacy is the outward sign of what is supposed to be occurring in our hearts—it is a sharing of self. When we teach our children that it's okay to have sex outside of marriage, or even if we encourage it through our silence, then we are teaching them that it is all about this physical feeling when nothing could be further from the truth.

The intimate act of intercourse was designed for, and is a model of, the desire of heart. If commitment is not going to be there for them when they share themselves, then they are making a great error in partaking in premarital sex. Sex is best stated as intimacy, and it is best to be kept between two truly committed people—typically married—a Husband and a Wife; and to make sure that we have a standard with no ambiguity in this regard, a husband is a male who is born with and retains his penis, and a wife is a female who is born with and retains her vagina.

Raising Valueless Children through Promiscuity

We can have a good time with sex and have many random partners, but to do so we must disconnect from what is true within ourselves by turning a blind eye to what we are truly seeking. *Uncommitted* sex is like whitewash, or like the walls of our fortress-prisons that we build to hide behind. It is also like hiding behind our money and the status that the money brings us. Sex works the same way, but with sex there is a certain irony: Intimacy with our bodies is designed so that we learn to *expose* ourselves to our spouse. However, in open uncommitted sex, it is used to *hide* behind. Saying "Oh it's just sex" allows us to believe that no one is negatively affected by the sexual free-for-all that too many people partake in.

When we encourage our children to partake in premarital sex, and when we allow them to believe that it does not matter, then we devalue them and allow them to be devalued by others and themselves. When we give ourselves away to anyone for free, then we become worthless. But when we properly value ourselves and reserve this gift only for *true* commitment, then we become priceless!

To better illustrate this point with clear proof to make it more evident, we even see people trying to play hard-to-get so that they are wanted. If this does not speak of the value of using restraint, then nothing does! The world will have its eye on our children to destroy them as it is, we need not encourage them to devalue themselves through encouraging them to partake in premarital sex.

As a society, we have brought ourselves to a point where we are *required* to freely distribute birth control in our public schools, because we have taught and have been taught, that there are ways of birth control other than abstinence. It is believed by many that if we do not teach using contraceptives, then the teen pregnancy rate will explode. This is not a good position for a family or society to be in. Recklessly promoting birth control and free sex will not solve our children's problems, it will only add to those problems. But teaching our own children truths about this subject and giving *them* the power to *choose* to *not* partake in premarital sex, gives them the true power.

Abstinence is the only true way to avoid pregnancy, and it works one-hundred percent of the time. However, because so many children fail to abide by abstinence, due to what we taught them, contraceptives have become common amongst our children, as have unwanted pregnancies, often times even when they have used birth control.

Physical intimacy is often used by people as a form of acceptance, just as money is. We throw money and sex around so that people will like us. While this may gain us some temporary friends, it lowers our worth to others, and our worth to our own selves. When the money or status goes away then the friends who are based upon it will also go away. The same is true for sex, when the sex goes away then the partners who are based upon that premarital sex will also go away. This clearly is **not** love.

Teaching our children to be promiscuous devalues them whether it is specifically done with our words or indirectly supported from our fear of speaking up about it. When their sexuality is devalued, then their self-worth will follow, as will the value that others perceive in them. If you doubt this, just consider how many instances there are where when the boy finally achieves his premarital conquest, then, suddenly, he no longer is interested in the girl he sought to conquer. And often, in such cases, he will go about defaming her by derogatorily referring to her as a "slut" or a "whore." Then, often, she will feel used and devalued, and will subsequently seek acceptance through sexuality because it is fairly easy to get young hormonal men to pursue her. Thus, she becomes what the first boy unfairly accused her of. Such unfair and unkind situations for young girls/women can easily be avoided when parents actively teach their children to pursue what is true.

Our time alive is the most valuable thing that we each have here on Earth. To toss this away to people who are not fully committed to us is foolish. It is like throwing gold coins to the dogs. The dogs simply do not understand how to appreciate what the value is or how to appreciate the luxury of the deliberate happiness that can be obtained through the value of the gold. Let us build our children's self-worth by teaching them what their true value is!

Chapter 24

Life Goes Quickly, Take Time to Enjoy it!

It seems that the more we age, the faster life appears to have gone. When we are forty or fifty we look back and wonder what happened, and, all too often, we wonder where we went wrong with our children.

We get one chance to build a great family; let's not miss our opportunity! Our family will affect the rest of our lives no matter what our age is. Our teaching never ends as parents, and it goes on long after we are gone. All of our words and actions will have affected us and our children. And what our children learn from us will affect their children and will pass from generation to generation.

Our parental teaching can be done at any age and it never ends. Our power as parents, to teach good things, is proportional to our commitment and understanding of what is true. Whether we try or not we will teach them, no matter what. The question is, **what** will we teach them? Will we accidentally teach them lies, or will we choose to specifically and deliberately teach them what truth is. Sometimes people get very lucky, and, out of pure chance, teach their children truth. But how much better is it if we teach truth *intentionally*!

Life Changes Rapidly

We have a tendency to believe that life does not, or should not, change, but life changes rapidly—always! Teach your children to embrace those changes.

There is nowhere that this feeling about change is more evident than in the opinions of naturalists or the followers of evolution. It is interesting to observe people in this regard. We insist that there is no Creator and that all life evolved over long periods of time. We will also insist that there have been multiple ice ages at regular intervals over thousands or millions or billions of years. Yet, we attempt to *stop changes* from occurring. We claim we are due for a *cyclical* ice age, but insist that we must do something to stop this *natural cyclical* occurrence from occurring again.

With regard to the survival of the fittest, humans (who seem to be winning that battle) want to stop the survival of the humans and often favor other species. This manner of thinking is inconsistent and contrary, and is not the "survival of the fittest!" Rather, it is the destruction of the fittest and it goes against all things good. Teaching these inconsistent perspectives to your children causes them tremendous doubt and obscures their view to the clear and perfect path that truth has prepared for them. Learn to accept good changes because life changes rapidly, but truth is constant and reliable and never changes.

Embracing Changes

We must embrace life and the changes that occur within it. When we have no index of what is good then we lose sight of anything good, and, in the end, it causes us to fail in life. The previous section shows our inconsistent state of mind and resistance to natural change. We should certainly take care of our environment and the people within it. But life changes rapidly as we learn new things. We must learn to embrace the changes in life and the newly revealed everlasting true information that changes it.

Hanging onto past errors will not improve our future. We can learn from our mistakes, but we can do so only by looking back at them *as mistakes* and as points of reference and a map of what **not** to do in our future. However, even this becomes rarely needed when we embrace the things that are true. Truth is the most important reference point on anyone's personal life-map. Once we have found what is true, then the changes in life that often feel confusing will occur less often, and life will become less chaotic and more certain for us. Then the changes we encounter in our future will mostly be good! Anything that cannot adapt to what is true **will** someday perish. Embrace *true* changes!

Your Children and Your Grandchildren

We are the teachers of our children *and* of our grandchildren. We are their past and we are their future. Our teachings and our words to them will live on in their hearts, minds, and actions for generations to come.

We can teach our children to teach their grandchildren by teaching our own grandchildren and our own children. When we do this *properly*, then our children will understand the importance of teaching subsequent generations what is true. Humanity's stumbling block has always been the belief in things that are wrong. We can choose to teach things that are good and true directly to our children, and directly to our grandchildren. Or, we can choose to do nothing, and in so doing, we teach them to do nothing, leaving them without direction and highly susceptible to the predatory lies of error.

The disease that has caused so many generations to fail is that true information is not passed on to the next generation. The *failure* to pass truth on is done of our own free will.

All of our fortresses and our masks of fear and arrogance stop us from being able to see and share good things. If we are too embarrassed to admit to our own errors, then we cannot help our children and grandchildren from making similar errors.

Not one of us is perfect. We *all* have made errors. We cannot go back and undo those errors. However, we can go back and change their value by admitting to our errors and using our own errors as an example of what must be avoided, and as an example and explanation as to why it is so destructive.

But there is something that is more important than changing the value of our past, and that is to define the value of our future by sharing things that are good and true with our children and our grandchildren.

Grandchildren seem to grow even faster than our own children. We cannot afford to sit idle and do nothing. Because before we know it, they too, will have children of their own. Our opportunity is **now**!

Let us begin today to change our own tomorrows and all of the tomorrows of our family for generations to come. Take time for your children, and your grandchildren when those days come, and then be there with them to enjoy them and their company. Share your life with them, and share in their lives!

Making it too Easy for Your Children by Raising Their Children

Grandparents, and especially grandmothers, are often available to lend a helping hand to their children when a babysitter is needed. This is a good opportunity to spend time with the grandchildren and to teach them good things. However, if we make it too easy for our children when they are raising their own children, they likely will not be of much help for their own children when their grandchildren come along.

This is exactly the same as when we allow a child to be dependent upon being *demanding,* by us submitting to their demands. So, too, will we create dependency for them to set aside their children for their own (the parents) benefit when we submit to becoming regular daytime caregivers to their children every day.

A grandparent who takes care of grandchildren every day for years while the parent runs off to have their own desires met by making more money, will likely find that if they live long enough, that their children will *not* be of much help with their grandchildren (your child's children.) Bailing out your children by taking care of their kids on a regular daily basis, so that your children can selfishly have a more luxurious life, sets up a precedent of selfishness.

When we make life too easy for others by doing the work that is due of them, then we are cheating them out of a wonderful future.

Assisting our children in a brief time of need and occasionally caring for their children is good and proper. However, when we allow our children to avoid their duty by raising their children *for them*, then we are creating a dependency on this behavior, and by allowing them to have their way, we have met their demands once again.

Meeting these demands is a disservice to them and to their children. If this is what our children are asking of us, then it is our own fault for allowing them their demands as children. Any parent who does not want to be with their own children should not have had them to begin with. With regard to our own families, our children and what we teach them are the only things from us that have any true and lasting value *when* we do it right. How our children turn out when they are older is directly due to the way we taught them as they grew up. If we decide that for some reason, we do not like our children when they are grown, then we must acknowledge that we have failed in a very deep and profound manner when they were young. And if that is the case, then today is the day to begin to turn it around for your joy and for the joy of your entire family!

Grandchildren

People are vessels, and all of our experiences in life are gathered and poured into our grandchildren by our own children and by ourselves. We fill the lives of our grandchildren through the thoughts, words, and actions of our own lives. Whether they are to be thirty years in the future or they are thirty years of age, think of your grandchildren (and children) as a vessel or a vase in which you will pour the experiences of your life, both through your own children, and directly from you into your grandchildren.

What *we* live determines what will be poured into the vessel, and then it will be saved up and poured into the next generation blended with all of our children's experiences. *We* get to decide what will be poured into both our children and our grandchildren by the choices we make today and tomorrow and by how we utilize our past errors.

If what we have poured into those vessels, so far, is not good, then we can reach into our past and change its meaning by changing what we do today. Changing our today will change our tomorrows and will empty those vessels of that old dirty water and will replace it with the new pure fresh water of truth. If you do not have children yet, then now is a great time to begin to redirect your life for the sake of all of your offspring and subsequent generations.

When we are with our grandchildren we must recall the errors that we made with our own children and refuse to make those mistakes again. Be there with your grandchildren when you are with them. Look into their eyes and tell them wonderful and true things.

Listen to their beauty and innocence, and hear their words and consider those words. Doing so will teach them to teach their own grandchildren. In the process of doing this, we have spent real time with them and have spread our joy all the way to their grandchildren (our great-great-grandchildren) whom we might never meet.

Finale

What we do in our lives matters. The words matter, our thoughts matter, and our consistency matters. There is much in the world that will try to trip us up and invade our family in an attempt to undermine and destroy it. Whether or not that happens is up to us. We will struggle in life until we have embraced what is true.

If you think back to the bad times in your life, then you *will* find that wrong-thinking, lies, and things that are not true will be lurking in the shadows of your past. This includes those times where it was not us, but rather someone else who caused us a great deal of pain; we need not look very far into their lives and we will find lies and the departure from what is true lurking in the darkness in their lives also.

All true joy comes from staying on and following a path that is true. The benefits are good health, a robust and joyous life, good and healthy children, creativity, personal rest, contentment, satisfaction, abundance, wealth, and on and on the list goes! The power is yours to shape and mold the life of your children and family. We can only lose that power through being blind to seeing what is true.

Today is your day to decide that you will only accept things that are *real* into your life and into your family. It is also your day to decide that you will reject all else and that you will reveal your own truth about you and your own errors. Doing so reveals to you how to no longer make those same errors. This is a new day for you to shape and form and cause to be excellent! You might have a few battles ahead, but these battles will each be more quickly defeated than the previous as you learn the skill of allowing what is true to fight your battles for you.

Let's take our stand now and change the rest of our lives by building families that will no longer accept untrue things. Let us build our family on a foundation of understanding, built with stones cut and shaped from perfect truth. And let us cast away all of the excess scraps of lies that contaminate our families.

Our world thrives on the perception of power. People kill to maintain their own *perception* of power. If we must harm someone in order to maintain our own power, then we truly have no power at all, and we can only maintain our lie by destroying others. If we do this, then *we* have instantly and automatically made everyone better than us through our own thoughts and actions. This is what the serpent did in the Garden.

If someone is trying to destroy us, then they believe we are a threat to them, and they are afraid of us and believe that we are better than they are. This is not power at all, rather it is their fear of what is true and good—they fear exposure by truth and are trapped within the walls of their own fortress-prison built with the mortar of lies.

Anyone who wants real power will embrace what is true and then the truth will fight their battles for them and set an unshakable foundation of understanding and truth for their family. Truth will protect and lead us to a life filled with strength, power, and joy!

Your family is your Garden of Paradise. Just as your yard needs to be maintained to be weed-free and beautifully planted with rich and vibrant colors, so too it is with your family. If you allow the weeds to grow in your family, then you will be constantly stepping on thistles and other noxious weeds that will choke out the beauty of your joy. You must choose to plant flowers and fruit trees bearing joyous delicious fruit in vibrant colors within your family. Remember though, to take care to weed your Garden regularly, or you will pay the price of your neglect.

In a family, the father is the main vine and his children are the fruit. If no one cares for the vine, then the vine cannot produce good fruit. The mother and the father are the keepers in the Garden of their own family.

Embrace Truth and teach it to your children so that you and your family can go on to live a life filled with Abundance, Love, True Joy, and Truth!

Today is always *your* day—Live it Well!

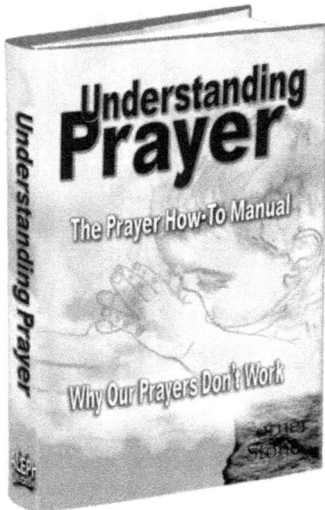

Volume 1 - The First Four Days

Is there a God? Did we evolve? Did everything start from a big bang? These questions have been plaguing our minds for many years. Only science-minded people and clergy seem to have the answers. But do they really have any true answers?

Is what we are told by science true? Is what we are told by the Church true? Or are there other better explanations for everything? Did we hitch a ride from Mars, or is that all fantasy science? Was everything Created in six twenty-four hour days, or did it all take billions of years to happen? Few people are willing to even fully consider these questions, and even fewer have any coherent answers. *The Science of God* challenges your current beliefs while asking tough questions of science and of the Church.

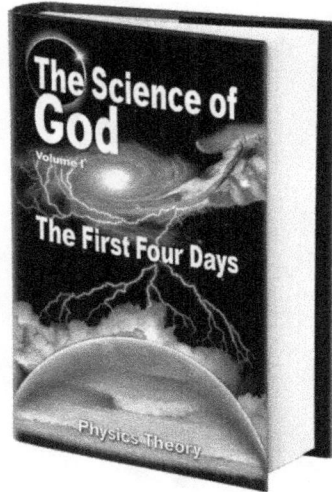

For years, Christian after Christian has attempted to argue for God and the Bible's Creation only to fail miserably. Why is this, why is it that Christians cannot seem to win this debate? Often Christians think they are winning the debate only to find themselves at a loss to answer the real questions, and then they get mocked for their poor answers.

Whether you are a scientist or an average Christian and want to discuss the Creation debate, *The Science of God* is a mandatory read for you. *The Science of God* takes you through the thought process to enable you to speak intelligibly about Creation, the cosmos, evolution, and astrophysics.

Search: The Science Of God Book
SayItBooks.com

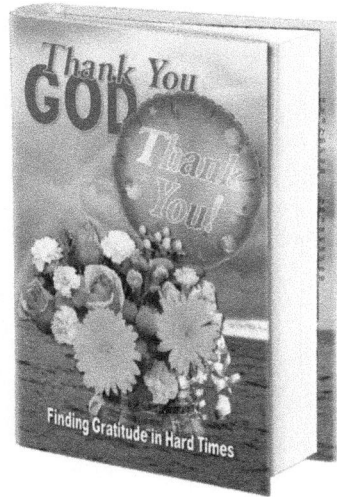

Notes

Notes

Notes

www.ingramcontent.com/pod-product-compliance
Lightning Source LLC
Chambersburg PA
CBHW020148090426
42734CB00008B/735